Francis Adelbert Blackburn

The Essentials of Latin Grammar

Francis Adelbert Blackburn

The Essentials of Latin Grammar

ISBN/EAN: 9783741183683

Manufactured in Europe, USA, Canada, Australia, Japa

Cover: Foto ©Andreas Hilbeck / pixelio.de

Manufactured and distributed by brebook publishing software (www.brebook.com)

Francis Adelbert Blackburn

The Essentials of Latin Grammar

# THE

ESSENTIALS

OF

LATIN GRAMMAR

BY

F. A. BLACK

Nobis prima sit virtus perspicuitas, … ordo; … nihil
neque desit neque super… 2, 22.

PUBLISHED BY GINN, HEATH, & CO.

1883.

Entered according to Act of Congress, in the year 1883, by

F. A. BLACKBURN,

In the Office of the Librarian of Congress, at Washington.

745.24

J. S. CUSHING & CO., PRINTERS, BOSTON.

PREFACE.

THIS book is the outgrowth of several years' experience in teaching Latin to beginners. Portions of it were drawn up some years ago for the use of my own classes; the success that has followed the use of them has led to the completion of the lacking portions and the publication of the whole.

The objects kept in view in compiling the book were two: without omitting essentials, to make a book small enough to be mastered by a beginner, and to arrange the principles of grammar contained in it as systematically as possible, thus making them easy to learn and easy to keep. The first object I have tried to secure by studied conciseness of statement and by the omission of all that Latin has in common with English, *e.g.*, definitions of the parts of speech, kinds of sentences, subject, object, etc.; rules for the use of adverbs, conjunctions, and the like. The object of these omissions, however, was not brevity alone, but rather simplicity. I have assumed that the book will be put into the hands of pupils who have already studied English Grammar, and I believe that loss of time is only a part of the harm of requiring a pupil to relearn a grammatical definition or principle couched in new words. The book will not be found suitable, therefore, for pupils who have not mastered the elements of grammar, unless the teacher shall supplement it with the needed definitions.

The second point aimed at is partly a matter of grammatical system, partly of typography. Whether my classification of the facts and principles of the Latin tongue is any help to the pupil in learning them and keeping them, is a question for the teacher who may use the book. The arrangement of these facts and principles on the page, however, will commend itself, I hope, to all. The coarser print contains those portions of the grammar of the language, which, in my judgment, should be absolutely mastered; the smallest amount to which memorizing can be limited. The notes contain illustrations, explanations, and those limitations of grammatical principles which are the outgrowth of usage, and which should be gradually learned by daily reference in the course of reading a Latin author. Much that is in the notes should be memorized; how much, is a question left to the judgment of the teacher, and the answer will depend on circumstances: the amount of time at the disposal of the class, the age and character of the pupils, the requirements of the college they have in view, etc. The duplicate numbering serves to connect the notes to the statements they illustrate or explain, and is simple enough, I hope, to save the vexation and loss of time incurred in trying to find a reference in a book systematically sub-divided and classified. The numbering answers the same purpose as paging: convenience of reference. A bracketed reference refers to a note; such a reference, given orally, may be called simply "*note*," *e.g.* [142] may be read "note 142."

It is not claimed, of course, that so small a book contains a complete exposition of the principles of the Latin tongue, or a complete history of the growth of the forms and usage of Latin speech, and the book is not intended for those who pursue the study of the language so far. Such should provide themselves with larger and fuller treatises. It is intended for that class of pupils who study Latin in school and college for the training it gives in clearness of thought and exactness of speech, but whose tastes or plans of life and work do not lead them to the higher and more attractive study of the life and growth of the language. I have, therefore, omitted discussions of the origin and growth of forms and idioms, or of the development of syntactical usages, as well as all illustrations drawn from comparative grammar. I have tried to include, however, all the grammatical information needed for a high school or for the early years of a college;

to the point, in fact, where the better colleges now give the pupil the option of continuing classical studies, or substituting other branches more to his taste. I have tried, moreover, to so arrange the facts and usages of Latin speech, that the pupil who carries his studies beyond the limit of the book, shall not be obliged to unlearn, but only to supplement, what he has already mastered.

It is proper to add that I put forth no claim to original research, my object being to make a school-book. If the plan and arrangement do not justify its publication, there is nothing else in it to do so. I have not tried, moreover, in seeking for the best and clearest arrangement, to avoid what has been already used by others. I have freely taken from every source, whatever, in the way of expression or classification, seemed good for my purpose. The teacher who is familiar with the various Latin grammars issued within the last twenty years, will find much taken directly from them; more than I can acknowledge in detail. On questions of fact and usage, I have depended almost entirely on Roby's Latin Grammar, and have drawn freely on his citations from Latin authors, for illustrative examples. His full collections of illustrative words and sentences have saved a great amount of labor that would have been needed to find appropriate illustrations.

I shall be grateful for criticism from any source, especially for corrections or suggestions from teachers who may have occasion to test the value of the book by actual use with classes.

F. A. BLACKBURN.

SAN FRANCISCO, CAL., *Feb.* 17, 1883.

CONTENTS.

PART I. — SOUNDS.

Alphabet and Pronunciation 1–13
   Alphabet 1
   Vowels, their sounds 2
   Open and close vowels 3
   Diphthongs 4
   Sounds of diphthongs 5
   Sounds of the consonants 6–11
   Classification of consonants 12
   Double consonant x 13

Quantity and Accent 14–20
   Long syllables 14, 15
   Short syllables 16, 17
   Common syllables 18
   Accent 19, 20

PART II. — FORMS.

Inflection 21–26
   Inflection 21, 22
   Inflection of nouns 23
   Inflection of adjectives 24
   Inflection of pronouns 25
   Inflection of verbs . . . 26

Stem and Suffixes; Theme and Endings . . . 27–29
   Stem and suffixes 27
   Theme and endings 28, 29

CONTENTS.

Gender 30–40
   Three genders 30
   Natural and grammatical gender 31
   Naturally masculine nouns 32, 33
   Naturally feminine nouns 34–36
   Naturally neuter nouns 37, 38
   Naturally common nouns 39, 40

Person, Number and Case 41–49
   Person and number 41
   Cases 42
   Nominative case 43
   Genitive case 44
   Dative case 45
   Accusative case 46
   Vocative case 47
   Ablative and locative cases 48
   Direct and oblique cases 49

The Declensions 50–53
   Six forms of declension 50
   Two groups 51
   Open-vowel declensions 51
   Close-vowel and consonant declensions . . . 51

The a-declension 52–56
   Theme and stem 52
   Endings 53, 54
   Locative of a-stems 55
   Gender of a-stems 56

The e-declension 57–60
   Theme and stem 57
   Endings 58
   Gender of e-stems 59, 60

The o-declension 61–69
   Theme and stem 61
   Endings 62, 63
   Vocative of o-stems 64
   Locative of o-stems 65
   Stems in -čro 66
   Stems in -io 67
   deus, its irregularities 68
   Gender of o-stems 69

CONTENTS. ix

Adjective stems in -*a* and -*o*	**70-72**
Declension of a- and o-stem adjectives	70
Irregular adjectives	71
duo and ambo	72
The Consonant-declension	**73-90**
Theme and stem	73
Endings	74, 75
Weakening of stem-vowel	76
Locative of consonant-stems	77
Loss of ending in semi-vowel stems	78
Loss of n in nominative singular	79
Stems in -ĕr	80
Irregularities	81
Gender of consonant-stems	82-90
Adjectives with Stems in a Consonant	**91-93**
Declension of consonant-stem adjectives	91
Adjectives comprised	92, 93
The *i*-declension	**94-105**
Theme and stem	94
Classes of i-stems	95-98
Endings	99-101
Stems in -ĕri	102
Gender of i-stems	103-105
Adjectives with Stems in -*i*	**106-108**
Declension of i-stem adjectives	106
Adjectives comprised	107, 108
The *u*-declension	**109-113**
Theme and stem	109
Endings	110, 111
Monosyllabic u-stems	112
Gender of u-stems	113
Irregular Declension	**114-117**
Numeral Adjectives	**118**
Comparison of Adjectives	**119-123**
Suffixes of comparison	119, 120
Stems in -ĕr, -ĕro, -ĕri, -īli	121
Compounds of -dĭcus, -fĭcus, -vŏlus	122
Comparison by the use of **magis, maxime**	123

CONTENTS.

Forms of Pronouns 124–141
    The personal pronouns 124
    Declension of the personal pronouns 125
    Possessive pronouns 126
    Demonstrative pronouns 127, 128
    Declension of is, ea, id 129
    Declension of iste, ista, istud . . . 130
    Declension of ille, illa, illud . . 131
    Declension of ipse, ipsa, ipsum . 132
    Declension of hic, haec, hoc . . 133, 134
    Strengthened forms of ille and iste . 135
    Declension of idem, eadem, idem . . . 136, 137
    Declension of the relative pronoun, qvi, qvae, qvod . 138
    Declension of the interrogative pronoun, qvis, qvae, qvid . 139
    Declension of the indefinite pronoun, qvi or qvis . . 140
    Declension of the indefinite compounds of qvi or qvis . 141

Forms of the Verb 142–154
    Tenses and moods of the finite verb . 142–147
    Non-finite verb-forms 148–152
    Passive verb-forms 153
    Deponent verbs 154

Verb-stems 155–169
    Forms of verb-stems 155
    Simple stem; present stem; perfect stem . . 156
    Formation of present stem 157–162
    Formation of perfect stem . . . 163–167
    Principal parts of the verb 168, 169

Verbal Suffixes 170–190
    Two elements of verb-suffixes 170
    Mood-and-tense signs 171–177
    Tense-base 178
    Suffixes of finite verb-forms . . . 179–182
    Suffixes of non-finite verb-forms . . . 183–187
    Endings of perfect active indicative and infinitive 188–190

The Conjugations 191–214
    Five conjugations 191
    Theme of the incomplete tenses . 192
    Inflection of the incomplete tenses . . . 193
    Endings of the incomplete tenses; a-stems . 194, 195
    Endings of the incomplete tenses; e-stems . . 196, 197

CONTENTS.   xi

Endings of the incomplete tenses; consonant and u-stems   198, 199
Two forms of inflection of i-stems 200
Endings of the incomplete tenses; short i-stems . . 201, 202
Endings of the incomplete tenses; long i-stems . 203, 204
Theme of the complete tenses 205
Endings of the complete tenses 206
Formation of the complete tenses; passive voice . 207
Theme of simple stem forms 208
Endings of simple stem forms 209
Periphrastic forms made from the participles . . 210–214

Irregular Verb-forms **215–229**
   Loss of v in perfect stem 215
   Loss of imperative ending in dic, duc, fac . 216
   Specially irregular verbs 217–220
   sum, esse, fui 221
   Compounds of sum 222
   edo, edere, edi, esum 223
   fero, ferre, tuli, latum 224
   volo, velle, volui; nolo, nolle, nolui; malo, malle, malui   225
   do, dare, dedi, datum 226
   eo, ire, ivi, itum 227
   qveo, qvire, qvivi, qvitum; neqveo, neqvire, neqvivi,
     neqvitum 228
   fio, fieri 229

Impersonal and Defective Verbs . . **230–235**

PART III. — WORD-FORMATION.

Roots and Stems **236–238**
   Roots 236
   Stems 237, 238

Formation of Nouns **239–241**
   Nouns from nouns 239
   Nouns from adjectives 240
   Nouns from verbs 241

Formation of Adjectives **242–244**
   Adjectives from nouns 242
   Adjectives from adjectives 243
   Adjectives from verbs 244

CONTENTS.

Formation of Verbs 245–247
    Verbs from nouns and adjectives 245, 246
    Verbs from verbs 247
Formation of Adverbs 248, 249
    Case forms used as adverbs 248
    Adverbs from nouns, adjectives and verbs 249
Formation of Prepositions, Conjunctions and Interjections
    250, 251
Composition 252

PART IV. — SYNTAX.

Person, Number, Voice, Concord 253–257
    Person, number and voice 253
    Agreement of the appositive 254
    Agreement of the adjective 255
    Agreement of the pronoun 256
    Agreement of the finite verb 257
Use of the Cases 258–308
    Nominative 258–260
    Vocative 261
    Accusative 262–268
    Dative 269–272
    Locative 273, 274
    Genitive 275–291
    Ablative 292–308
Use of the Tenses 309–312
    General use 309
    Perfect definite and indefinite 310
    Primary and secondary tenses 311
    Sequence of tenses 312
Use of the Moods 313–333
    Indicative of statement 313
    Indicative of question 314
    Imperative of command 315
    Subjunctive of doubtful statement 316
    Subjunctive of doubtful question 317
    Subjunctive of doubtful command 318–321

Subjunctive of dependent statement	322
Subjunctive of dependent question	323
Subjunctive of dependent command	324
Subjunctive in purpose clauses	325
Subjunctive in result clauses	326
Subjunctive in conditions impliedly false	327
Subjunctive in causal clauses	328
Subjunctive in concessive clauses	329
Subjunctive in temporal clauses	330
Subjunctive in future conditions	331
Subjunctive in general conditions	332
Subjunctive by attraction	333
Use of the Non-finite Verb-forms	**334–352**
The infinitive	334
Uses of the infinitive	335–342
The participles	343
Uses of the participles	344–346
Peculiar force of the passive participles	347
The gerund	348
The gerundive	349
The supine	350–352

PART V. — THE LAWS OF LATIN VERSE.

Quantity	**353–397**
Latin versification	353
General rules of quantity	354
Special rules of quantity	355
Tendencies affecting quantity	356–363
Quantity of stem-vowels and suffixes of nouns	364–373
Quantity of stem-vowels and suffixes of pronouns	374–379
Quantity of nominative singular of consonant-stems	380–384
Quantity of verb-forms	385–394
Quantity of uninflected monosyllables	395
Quantity of uninflected polysyllables	396, 397
Versification	**398–421**
Long and short syllables	398
Feet	399
Fundamental feet	400–404

Substitute feet	405
Dipodies	406
Verses and their names	407, 408
Most common kinds of verse	409
Dactylic hexameter	410, 411
Dactylic pentameter	412, 413
Iambic and trochaic verse	414–416
Laws of the structure of Latin verse	417–421

Supplement to Syntax

A. Negative particles	422–425
B. Interrogative particles	426–434
C. Use of the pronouns	435–445
D. Forms of conditional sentences	446–456
E. Reported speech	457–478
F. Order of words and clauses	479–486
G. Dates	487–497

Appendix.— List of Verbs	**498**
Index of Topics	**499**
Index of Words	**500**

ESSENTIALS OF LATIN GRAMMAR.

PART I.—SOUNDS.

1. Alphabet and Pronunciation.

The Latin alphabet has no **w**; otherwise it is like the English. | **1**

The vowels are **a, e, i, o, u.** They are sounded, when long, like the same vowels in the English words, *father, they, pique, ore, rude.* When short, they have the same sound, but more shortly uttered; nearly like the same vowels in *half, them, pick, obey, full.* | **2**

---

[1] K is found in Old Latin, but is rare in the later language, being replaced by c. Q is used for c before v. I was used for both **i** and **j**, and u for both **u** and **v**; but they are often distinguished in modern print, except that u is used for v after q, g, and s. (For the sake of exactness, they are distinguished in this book, j and v being always consonants, i and u vowels.)

Y and z are, strictly speaking, not Latin letters, but were borrowed from the Greek. They are found only in Greek words.

[2] Long vowels are marked ā, ē, ī, ō, ū; short, ă, ĕ, ĭ, ŏ, ŭ. Sometimes in manuscripts and inscriptions long vowels are indicated by writing them double. For long **i**, ei is written in such cases (not ii).

EUPHONIC CHANGES OF VOWELS.

(*a*) Before final consonants, except s, long vowels are often shortened.

(*b*) Before ns and nf short vowels are lengthened.

(*c*) The short vowels are often "weakened," sometimes from a shifting of the accent, often without any apparent reason. The tendency in vowel-weakening is from "open" to "close." (See 3.) Thus a weakens to o and u, or to e and i; o weakens to u, e to i. Less often o weakens to e, u to i.

(*d*) The same weakening sometimes takes place in long vowels and diphthongs, but rarely.

(*e*) This tendency is checked and modified by various causes, a common one being the character of the following sound. Thus the open vowels (see 3) are favorites before two consonants, the close ones before single mutes; the open vowels before liquids and spirants, the close ones before nasals and s.

PART I.—SOUNDS.

3 A, e, o, are *open* vowels; i, u, *close* vowels.

4 The diphthongs are made up of an open vowel-sound, followed by a close one. Each sound is uttered, but the two are run into one syllable in pronunciation.

5 The diphthongs are **ae, oe, ei, au, eu.** Ae is sounded like English *ay* (= *yes*); oe like *oi* in *toil;* au like *ou* in *loud;* ei as in *eight;* eu as in *feud.*

6 The consonants are sounded as in English, except that

7   C and g are always "hard," as in *cave, give.*
8   J sounds like *y* in *young.*
9   T sounds like *t* in *tongue.*
10 S sounds like *s* in *sin.*
11 V sounds like *w* in *win.*

[3] So named from the fact that the organs of speech are more open, or less open in uttering them. A is more open than e or o; the latter are, therefore, sometimes called "medial" vowels.

[4] In Old Latin is found the complete schedule of diphthongs, ai, ei, oi, au, eu, ou. In the later language ai becomes ae; ei usually becomes ē or ī; oi becomes oe; ou becomes ū. In some cases this weakening tendency has gone still further, weakening ae and oe also to ē and ū. The simple vowels which thus replace the older diphthongs then become subject to the same weakening tendency as single vowels.

[6] H is sounded as in English, but seems to have originally had a stronger sound, as it stands in place of an older guttural mute. Before s and t it changes or reverts to c.

M and s in Old Latin seem to have been but slightly sounded, and, when final, are often dropped.

Y and z of Greek words are generally sounded as in English, but it is supposed that y had the sound of French u.

The compounds ch, th, ph, are also found in Greek words. It is customary to sound them as in English *chasm, thin, phase,* although it is believed that the Romans sounded them in such a way as to give each letter its own sound; *i.e.*, as c, t, and p, followed by an h-sound.

ALPHABET AND PRONUNCIATION.

The consonants are classified as follows:— **12**

	Mutes.		Semi-vowels.			
	Breathed.	Voiced.	Nasal.	Liquid.	Spirant.	Sibilant.
Guttural . . .	c (k, q)	g	n		h	
Linguo-palatal .					j	
Linguo-dental .	t	d	n	l, r		s
Labio-dental . . .					f	
Labial	p	b	m		v	

X (called a double consonant) is a short way of writing *cs*. **13**

[12] The name "voiced" is given to those sounds, the utterance of which is attended by a vibration of the vocal chords, thus making "voice"; the others, consisting of mere expulsion of breath, are called "breathed." Of the semi-vowels, f and s are breathed; the others are voice-letters, as are also all the vowels. The names "guttural," etc., refer to the organs used in uttering the sounds.

Qv and gv are treated as single consonants by the Latins, like single c and g. In many words the spelling varies between qv and c.

EUPHONIC CHANGES OF CONSONANTS.

(*a*) The sounds of j and v are so much like those of i and u that they are not only represented by the same letters, but, in poetry, are sometimes interchanged. Thus ablete becomes abjete; Gajus becomes Gaius; cui becomes cvi; silvae becomes siluae, etc. V regularly becomes u when brought before a consonant; sometimes qv becomes cu, but usually c.

(*b*) Doubled consonants at the end of a word are not found in Latin, but one is dropped. Often, also, in the middle of a word, one consonant is written where the derivation or formation would require two.

(*c*) Between two vowels s usually changes to r, and h and v are often dropped. J sometimes drops before i, and s sometimes changes to r in other positions than between vowels.

Consonant sounds are often modified when brought together in inflection or word-formation. Usually the preceding sound adapts itself more or less fully to the following. Thus:

(*d*) Before s, t and d become s. [ss thus formed is often changed to s. See (*b*) above.]

2. Quantity and Accent.

A syllable is long

14 (*a*) When it contains a long vowel or a diphthong.
15 (*b*) When its vowel, naturally short, is followed by two consonants.

(*e*) Before a liquid, n is often changed to that liquid.

(*f*) In the prepositions **ab, ad, ob, sub, com, in,** this tendency goes much further, and the final sound of these words is assimilated to various sounds. (Assimilation of a preceding to a following sound also occurs in many other cases, which cannot be enumerated or classified in an elementary work.)

In cases (*d*), (*e*), and (*f*), there is entire assimilation of the preceding sound to the following one. In the following, partial assimilation takes place.

(*g*) Before a breath-consonant, the voice-mutes change to the corresponding breath-mutes. But assimilation often takes place, especially of the final mutes of prepositions, and **dt** and **tt** often change to **st, ss,** or **s. G, h, gv,** and **qv** change to **c** before a following **s,** and make **x,** *i.e.*, **cs. Bs** is generally written, but is always pronounced as **ps.**

(*h*) Before a mute the nasals become of the same character as the mute, **m** before labials, **n** before palatals and dentals. (N has two sounds, as in English; that of a palatal nasal (Eng. *sing*) before palatal mutes, and that of a dental nasal (Eng. *sin*) elsewhere.) M before **s** is changed to **n** or assimilated, but in some cases a parasitical **p** is inserted between **m** and **s**; *e.g.*, **hiemps** (for **hiems**), **sumpsi** (for **sumsi**), etc.

(*i*) In combinations of consonants difficult to utter, one is often dropped.

(The changes given here are not always made in writing, and it is not easy to decide how fully they were made in speaking. Perhaps it would be the wisest course for a beginner to pronounce the words as he finds them written.)

[14] Whether any particular vowel is long or short, must often be learned by consulting a lexicon, but vowels formed by contraction are long.

[15] A mute or **f** followed by **l** or **r** does not make a long syllable, but a common one. See 18. **X** and Greek **z** are two consonants, and **qv, gv** are single consonants. See [12]. To make a long syllable, one of the consonants must be in the same word with the preceding short vowel; a

QUANTITY AND ACCENT.

A syllable is short
  (*a*) When it contains a short vowel. | **16**
  (*b*) When its vowel, naturally long, is followed by another vowel. | **17**

A syllable is common
[*i.e.*, long or short at the option of the writer]
  (*a*) When its vowel, naturally short, is followed by a mute or f with l or r. | **18**

---

final short vowel seldom makes a long syllable with two consonants of the following word. Ch, th, ph also are single consonants in Greek, and do not make a long syllable, though two consonants are used in Latin to represent them.

[17] An interposed h has no effect, and the rule applies to diphthongs as well as to single vowels. But in a few cases a vowel remains long or common, though followed by another vowel; viz.:—

  (*a*) The genitive singular endings, āī, ēī, īus, and the dative singular pronoun ĕī.
  (*b*) The syllable fī in the verb fīo, except before -ĕr.
  (*c*) Proper names in -āīus, -ēīus [poetical forms for -ājus, -ējus. See [12] (*a*)].
  (*d*) ōheu, dīŭs, Dīānă, ŏhe, Rhēa.
  (*e*) Many Greek words, which usually keep their own quantity.

[18] The following combinations occur: pr, br, cr, gr, tr, dr, fr; pl, cl, fl. But both consonants must be in the same word with the preceding vowel; in different words (or in different parts of a compound) they make a long syllable. In Greek words, a mute followed by a nasal may make a short syllable with a preceding short vowel.

(The vowels of 16, 17, and 18 are often called long, short, or common *by position*. The expression, though convenient, is inexact as regards long and common syllables; for the syllable, not the vowel, is long or common. Such vowels should have their short sound; but a *long* vowel before two consonants (*e.g.*, before ns or nf) should, of course, have its long sound. In many cases, however, there is little or no evidence to show the natural quantity of the vowel; but the pupil is more likely to be right in sounding it short.)

19 **20**	The accent in Latin is (*a*) In words of two syllables, on the first syllable. (*b*) In words of more than two syllables, on the *penult*, if that syllable is long; otherwise, on the *antepenult*.

[19] The rules for the accent of Latin words are given by the Latin grammarians, who add also the following statements:—

(*a*) Prepositions, when standing directly before their nouns, or before an adjective or genitive limiting their nouns, have no accent, but are pronounced as one word with the following. In other positions they are accented, with the exception of **cum** when it is attached enclitically to the ablative of pronoun forms.

(*b*) The enclitic particles **-ne, -ve, -ce, -met, -pte, -dum** (also **-qve** when it means *and*, and **cum, inde** and **qvando** when attached to a preceding word) have no accent, but cause the accent to fall on the last syllable of the word to which they are attached; *e.g.*, **itáqve**, *and thus*; **éxinde**, *thenceforth*; **écqvando, manédum**, etc.

(*c*) The accent may stand on the last syllable, or on a short penult, if a syllable has been lost; *e.g.*, **vidén** (for **vidésne**), **illíc** (for **illíce**), **nostrás** (for **nostrátis**), **Vergíl** (for **Vergílí**), etc.

It is customary also, in words of several syllables, to put a secondary accent on the second or third syllable before the accented syllable.

[20] *Penult*, last syllable but one; *antepenult*, last but two.

PART II.—FORMS.

Inflection.

21. Inflection is a change in the form of a word to denote some modification of its meaning or to show its relation to other words. Nouns, adjectives, pronouns and verbs are inflected in Latin.

22. Inflection in Latin, as in English, consists either in a change in the vowel of the word or in the addition of syllables; far more often the latter. Sometimes both methods are used.

23. Nouns have inflections to denote *number* and *case*.

24. Adjectives have inflections to denote *gender*, *number* and *case*.

25. Pronouns, when used substantively, have the inflections of nouns; when used adjectively, those of adjectives.

26. Verbs have inflections to denote *tense*, *mood*, *person*, *number* and *voice*.

Stem and Suffixes; Theme and Endings.

27. Inflection, in Latin, usually consists in adding certain syllables to the ground-form or basis of the inflected word. This ground-form or basis is called a *stem*, and the added syllables are called *suffixes*.

---

[21] *E.g.*, **servus**, slave; **servi**, slave's; **pastor**, shepherd; **pastores**, shepherds; ama-s, love-st; ama-t, love-s; ama-vit, love-d; etc.

The inflection of nouns, adjectives and pronouns is often called *declension*; that of verbs, *conjugation*.

28 When the stem ends in a vowel and the suffix begins with a vowel, the resulting contraction often obscures both stem-ending and suffix. For convenience of memorizing we therefore divide inflected words not only into stem and suffix but also into *theme* and *ending*.

29 The *theme* is that part of the word which remains unchanged in inflection. The *endings* are the letters or syllables added to the theme to make the various forms of the word.

Forms of Nouns and Adjectives.

GENDER.

30 There are three genders: *masculine, feminine, neuter*.

31 Gender, in Latin, is fixed either by the meaning or by the form. When fixed by the meaning, it is called *natural* gender; by the form, *grammatical*.

Rules of natural gender: —

32 (a) { Names of *male* beings
33   { Names of *rivers* and *mountains* } are masculine.

34   { Names of *female* beings
35 (b) { Names of *trees* and *plants*
36   { Names of *countries, towns* and *islands* } are feminine.

37 (c) { Indeclinable nouns
38   { *Phrases* or *clauses* used as nouns } are neuter.

39 (d) { Names that may be used of *either* sex
40   { Some names of *beasts, birds, fishes* and *insects* } are common.

[29] The theme is always the same as the stem with its final vowel removed, and the endings consequently contain the final vowel of the stem and the suffixes, both often obscured by contraction. If the stem ends in a consonant, the stem and theme are the same, and the endings are the simple suffixes.

[31] The rules of grammatical gender will be given with the various declensions.

PERSON, NUMBER, AND CASE.

In *person* and *number* the Latin is like the English.	41
There are five cases in common use; viz.: *nominative, genitive, dative, accusative, ablative.* Two other cases, a *locative* and a *vocative*, are found in a few words.	42
The nominative corresponds to the English nominative, being the case of the subject.	43
The genitive corresponds to the English possessive.	44
The dative corresponds to the English indirect objective.	45
The accusative corresponds to the English direct objective.	46
The vocative corresponds to the English nominative in direct address.	47
The ablative and locative have no corresponding cases in English.	48

[33] **Hadria**, the *Adriatic*, is masculine, like names of rivers.

The gender of *rivers, trees, countries*, etc., is the result of the simplicity of primitive thought and conception, which gave life and feeling to inanimate objects. In many of these, however, the gender is fixed by the form, and they come under the rules of grammatical gender. In most words, also, there is no contradiction of form and meaning.

[37] Strictly speaking, the neuters of 37 and 38 fix their gender neither by meaning nor by form, but they are put here for convenience. Words quoted only for their form, without regard to meaning, come under the head of indeclinable nouns; *e.g.*, **pater dixi**, *I said "pater"*; **pater est dissyllabum**, *"pater" is dissyllabic.*

[39] Common; *i.e.*, sometimes *masculine*, sometimes *feminine*.

[40] But in most of these sex is not thought of, and they are either masculine or take grammatical gender.

Words borrowed from the Greek keep the gender they have in that language.

49 The nominative and vocative are sometimes called *direct* cases, the others *oblique*. The oblique cases are often rendered into English by prepositions. The genitive is most often rendered by *of;* the dative, by *to* or *for;* the locative, by *at* or *in;* the ablative, by *from, by, in* or *with*.

The Declensions.

50 Nouns and adjectives are inflected by adding to the stem the proper case-suffixes. As these suffixes differ in certain cases and are often obscured in form by contraction with the final vowel of the stem, we have six forms of declension, as the stem ends in a consonant or in one of the vowels, a, e, i, o, u.

51 These six forms fall naturally into two groups; viz.:
A. Stems in an open vowel (a, e, o).
B. Stems in a consonant or a close vowel (i, u).

---

[49] The details of the use of the cases must be learned from the Syntax. Only enough is given here to enable the pupil to master elementary exercises.

[51] These groups are distinguished by different case-suffixes in certain cases; most clearly in the genitive, where A has sg. -ī, pl. -rūm; B, sg. -is, pl. -ūm.

Nouns and adjectives are usually classified into declensions according to the ending of the genitive singular; and lexicons give, therefore, not the stem, but the nominative and genitive singular. That the pupil may be able to refer each word to its proper declension, the usual method of classification is here added.

First Declension, gen. sg. ending -ae = a-stems.
Second " " " " -ī = o-stems.
Third " " " " -is = consonant and i-stems.
Fourth " " " " -ūs = u-stems.
Fifth " " " " -ēī = e-stems.

The ending of the genitive singular, therefore, distinguishes all vowel-stems except those in -i. Rules for distinguishing i-stems from consonant-

THE DECLENSIONS.

THE *A*-DECLENSION. STEMS ENDING IN -*A*.

52 The theme of any a-stem may be found by dropping the ending of the genitive singular, -ac. The stem is found by adding a to the theme.

53 The final a of the stem combines with the case-suffixes to make the following case-endings, by adding which to the theme any a-stem may be declined: —

Sg. N. -ă	Pl. N. -ae	E.g., mensă	mensae
G. -ae	G. -ārŭm	mensae	mensārŭm
D. -ae	D. -īs	mensae	mensīs
Ac. -ăm	Ac. -ās	mensăm	mensās
Ab. -ā	Ab. -īs	mensā	mensīs

54

55 The locative singular of a-stems has the ending -ac.

56 The gender of a-stems is feminine.

stems, by the forms of the nominative and genitive singular, will be found under the I-declension.

[54] The uncontracted ending -āī is sometimes found in the genitive singular; also -um for ārŭm in the genitive plural.

Familia, in combination with pater, mater, filius, or filia, sometimes has the ending -ās in the genitive singular. The same ending is found in a few other words in old Latin.

Dea and **filia** usually form the dative and ablative plural with the ending -ābŭs; a few others rarely.

In poetry, words borrowed from the Greek often keep Greek endings in the singular. The following are found: nom. -ē, -ās, -ēs; gen. -ēs; acc. -ān, -ēn; abl. -ē. But the regular Latin endings are common.

Various old endings are found in inscriptions and old Latin; viz.: gen. sg. -aes; dat. sg. -ai (diphthong?); abl. sg. -ād (the original abl. ending); nom. pl. -as; dat. and abl. pl. -eis (another spelling of -is. See [2]). In a few instances stems in -ia contract -iis in the dat. and abl. pl. to -īs.

[56] The rules of grammatical gender given with the declensions apply only to such nouns as do not come under the rules of natural gender, 32–40.

THE E-DECLENSION. STEMS IN -E.

57 The theme of any e-stem may be found by dropping the genitive singular ending, -ēī. The stem is found by adding e to the theme.

The case-endings are: —

58

	Sg.		Pl.		E.g.,		
	N. -ēs		N. -ēs		di ēs	di ēs
	G. -ēī		G. -ērŭm		di ēī	di ērŭm
	D. -ēī		D. -ēbŭs		di ēī	di ēbŭs
	Ac. -ĕm		Ac. -ēs		di ĕm	di ēs
	Ab. -ē		Ab. -ēbŭs		di ē	di ēbŭs

59 Stems in -e are feminine,

60 But **dies** is usually masc.; **meridies**, always so.

THE O-DECLENSION. STEMS IN -O.

61 The theme of any o-stem may be found by dropping the genitive singular ending, -ī. The stem is found by adding o to the theme.

The case-endings are: —

FOR MASCULINES.

62

	Sg.		Pl.		E.g.,		
	N. -ŭs		N. -ī		hort ŭs	hort ī
	G. -ī		G. -ōrŭm		hort ī	hort ōrŭm
	D. -ō		D. -īs		hort ō	hort īs
	Ac. -ŭm		Ac. -ōs		hort ŭm	hort ōs
	Ab. -ō		Ab. -īs		hort ō	hort īs

---

[58] The ending of the genitive and dative singular is commonly -ĕi when the theme ends in a consonant; viz.: in **fides, plebes, res, spes**.

Old or unusual endings are found; viz.: gen. sg. -ēs, -ē, -ī; dat. sg. -ē, -ī. Stems in -e lack the plural except **dies** and **res**, and a few found in the nom. and acc. pl.; viz.: **acies, effigies, facies, series, species, spes**; with **eluvies** (nom.) and **glacies** (acc.). Other forms are cited by grammarians, but not found in literature.

A locative **diē** is found in old Latin, and in certain (so-called) adverbs of time: **postridiē, pridiē,** etc.

THE DECLENSIONS.

				FOR NEUTERS.		
Sg. N.	-ŭm	Pl. N.	-ă	E.g., dōn ŭm	don ă	
G.	-ī	G.	-ōrŭm	don ī	don ōrŭm	
D.	-ō	D.	-īs	don ō	don īs	63
Ac.	-ŭm	Ac.	-ă	don ŭm	don ă	
Ab.	-ō	Ab.	-īs	don ō	don īs	

Masculine o-stems have a vocative singular with the ending -ĕ. | 64

The locative singular of o-stems has the ending -ī. | 65

Most masculine stems in -ĕro drop the endings of the nominative and vocative singular, and many of them syncopate ĕ in all the other cases. | 66

Stems in -io contract -iĕ of the vocative singular to ī, often also -iī of the genitive singular to ī. | 67

Deus has no vocative singular. In the plural, | 68

---

[62] The older endings -ŏs, -ŏm, are sometimes found for -ŭs, -ŭm, especially after v; also -um (or, after v, -om) for -ōrum.
Old endings, found in inscriptions, etc., are gen. sg. -oe (¹), -ei (see [2]); dat. sg. -oi; abl. sg. -ōd; nom. pl. -ēs, -ē, -oe; also -ei (see [2]); dat. and abl. pl. -oes, -ōbus (in duo and ambo, see [72]).
Nouns borrowed from the Greek sometimes keep Greek endings. The following are found: nom. sg. masc. -ŏs; neut. -ŏn; gen. sg. -ū; acc. sg. -ŏn, -ō; nom. pl. masc. -oe; gen. pl. -ōn. Many Greek words are confused in their forms, taking, in certain authors, or in certain cases, the endings of o-stems; at other times, or in other cases, the endings of consonant-stems.

[66] Thus (from the stem puĕro) puer, puĕri, puĕro, etc.; (from the stem agĕro) ager, agri, agro, etc. Vir (stem vĭro) drops the nom. and voc. sg. endings. In old Latin, however, these endings are sometimes kept.

[67] The voc. sg. of Tullius, for example, is Tulli. The accent in these shortened forms remains unchanged; e.g., Domĭti (gen. or voc.); Impĕri (gen.). See [19], (c). Other cases of stems in -io sometimes contract ii to ī. Stems in -ājo, -ējo, when j changes to i [see [12] (a)], suffer a similar contraction.

[68] Some editors print dii and diis also.

PART II.—FORMS.

	besides the regular forms, it has also nominative **dī**, dative and ablative **dīs**.
69	Stems in -o with nominative singular ending -ŭm are neuter; others are masculine.

ADJECTIVE-STEMS IN -A AND -O.

70	Adjective-stems in -a and -o are declined like noun-stems of like form. (The feminine is an a-stem; the masculine and neuter, o-stems.)
71	A few adjectives have in all genders **-īŭs** for genitive singular ending, and **-ī** for dative singular.
72	**Duo** and **ambo** have special irregularities.

[69] But **carbăsus, humus,** and **vannus** are feminine; **alvus** and **colus** usually so. **Domus** (see [115]) is feminine.
For **pelăgus, virus, vulgus,** neuter, see [115].

[70] Adjective stems in -lo are regular, and are not shortened in the genitive and vocative singular.

[71] Viz., **alius, nullus, solus, totus, ullus, unus, alter, uter,** neuter. In poetry **-ĭus** is found, and, rarely, the regular endings.
Alius has an ending **-ŭd** for **-ŭm** in the neut. sg. nom. and acc., and contracts **-ilus** of the gen. sg. to **-īŭs**. (An older stem **ali** is found in compounds and derivatives, and in the rare forms of the nom. sg. **alis, alid.** See under the I-declension, 94 ff.)
Satur drops the nom. sg. masc. ending (like stems in **-ěro**).

EXAMPLES FOR PRACTICE.

altŭs	altă	altŭm	totŭs	totă	totŭm
altī	altae	altī	totīus	totīus	totīus
altō	altae	altō	totī	totī	totī
altŭm	altăm	altŭm	totŭm	totăm	totŭm
etc.	etc.	etc.	etc.	etc.	etc.
tenĕr	tenĕră	tenĕrŭm	altĕr	altĕră	altĕrŭm
tenĕrī	tenĕrae	tenĕrī	alterīus	alterīus	alterīus
tenĕrō	tenĕrae	tenĕrō	altĕrī	altĕrī	altĕrī
etc.	etc.	etc.	etc.	etc.	etc.

THE DECLENSIONS.

THE CONSONANT-DECLENSION. STEMS IN A CONSONANT.

The theme of any consonant-stem may be found by dropping the genitive singular ending, -ĭs. The stem is the same as the theme.

The case-endings are: —

FOR MASCULINES AND FEMININES.

Sg. N. -s	Pl. N. -ēs	E.g., dux (= duc s)	duc ēs	
G. -ĭs	G. -ŭm	dŭc ĭs	duc ŭm	
D. -ī	D. -ĭbŭs	duc ī	duc ĭbŭs	**74**
Ac. -ĕm	Ac. -ēs	duc ĕm	duc ēs	
Ab. -ĕ	Ab. -ĭbŭs	duc ĕ	duc ĭbŭs	

FOR NEUTERS.

Sg. N. —	Pl. N. -ă	E.g., căpŭt	capĭt ă	
G. -ĭs	G. -ŭm	capĭt ĭs	capĭt ŭm	
D. -ī	D. -ĭbŭs	capĭt ī	capĭt ĭbŭs	**75**
Ac. —	Ac. -ă	căpŭt	capĭt ă	
Ab. -ĕ	Ab. -ĭbŭs	capĭt ĕ	capĭt ĭbŭs	

ātĕr	ātră	ātrŭm	ŭtĕr	ŭtră	ŭtrŭm
atrī	atrae	atrī	utrīŭs	utrīŭs	utrīŭs
atrō	atrae	atrō	utrī	utrī	utrī
etc.	etc.	etc.	etc.	etc.	etc.

[72]
duŏ	duae	duŏ			
duōrum	duārum	duōrum	ambŏ	ambae	ambŏ
duōbŭs	duābŭs	duōbŭs	ambōrŭm	ambārŭm	ambōrŭm
duōs, duŏ	duās	duŏ	etc.	etc.	etc.
duōbŭs	duābŭs	duōbŭs			

[74]   **EXAMPLES FOR PRACTICE.**

[(m), (f), (n), and (c) show the gender.]

princeps (c)	consŭl (m)	hiems (f) [78]	gĕnŭs (n)	mĕl (n) [12] (b)
princĭpĭs	consŭlĭs	hiĕmĭs	gĕnĕrĭs	mellĭs
princĭpī	consŭlī	hiĕmī	gĕnĕrī	mellī
etc.	etc.	etc.	etc.	etc.
mīlĕs (m)	actŏr (m)	leō (m) 79	corpŭs (n)	făr (n) [12] (b)
mīlĭtĭs	actōrĭs	leōnĭs	corpŏrĭs	farrĭs
etc.	etc.	etc.	etc.	etc.

76	The last vowel of the nominative singular is often weakened in other cases when a syllable is added. See [2] (c). But in s-stems the stronger vowel is retained before r, though weakened before s in the nominative singular.
77	The locative singular of consonant-stems ends in -ī.
78	Masculine and feminine semivowel-stems drop the ending of the nominative singular.
79	Final n of a stem falls after o in the nominative singular.

pĕcŭs (*f*)	ĕbŭr (*n*)	hŏmō (*c*) 79	mōs (*m*)
pecŭdĭs	ebŏrĭs	homĭnĭs	mōrĭs
etc.	etc.	etc.	etc.
sĭlex (*c*)	aggĕr (*m*)	nōmĕn (*n*)	tellūs (*f*)
silĭcĭs	aggĕrĭs	nomĭnĭs	tellūrĭs
etc.	etc.	etc.	etc.
rex (*m*)	pătĕr (*m*) 80	cărō (*f*) [115]	aequŏr (*n*)
rēgĭs	patrĭs	carnĭs	aequŏrĭs
etc.	etc.	etc.	etc.

In Greek words the Greek endings are sometimes kept. The following are found; viz.: gen. sg. -ŏs; dat. sg. -ī; acc. sg. -ă; nom. pl. -ĕs; gen. pl. -ōn; dat. pl. -sī; acc. pl. -ăs; nom. and acc. pl. neut. -ē (contracted from -ĕă). Greek stems in -ăt sometimes take a dat. and abl. pl. ending -ĭs like o-stems, though this is not a Greek ending in consonant-stems. See [62].

Old case-endings of consonant-stems are gen. sg. -us, -es; dat. sg. -e; abl. sg. -ed, -id, -i; dat. and abl. pl. -ebus.

[76] S-stems (except vas, see [115]) regularly become r-stems when a case-suffix is added. See [12] (c). Sometimes the final s of the nom. and acc. sg. becomes r, thus making them r-stems throughout. This change seems to have taken place in jecur and robur, which show the weaker vowel in the nominative, though the stronger ŏ appears in the other cases; and perhaps ebur and femur, which show the same peculiarity, may be explained in the same way.

[78] Except hiem (the only stem in -m), nom. hiems [or hiemps. See [12] (h)].

[79] Not always, however, in nouns borrowed from the Greek.

THE DECLENSIONS.

80 A few stems in -ĕr syncopate ĕ, except in the nominative singular. (Compare stems in -ĕro, 66.)

81 A few cases occur where consonant-stems take the endings of i-stems. Such forms are irregular, a result of the confusion caused by the close likeness of the two declensions.

82 Most mute-stems are feminine,

83 But { stems in -ĭc with nom. in -ex } are masculine.
           {   "   -ĭt   "   "   -ĕs }

84 Stems in -ōn are masculine,

85 But abstracts in -iōn are feminine.

86 Stems in -ĭn with nominative in -o are feminine.

87 Stems in -ĭn with nominative in -ĕn are neuter.

88 Stems in -l are masculine.

89 Stems in -r and -s are neuter,

90 But stems in -ōr and -ōs are masculine.

---

[80] Viz.: pater, mater, frater, accipiter.

[81] Viz.: an abl. sg ending -ī, or gen. pl. -ium. The latter is not unusual in stems in -tāt, which seem to have once been i-stems.

The following exceptions to the rules of gender are added for completeness, the more usual words being printed in larger type. **Hiems** (the only stem in -m) is feminine.

[82] **grex, paries, pes,** calix, fornix, are masculine.
    lapis, adeps, forceps, larix, varix, are common.
    caput, cor, are neuter.

[83] **silex, cortex,** forfex, imbrex, obex, rumex, are common.

[86] **ordo, cardo, turbo,** are masculine.
    cupido, margo, are common.

[87] **pecten** is masculine; (sangvis, see [115], is masculine).

[88] **fel** and **mel** are neuter (also sal sometimes in singular).

[89] **agger, carcer,** asser, later, vesper, vomer, are masculine.
    arbos, tellus, are feminine; **cinis, pulvis,** common; **cucŭmis,** masculine.

[90] **os** is neuter.

CONSONANT-STEM ADJECTIVES.

91 Adjectives with consonant-stems are declined like noun-stems of like form, but most of them take -ī as well as -ĕ for the ablative singular ending, — a result of their likeness to i-stems. They comprise: —

92 (*a*) Adjectives in the comparative degree.

93 (*b*) Imparisyllabic adjectives with themes ending in a *short* syllable.

[92] Comparatives are thus declined: —

Sg. M. and F.	N.	Pl. M. and F.	N.	Sg. N.	Pl. M. and F.	N.
altiŏr	altiŭs	altiores	altiora	plūs	plures	plura
altiōris		altiorum		(plūris)	plurium	
altiori		altioribus			pluribus	
altiorem	altius	altiores	altiora	plus	plures	plura
altiore(ī)		altioribus		(plure)	pluribus	

Plus is defective in the sg., and the forms **pluris** and **pluro** are rare. In the gen. pl. it takes the ending -ium of i-stems. Its compound com-**plūres** (only plural) has in old Latin **complur-ia** as well as the regular **complūra**.

[93] Parisyllabic, having the same number of syllables in all cases of the singular. Those a- and o-stem adjectives which have become imparisyllabic by the loss of the nominative singular ending (*i.e.*, stems in ĕro and satur) are, of course, not included.

The adjectives included in (*b*) are few, and their meanings usually cause them to be used only of persons. They have no separate form in the singular for the neuter gender, but when necessary use the masc. and fem. form of the nom. as nom. and acc. neuter sg. They are declined as follows: —

Sg. M. and F.	N.	Pl. M. and F.	N.	Sg. M. and F.	N.	Pl. M. and F.	N.
divĕs		divites	[divita]	pauper		pauperes	paupera
divĭtis		divitum		pauperis		pauperum	
diviti		divitibus		pauperi		pauperibus	
divitem	dives	divites	[divita]	pauperem	pauper	pauperes	paupera
divite		divitibus		paupere		pauperibus	

As exceptions to (*b*), must be set down a few i-stems; viz.: **par** and **celer**, which drop the nom. sg. ending (see [102]); also **hebes, teres,**

THE I-DECLENSION. STEMS IN I.

The theme of any i-stem may be found by dropping the genitive singular ending, -ĭs. The stem is found by adding i to the theme. | 94

The following classes contain all the i-stems in common use; viz.:— | 95

---

praecox, and compounds of -plex (except supplex). See [108]. A few adjective compounds of noun-stems have themes ending in a *long* syllable, but are declined, of course, like the nouns from which they are made; *e.g.*, discŏlor, discolōrĭs, etc. Only a few forms of such are found, and it has not seemed necessary to add a third class to contain them.

[94] I-stems have become much confused with consonant-stems through their close likeness in declension, and have been changed into consonant-stems in certain cases by the loss of i. They cannot, therefore, be distinguished by the ending of the gen. sg. as other vowel-stems can, since the i is always lost in that case.

A comparison of i-stem nouns with more primitive forms in Latin or kindred languages, shows that the i has arisen in many cases from an older a, e, o, or u, by weakening. Some i-stems show the older e in certain cases. In other words, the i is not found in kindred words in other languages, and seems to be added in Latin.

The i is kept or lost as follows:—

In Class I., kept in nom. sg. (sometimes as e); also in some words in acc. and abl. sg.; lost in gen. sg., and usually in abl. sg. The form of the dat. sg. would be the same whether i be kept or lost, and the acc. sg. ending -em may be considered an older form for -ĭm (like -ēs for -ĭs in the nom. sg.), or a consonant-stem ending after i is lost.

In Class II., kept in the abl. sg.; also in a few words (as e) in the nom. and acc. sg.; lost in gen. sg., usually in nom. and acc. sg. The dative may be either, as in Class I.

In Class III., lost throughout the singular.

In the plural of all three classes, i may be kept throughout; but it is usually lost in the nom. and often in the acc. of masc. and fem. nouns.

Occasionally, however, i is kept in cases where it is usually lost, or lost in cases where it is usually kept. This occurs more often in poetry for metrical convenience.

PART II.—FORMS.

96 I. Parisyllabic nouns in -es and -is.
97 II. Neuters in -e, and neuters with themes in -āl or -ār.
98 III. Nouns with themes ending in an impure mute. These, however, are i-stems only in the plural, having lost i in the singular.
99 The case-endings of i-stems of Class I. (masculine and feminine) are:—

	Sg. N.	-ēs	-ĭs	*Pl.* N.	-ēs (-īs)
	G.	-ĭs	-ĭs	G.	-ĭŭm
	D.	-ī	-ī	D.	-ĭbŭs
	Ac.	-ĕm	-ĭm, -ĕm	Ac.	-īs, -ēs
	Ab.	-ĕ	-ī, -ĕ	Ab.	-ĭbŭs
E.g.,	N.	nūbēs	nubēs	turrīs	turrēs
	G.	nubĭs	nubĭŭm	turrĭs	turrĭŭm
	D.	nubī	nubĭbŭs	turrī	turrĭbŭs
	Ac.	nubĕm	nubīs (ēs)	turrĭm (ĕm)	turrīs (ēs)
	Ab.	nubĕ	nubĭbŭs	turrī (ĕ)	turrĭbŭs

[96] Of Class I., canis and juvĕnis lose i and become consonant-stems in the plural; sedes and vates usually; occasionally, also, a few others.

[98] Impure mute; *i.e.*, a mute preceded by a consonant. Of course nouns of this kind are not included if the gen. sg. ending shows them to be a-, o-, or u-stems.

Cor, though an i-stem in compounds, loses i in the plural also, and becomes a consonant-stem throughout. Many other monosyllables, especially those with a long stem-syllable, give evidence of having once been i-stems, and though the i is usually lost, it sometimes appears, especially in the abl. sg. or gen. pl. The Latin writers and grammarians were evidently uncertain as to the proper form in these words. All such words are put by the classification here given in the consonant declension, where the preponderance of evidence places them; but a list is subjoined, containing those words in which a pupil may occasionally meet with i-stem forms; viz.:—

cos, dos, faex, fraus, glis, lis, lux, mas, mus, pax.

as, nix, plebs, scrobs, trabs, have a greater claim to be classed as i-stems; the older forms, assis, ningvis, plebes, scrobis, trabes, show that they once belonged to Class I.

THE DECLENSIONS.

The case-endings of i-stems of Class II. (neut.) are: **100**

	Sg. N.	-ĕ or —	Pl. N.	-iă
	G.	-ĭs	G.	-iŭm
	D.	-ī	D.	-ĭbŭs
	Ac.	-ĕ or —	Ac.	-iă
	Ab.	-ī (ĕ)	Ab.	-ĭbŭs

E.g.,	N.	măr ĕ	mariă	ănĭmăl	anĭmăliă
	G.	marĭs	mariŭm	anĭmălĭs	anĭmăliŭm
	D.	marī	marĭbŭs	anĭmălī	anĭmălĭbŭs
	Ac.	marĕ	mariă	anĭmăl	anĭmăliă
	Ab.	marī ·	marĭbŭs	anĭmălī	anĭmălĭbŭs

I-stems of Class III. have in the plural the same **101**
endings as those of Classes I. and II., but the endings
of consonant-stems in the singular. (See 74 and 75.)

[99] As acc. sg. ending, -ĭm is found in
  Arārĭm, Lĭgĕrĭm, puppĭm, sĭtĭm, Tĭbĕrĭm, vĭm,
  amussim, burim, cucŭmim, praesēpim (?), ravim, tussim.
As acc. sg. ending, both -ĭm and -ĕm are found in
  febrĭm, messĭm, navĭm, turrĭm (or febrem, etc.).
  cravim, cratim, lentim, pelvim, restim, sementim, secūrim (or
  cravem, etc.).
As abl. sg. ending, -ī is found in
  sĭtī, vī.
  Aprīli, cucŭmi, Qvintīli, ravi, rumi, secūri, Sextīli, tussi.
As abl. sg. ending, both -ī and -ĕ are found in
  aedīlĭ, amnĭ, angui, Arārĭ, avĭ, civĭ, classĭ, collĭ, febrĭ,
  fĭnĭ, ignĭ, imbrĭ, Lĭgĕrĭ, navĭ, orbĭ, puppĭ, turrĭ (or
  aidīle, amne, etc.).
  axi, corbi, fusti, pelvi, posti, sodāli, strigĭli, ungvi (or
  axe, etc.).
The nom. pl. ending -is (or -eis, see [2]) is rare; in the acc. pl., modern
editions usually give one ending in all words to the exclusion of the other.
Which one is given is a matter of indifference as a question of grammar.

[100] The abl. sg. ending -ĕ is rare, except in names of towns.

[101] In Class III., only **partĭm** shows the i kept in the acc. sg., and
partĭ, lactĭ, sortĭ, in the abl. sg. As an adverb, the form **partĭm** is

102	A few stems in -ĕri drop the ending of the nominative singular, and syncopate ĕ in all other cases. (Compare stems in -ĕro, 66, and -ĕr, 80.)
103	I-stems of Class I. with themes in n or s are masculine; other i-stems of Class I. are feminine.
104	I-stems of Class II. are neuter.
105	In Class III. polysyllables are masculine; monosyllables are feminine.

ADJECTIVES WITH STEMS IN *I*.

106	Adjectives with i-stems are declined like noun-stems of like form, but those of Class I. have only -ī, the regular ending, in the ablative singular; those of Class III. have both -ī and -ĕ.

common; the other forms are very rare, the I being regularly lost in the singular of Class III.

[102] Viz.: imber, linter, uter, venter, and a few adjectives in the masculine. Arar, Liger, and the adjective par drop the nom. sg. ending (also celer in the masculine), but do not syncopate.

[103] The exceptions in Class I. are:—
(Theme in a mute)   orbis; fascis, unguis; antes, fustis, postis, sentis, vectis; *masculine*.
  corbis, scrobis, torqvis; *common*.
(Theme in a liquid) collis, imber; caulis, follis, buris, torris, uter, venter; *masculine*.
  callis, linter; *common*.
(Theme in a nasal) finis, clunis; *common*; cucumis, *masculine*.
(Theme in -s)   classis, messis, tussis; *feminine*.

[105] The exceptions in Class III. are:—
  dens, fons, mons, pons; *masculine*; cohors, *feminine*; lac, *neuter*.

[106] Adjective-stems in -ĕri (except celer) generally syncopate ĕ in all forms, except in the nom. sg. masc., and drop the ending of that case, thus gaining different forms for masc. and fem. nom. sg. This differen-

THE DECLENSIONS.   23

To Classes I. and II. belong Parisyllabic adjectives in -ĭs (M. and F.), -ĕ (N.).	107

To Class III. belong
   Imparisyllabic adjectives, with themes ending in
   a *long* syllable.
	108

tiation of form is not strictly observed, however; acer, for example, is *fem.* as well as *masc.* in old Latin, and acris *masc.* as well as *fem.*

There is, in general, a stronger tendency toward i-stem forms in the adjective than in the noun. This is shown not only in i-stem adjectives, which retain the ĭ more often than nouns, but also in consonant-stem adjectives, which often take ī as the ending of the abl. sg. In spite of this tendency, however, the acc. sg. of adjectives has regularly the consonant-stem ending -ĕm.

[108] To Class III. belong also the numeral multiplicatives in -plex (*e.g.*, duplex, *two-fold*; qvintŭplex, *five-fold*; etc.), and the adjectives hebes, teres, par, praecox. See [93]. The comparative plus is peculiar. See [92].

Adjectives of Class III. have no separate form for the neuter singular, but use the nom. masc. as nom. and acc. sg. neut. To this class belong tribal names in -ātes and -ītes, and a few other words of like formation, generally found only in the plural, and used substantively (*e.g.*, Arpinātes, optimātes, etc.), and verbal derivatives in -trix (commonly used as feminine nouns of agency) when used as adjectives (*e.g.*, victrix).

Adjectives with i-stems are declined as follows: —

M. and F.	N.	M.	F.	N.	M. and F.	N.	M. and F.	N.
lĕvĭs	lĕvĕ	ācĕr	ācrĭs	ācrĕ	pār		āmans	
levĭs		ācris	acris	acris	părĭs		amantis	
levī		acri	acri	acri	pari		amanti	
levĕm	levĕ	acrem	acrem	acre	parem	par	amantem	amans
levī		etc.	etc.	etc.		pari(e)		amante(i)
levēs	leviă	cĕlĕr	cĕlĕrĭs	cĕlĕrĕ	pares	paria	amantes	amantia
levium		celĕrĭs	celeris	celeris		parium		amantium
levĭbŭs		celeri	celeri	celeri		paribus		amantibus
levīs(ēs) leviă		celerem celerem celere			parīs(es) paria		amantes(īs) amantia	
levĭbŭs		etc.	etc.	etc.		paribus		amantibus

A few compounds of consonant noun-stems have themes ending in a long syllable, but are consonant-stems of course, and may be regarded as exceptions. See [93]. Adjectives in the comparative degree are also consonant-stems. See [92] and [93].

THE *U*-DECLENSION.   STEMS IN -*U*.

109 The theme of any u-stem may be found by dropping the genitive singular ending, -ŭs. The stem is found by adding -u to the theme.

The case-endings are: —

FOR MASCULINES.

110

	Sg.		Pl.			
N.	-ŭs	N.	-ūs	E.g.,	currŭs	currūs
G.	-ūs	G.	-uŭm		currūs	curruŭm
D.	-uī (ū)	D.	-ŭbŭs, ĭbŭs		curruī	currĭbŭs
Ac.	-ŭm	Ac.	-ūs		currŭm	currūs
Ab.	-ū	Ab.	-ŭbŭs, ĭbŭs		currū	currĭbŭs

FOR NEUTERS.

111

	Sg.		Pl.			
N.	-ū	N.	-uă	E.g.,	cornū	cornuă
G.	-ūs	G.	-uŭm		cornūs	cornuŭm
D.	-ū	D.	-ŭbŭs, -ĭbŭs		cornū	cornĭbŭs
Ac.	-ū	Ac.	-uă		cornū	cornuă
Ab.	-ū	Ab.	-ŭbŭs, -ĭbŭs		cornū	cornĭbŭs

[110] The gen. sg. sometimes has the uncontracted ending -uĭs, the gen. pl. (rarely) the contracted ending -um.

The contracted ending -ū of the dat. sg. is regular in neuters; rare in masculines.

The fuller ending -ŭbŭs of the dat. and abl. pl. is found in **acus, arcus, partus, tribus**; usually in **artus, lacus, specus**; sometimes in **portus, veru**.

An ending -ĭ occurs a few times in the gen. sg., apparently from confusion with o-stems from the same root. O-stem forms occur occasionally in other cases also, and many names of plants and trees are confused in their inflection, having both o-stem and u-stem forms.

Old forms in inscriptions, etc., show the ending of gen. sg. -uos. For -ū and -ūs, -uu and -uus are sometimes written to show the length of the ū. See [2].

A locative **domuī** occurs rarely; no other u-stems form a locative.

IRREGULAR DECLENSION.

Monosyllabic stems in -u retain the suffixes uncontracted with the stem-vowel, and are therefore declined like consonant-stems.	112
U-stems with nominative singular ending -ŭs are masculine; the others are neuter.	113

Irregular Declension.

Nouns and adjectives are irregular in declension —	
(a) From the retention of old endings.	114
(b) From variation of the stem.	115

[112] Viz.: **grūs, sūs,** and **lues** (when it drops i); with the irregular stems **bū, Jū.** But **sūs** has **sūbus** and **sŭbus** as well as **suibus.**

The stems **bū** and **Jū** stand for the older diphthongal stems, **bou-, Jou-.** The diphthong changes u to v before a vowel (see [12] (a)), and passes into ō or ū before a consonant. The forms are: —

bōs	bŏves	Jūpĭter (Juppiter)
bŏvis	bŏvum, boum (see [12] (c))	Jŏvis
bŏvī	bōbus, būbus	Jŏvī
bŏvem	bŏves	Jŏvem
bŏve	bōbus, būbus	Jŏve

The nom. **Jupiter** (old form **Jupater**) is a compound of **pater.** Sometimes the second part is declined **Jupitĕris,** etc.

[113] **Domus, idus, manus, tribus,** colus, qvinqvātrus, and portĭcus are feminine.

Acus, arcus, penus, and specus are common.

[114] The irregularities under (a) have been already mentioned with the endings of the various declensions.

[115] The following are irregular from variation of stem : —

balneum (st. **balneo-**); pl. usually **balneae,** etc. (st. **balnea-**).
caro (st. **carŏn-**); all other cases from a syncopated stem **carn-** (**carnĭs, carnī,** etc.).
domus (st. **domu-**); a stem **domo-** is found also in all cases except the nom., dat., and abl. pl., and is more common in the loc. and abl. sg., where the u-stem forms are old.
epŭlum (st. **epŭlo-**); pl. **epulae,** etc. (st. **epula-**).

116	(*c*) From variation of gender.
117	(*d*) From lack of certain cases.

fames   (st. fame-); but gen. sg. usually famis (st. fam-).
femur   (st. femŏr-); except in nom. and acc. sg., a stem femĭn- is equally common.
iter   (st. itĕr-); except in nom. and acc. sg., a stem itinĕr- is used.
jugĕrum   (st. jugĕro-); pl. jugĕra, etc. (st. jugĕr-).
jecur   (st. jecŏr-); except in nom. and acc. sg., a stem jocinĕr- or jocinŏr- is equally common.
pelăgus   (st. pelăgus-); only nom. and acc. sg. and nom. and acc. pl. in Greek form pelăgē (contracted from pelageă); other cases from a stem pelăgo-.
sangvis   (st. sangvi-); only nom. sg. Other forms from a stem sangvĭn-.
senex   (st. senec-); only nom. sg. Other forms from a stem sen-.
supellex   (st. supellect-); only nom. sg. Other forms from a stem supellectĭli-.
virus   (st. virus-); only nom. and acc. sg. Other forms from a stem viro-.
vas   (st. vas-); pl. vasa, etc. (st. vaso-). In this noun *s* does not suffer the usual change to **r**.
vesper   (st. vespĕro-); but abl. sg. vespĕre (st. vespĕr-).
vulgus   (st. vulgus-); only nom. and acc. sg. All other forms from a masc. stem vulgo-, which is found also in nom. and acc. sg.
vis   (st. vi-); pl. vires, etc. (st. viri-).

The only adjectives irregular from variation of stem (except senex above, which is usually used as a noun) are the adjective compounds of caput, which form the nom. sg. from a syncopated stem; *e.g.*, praeceps (st. praecept-); but other cases from a stem praecipit-; praecipitis, etc.

[116] Nouns in which variation of stem has caused variation of gender are included in [115]. Aside from such, variation of gender causes irregularity of declension in the following:—

caelum   (st. caelo-), neut.; pl. (found only once), caelos, masc.
carbăsus   (st. carbăso-), fem.; pl. neut. carbăsa, etc.
frenum   (st. freno-), neut.; pl. neut. frena, etc., or masc. freni, etc.
jocus   (st. joco-), masc.; pl. neut. joca, etc., or masc. joci, etc.
locus   (st. loco-), masc.; pl. neut. loca, etc., or masc. loci, etc.
rastrum   (st. rastro-), neut.; pl. neut. rastra, etc., or masc. rastri, etc.

[117] Nouns that lack some of their forms are called defective. There are many such in Latin, some of which lack the plural or the singular on account of their meaning; in others, the lack of certain forms seems to be

Numeral Adjectives.

The cardinal numerals, from *one* to *ten*, with centum and mille, are primitive words; the others are formed from these. Unus, duo, tres, and the | **118**

purely accidental. A few neuters have only the nom. and acc. sg., and are called indeclinable.

It has not seemed necessary to add any list of defective nouns. Such a list would be of no practical value to the learner, and would be a very large one if it should contain all the nouns, except those all of whose forms are found in Latin writers. The lexicon must be consulted for such information.

[118] For the declension of **unus**, see 71; of **duo**, [72]. Tres is a regular i-stem. Mille is a regular i-stem, but is indeclinable in the singular. The hundreds are regular a- and o-stems. All cardinals except unus, of course, lack the singular, as do all the distributives. See the list below.

The combination of units, tens and hundreds to form the intermediate numbers is made as in English.

A list of numeral adjectives is added for reference. The corresponding numeral adverbs are also given: —

Cardinals.	Ordinals.	Distributives.	Numeral Advs.
1 unus, -a, -um, one;	primus, -a, -um, *first*;	singŭli, -ae, -a, *one by one;*	semel, *once.*
2 duo, -ae, -o, two;	alter, -a, -um / secundus, -a, -um	bini, -ae, -a, *two by two;*	bis, *twice.*
3 tres, tria	tertius, -a, -um	terni *or* trini, etc.	ter, *thrice.*
4 qvattuor	qvartus, -a, -um	qvaterni	qvater, *four times.*
5 qvinqve	qvintus, etc.	qvini	qvinqviens, etc.
6 sex	sextus	seni	sexiens
7 septem	septĭmus	septeni	septiens
8 octo	octāvus	octoni	octiens
9 novem	nonus	noveni	noviens
10 decem	decĭmus	deni	deciens
11 undĕcim	undecĭmus	undeni	undeciens
12 duodĕcim	duodecĭmus	duodeni	duodeciens
13 tredĕcim	tertius decĭmus	terni deni	terdeciens
14 qvattuordĕcim	qvartus decĭmus	qvaterni deni	qvaterdeciens
15 qvindĕcim	etc.	etc.	qvindeciens
16 sedĕcim			etc.
17 septemdĕcim			
18 octodĕcim			
19 novemdĕcim			

> hundreds except **centum**, are declined; also **mille**, when used as a noun. The other cardinals are indeclinable.

	CARDINALS.	ORDINALS.	DISTRIBUTIVES.	NUMERAL ADVS.
20	viginti	vicensĭmus	vicēni	vicies
21	viginti unus *or* unus et viginti	primus et vicensĭmus *or* unus et vicensĭmus	vicēni singŭli	semel et vicies
22	viginti duo *or* duo et viginti etc.	etc.	vicēni bini etc.	bis et vicies etc.
30	triginta	tricensĭmus	tricēni	tricies
40	qvadraginta	qvadragensĭmus	qvadragēni	qvadragies
50	qvinqvaginta	qvinqvagensĭmus	qvinqvagēni	qvinqvagies
60	sexaginta	sexagensĭmus	sexagēni	sexagies
70	septuaginta	septuagensĭmus	septuagēni	septuagies
80	octoginta	octogensĭmus	octogēni	octogies
90	nonaginta	nonagensĭmus	nonagēni	nonagies
100	centum	centensĭmus	centēni	centies
101	centum et unus	centensĭmus primus	centēni singŭli	centies semel
200	ducenti, -ae, -a	ducentensĭmus	ducēni	ducenties
300	trecenti	trecentensĭmus	trecēni	trecenties
400	qvadringenti	etc.	etc.	etc.
500	qvingenti			
600	sescenti			
700	septingenti			
800	octingenti			
900	nongenti			
1000	mille			
2000	duo millia			
3000	tria millia etc.			

For 18, 19, 28, 29, etc., *substractive* forms (**duodeviginti, undetriginta,** etc.) are more common than the regular forms. So also, **duodevicensĭmus, duodevicēni,** etc.

In the later language, the endings -ensĭmus and -iens drop n and become -ēsĭmus, -iēs.

The distributives, besides their regular meaning, *two by two, in twos,* etc., are also used with nouns plural in form but singular in meaning. Thus **castra,** *forts,* is the Latin word for a *camp.* **Bina castra** means *two camps* (lit. *forts by twos, two sets of forts*). They are also used in expressing multiplication; *e.g.,* **bis dena viginti sunt,** *twice ten is twenty.*

Comparison of Adjectives.

119 The stem of the comparative degree is formed by adding **-ios** to the theme of the positive. This suffix becomes **-iŭs** in the nominative and accusative singular neuter; **-iōr** elsewhere. (For the declension of the comparative, see [92].)

120 The stem of the superlative is formed by adding **-issĭmo-, -issĭma-** to the theme of the positive.

121 Stems in **-ĕr-, -ĕro-, -ĕri-,** add **-rĭmo-** to the theme for the superlative, and a few in **-ĭli-** add **-lĭmo-**.

122 Compounds of **-dĭcus, -fĭcus,** and **-vŏlus** add the suffixes of comparison to a theme in **-dĭcent-, -fĭcent-, -vŏlent-.**

123 Many adjectives are not compared. If a comparative or superlative of such is needed, it is formed by prefixing **magis** (*more*); **maxĭme** (*most*).

---

[119] Comparison is not inflection, but derivation; but is placed here for convenience.

[121] These stems, if syncopated in the positive, are also syncopated in the comparative, but not in the superlative. **Matūrus** sometimes adds **-rĭmo-** for the superlative.

Those which add **-lĭmo-** are **facĭlis, difficĭlis, simĭlis, dissimĭlis, gracĭlis, humĭlis.**

[122] The themes in **-nt** are participles in formation.

[123] The following have special irregularities:—

bonus	melior	optĭmus	infĕrus	inferior	infĭmus, imus
malus	pejor	pessĭmus	postĕrus	posterior	postrēmus, postŭmus
magnus	major	maxĭmus	supĕrus	superior	suprēmus, summus
multus	plus (neut.)	plurĭmus		citerior	citĭmus
parvus	minor	minĭmus		interior	intĭmus
senex	senior			prior	prīmus
juvĕnis	junior			propior	proxĭmus
extĕrus	exterior	extrēmus, or extĭmus	vetus	ulterior	ultĭmus veterrĭmus

Many adjectives lack the comparative or superlative. The lacking superlative of **senex** is supplied by the phrase **maxĭmus natu**; that of **juvĕnis** by **minĭmus natu.**

Forms of Pronouns.

124 The personal pronouns are ĕgo, tu, sui. They are peculiar in declension, partly from variation of stem, partly from the retention of older endings lost in the ordinary noun-declension.

They are thus declined: —

EGO (St. egon-, me-, nō-).

	Sg.		Pl.
N.	ĕgŏ		nōs
G.	(meī)		(nostrŭm, nostrī)
D.	mihĭ, mī		nōbĭs
Ac.	mē		nōs
Ab.	mē		nōbĭs

125

TU (St. te-, vō-).

	Sg.	Pl.
N.	tū	vōs
G.	(tuī)	(vestrŭm, vestrī)
D.	tĭbĭ	vōbĭs
Ac.	tē	vōs
Ab.	tē	vōbĭs

SUI (St. se-).

	Sg.	Pl.
G.	(suī)	(suī)
D.	sĭbĭ	sĭbĭ
Ac.	sē, sĕsē	sē, sĕsē
Ab.	sē, sĕsē	sē, sĕsē

126 The possessive pronouns meŭs, tuŭs, suŭs, nostĕr, vestĕr, are derived from the personal pronouns. They are regular a- and o-stem adjectives, except that meŭs forms its vocative singular masculine, mī, from an older form mĭŭs.

---

[125] Sui is often called the reflexive pronoun, because it refers to the subject of the sentence. For a personal pronoun not referring to the subject, a demonstrative (is, ille, iste) is used.

The gen. sg. of ego and tu was mis, tis. These forms were lost, and the gen. forms of all the personal pronouns in both numbers are borrowed from the possessives.

The personal pronouns are sometimes emphasized by appending -met, -te, or -pte. So also, at times, the possessives: egomet, nosmet, tute, suipte, suopte, etc.

Med, ted, sed, are old forms for me, te, se (acc. and abl.). The doubled form sese is common; tete for te occurs in old Latin; also vostrum for vestrum, and sibe or sibei for sibi.

FORMS OF PRONOUNS.

The demonstrative pronouns have the declension of adjectives, but take the pronominal suffix -d in the nominative and accusative singular neuter, and the pronominal endings -ius, -i, in the genitive and dative singular of all genders. Certain cases of some of them are regularly emphasized by appending a demonstrative or intensive syllable (ī, cĕ or c). **127**

The demonstratives are ĭs, istĕ, illĕ, ipsĕ, hĭc, īdem. **128**

Is (stem i-, usually lengthened to io-, eo-) is thus declined:— **129**

Sg.				Pl.			
N.	ĭs	eă	ĭd	N.	eī, iī	eae	eă
G.	ējŭs	ējŭs	ējŭs	G.	eōrŭm	eārŭm	eōrŭm
D.	ēī	ēī	ēī	D.	eīs, iīs	eīs, iīs	eīs, iīs
Ac.	eŭm	eăm	ĭd	Ac.	eōs	eās	eă
Ab.	eō	eā	eō	Ab.	eīs, iīs	eīs, iīs	eīs, iīs

[127] A few instances are found of the regular adj. endings in the gen. and dat. sg.

The forms strengthened by -i are those which end in -ŭ; viz.: nom. sg. fem., and nom. and acc. pl. neut. ŭ + i contracts to ae. This strengthening is found in hic; sometimes in ille and iste. (It occurs also in the relative pronoun. See 138.)

Ce is used to strengthen all the cases, but drops e except after s. It is used in hic; sometimes in ille and iste. In the older language various forms occur with an appended -ce or -c.

[128] A demonstrative stem, so-, sa-, is said to have been used by Ennius in the forms sum, sam, sas.

For ille an older spelling, olle, is found in poetry.

[129] From the stem i- are formed is, id; also the old forms em (or im) = eum, and ibus = eis. The rest is formed from the longer stem. Ei and eis are sometimes contracted into monosyllables; eae (dat. sg. fem.) and eābus (abl. pl. fem.) are found in Cato, and inscriptions show various forms with ei written for i (according to [2]), and the nom. pl. forms eis, eeis, ieis.

130 Istĕ (stem isto-) is thus declined:—

	Sg. N.	istĕ	istă	istŭd	Pl.	istī	istae	istă
	G.	istīŭs	istīŭs	istīŭs		istōrŭm	istārŭm	istōrŭm
	D.	istī	istī	istī		istīs	istīs	istīs
	Ac.	istŭm	istăm	istŭd		istōs	istās	istă
	Ab.	istō	istā	istō		istīs	istīs	istīs

131 Illĕ is declined like istĕ.

132 Ipsĕ is declined like istĕ, but has ipsŭm in the nominative and accusative neuter singular.

133 Hīc (stem hi- or ho-) is strengthened by both -i and -ce, but the latter is not usual except in certain cases.

134 The usual forms are:—

	Sg. N.	hīc	haec	hŏc	Pl.	hī	hae	haec
	G.	hūjŭs	hūjŭs	hūjŭs		hōrŭm	hārŭm	hōrŭm
	D.	huīc	huīc	huīc		hīs	hīs	hīs
	Ac.	hunc	hanc	hŏc		hōs	hās	haec
	Ab.	hōc	hāc	hōc		hīs	hīs	hīs

---

[130] A nom. sg. masc. istŭs is found once.

[132] For ipse, ipsŭs is found. Ipse is compounded of is and -pse, and a few forms occur in which the first part is declined while the second remains unchanged; viz.: eāpse, eumpse, eampse, eōpse, eāpse.

[133] The stem hī- is found in hīc, and in the old forms hīsce (= hī) and hībus (= hīs). Huīc is often monosyllabic (hvīc).

[134] Other forms of hīc, chiefly old or poetical, are:—

	Sg. N.	hīce		hoce	Pl. N.	hīsce	haec	haice
	G.	holusce / hujusce	holusce / hujusce	holusce / hujusce	G.	horunce / horunc	harunce / harunc	
	D.	hoīce	hoīce	hoīce	D.	hībus / hīsce	hībus / hīsce	hībus / hīsce
	Ac.		hunce		Ac.	hosce	hasce	haice
	Ab.		hāce		Ab.	hībus / hīsce	hībus / hīsce	hībus / hīsce

FORMS OF PRONOUNS.

Illĕ and **istĕ** are sometimes strengthened by **-i** and **-ce** in the same way as **hĭc**. | **135**

Idĕm is formed by appending **-dĕm** to the various forms of **is**. The forms **is** and **id** drop **-s** and **-d**. | **136**

Idĕm is thus declined:— | **137**

Sg. N.	īdem	eădem	idem	Pl. eīdem	eaedem	eădem
G.	ējusdem	ējusdem	ējusdem	eōrundem	eārundem	eōrundem
D.	eīdem	eīdem	eīdem	eīsdem	eīsdem	eīsdem
Ac.	eundem	eandem	idem	eōsdem	eāsdem	eădem
Ab.	eōdem	eădem	eōdem	eīsdem	eīsdem	eīsdem

The relative pronoun (stem **qvi-** or **qvo-**) has the strengthening **-i**. See [127]. It is thus declined:— | **138**

Sg. N.	qvī	qvae	qvŏd	Pl. qvī	qvae	qvae
G.	cūjŭs	cūjŭs	cūjŭs	qvōrŭm	qvārŭm	qvōrŭm
D.	cui	cui	cui	qvĭbŭs	qvĭbŭs	qvĭbŭs
Ac.	qvĕm	qvăm	qvŏd	qvōs	qvās	qvae
Ab.	qvō	qvā	qvō	qvĭbŭs	qvĭbŭs	qvĭbŭs

The same pronoun is also used as an interrogative pronoun, but when used substantively has **qvĭs**, **qvĭd** in the nominative singular for **qvī**, **qvŏd**. | **139**

---

[135] The forms thus produced are:—

Sg. N.	illic	illaec	illoc, illuc	Pl. N. illic	illaec	illaec
G.	illiusce	illiusce	illiusce	G.		
D.	illic	illic	illic	D. illisce	illisce	illisce
Ac.	illunc	illanc	illoc, illuc	Ac. illosce	illasce	illaec
Ab.	illoc	illac	illoc	Ab. illisce	illisce	illisce

So also istic, istaec, istoc, etc.

[138] From the stem **qvi-** is formed also an abl. sg. **qvī**, and the old nom. pl. **qves**. From the stem **qvo-** is formed also a dat. and abl. pl. **qvīs**. For **cujus, cui**, an older spelling, **qvojus, qvoi** (or **qvojei**), is found. **Cui** is often monosyllabic (**cvi**).

[139] A few cases of **qvi, qvod** used substantively occur, and **qvis, qvid**, are not rarely used adjectively; **qvis** and **qvem** are sometimes

140	The same pronoun is also used as an indefinite pronoun. When so used, it has the same forms as when used interrogatively, but usually does not take the strengthening -i.
141	Various indefinite pronouns compounded of **quĭs** or **qvī** occur, all of which have the same declension; but those in which **qvĭs** or **qvī** forms the second part usually do not take the strengthening -i.

Forms of the Verb.

142	The Latin verb has the following forms: —
143	(a) Three tenses for incomplete action: *present, imperfect, future.*
144	(b) Three tenses for completed action: *perfect, pluperfect, future perfect.*

---

feminine. **Qvīnam** or **qvīsnam** is a more emphatic interrogative; it has the same forms, with -nam appended.

From the stem qvo- is formed a possessive interrogative, **cūjus, a, um** (= *whose*). It is antiquated, and only a few forms occur; viz.: **cujā, cujum, cujam, cujā, cujae.**

[140] Qvī or qvīs is indefinite after **sī, nĭsĭ, ne, num,** rarely elsewhere.

[141] A list is added for reference: —

alĭqvī or alĭqvĭs	alĭqva	alĭqvod or alĭqvĭd	*some, any.*
ecqvī or ecqvĭs	ecqva, ecqvae	ecqvod or ecqvĭd	*any?*
qvīdam	qvaedam	qvoddam	*a, a certain.*
qvīcunqve	qvaecunqve	qvodcunqve	*whatever.*
qvīlĭbet	qvaelĭbet	qvodlĭbet	*which you like, any.*
qvīvĭs	qvaevĭs	qvodvĭs	*which you will, any.*

So **qvīvĭscunque,** etc.   *whichever you will, any.*

qvĭsqvĭs (once qvīqvī). Only a few forms are found.			*whosoever.*
qvĭsqvam		qvĭdqvam, qvĭcqvam	*any at all.*
qvĭspiam	qvaepiam	qvĭdpiam	*any.*
qvĭsqve	qvaeqve	qvodqve or qvĭdqve	*every.*

So **unusqvĭsqve,** etc.   *every single one.*

It should be noticed that **ecqvĭs**, being at the same time interrogative and indefinite, forms **ecqvă** and **ecqvae**, without the **i** and with it.

145 The present tense has three moods: *indicative, subjunctive, imperative.*

146 The imperfect, perfect, and pluperfect have two moods: *indicative, subjunctive.*

147 The future and future perfect have one mood: *indicative.*

148 These forms are often called, collectively, the "*finite verb.*" Beside these, certain derivative noun- and adjective-forms are usually treated in connection with the verb; viz.: —

149 (*a*) Three verbal nouns called *infinitives.*
150 (*b*) A verbal noun called the *gerund.*
151 (*c*) A verbal noun called the *supine.*
152 (*d*) Four verbal adjectives called *participles.*

153 Of the finite verb only the incomplete tenses form a passive voice. For the passive of the complete tenses the Latin, like the English, uses the verb "*be*" with a passive participle.

154 The passive voice of the incomplete tenses was originally reflexive in its formation and meaning, and

---

[149] Viz.: a present active infinitive, a present passive infinitive, a perfect active infinitive. The infinitives are indeclinable nouns.

[150] The gerund is a neuter o-stem used only in the oblique cases of the singular.

[151] The supine is a u-stem used only in the acc. and abl. sg.

[152] Viz.: a present active participle, a present passive participle, a future active participle, and a perfect passive participle. The first is an I-stem of Class III.; the others are regular a- and o-stems.

[154] The name "deponent" was given to these verbs by the old grammarians, because they were supposed to have "*laid off*" their active form. In many of them the reflexive force can be seen; *e.g.*, **fruor**, *I enjoy* (*myself*); **vescor**, *I eat* (*feed myself*); **cingor**, *I bind on* (*myself*), etc. That

the reflexive use still remains in some verbs; *e.g.*, **vertor,** *I turn* [*myself*]. Many verbs thus used have lost the active form entirely, and use only the passive. They are usually translated into English by active forms, and are called "*deponent*" verbs.

Verb-Stems.

155 Verb-stems, like noun-stems, may end in **a, e, i, o, u**, or a consonant. Of stems in -o only a few forms are found.

156 In most verbs two or three forms of the stem are found, — the verb-stem proper (*simple stem*), a modification of it used in the incomplete tenses (*present stem*), and another modification of it used in the complete tenses (*perfect stem*).

157 In many verbs the present stem is the same as the

---

they are not true passives, is shown by the fact that many of them are transitive and govern a direct object. In many of them it is not easy to see the reflexive meaning, possibly because the original meaning is not known, and they are apparently equivalent to active forms.

Deponent verbs form the gerund, supine, and participles of the active as well as the passive voice, and their passive participles are sometimes passive in meaning. In the tenses for completed action, though these are not reflexive in formation, the meaning follows that of the incomplete tenses, and these forms also are usually rendered into English by the active voice.

[155] Open vowel-stems, as in nouns, differ in certain points from close vowel and consonant-stems, but the division is not sufficiently marked to make the grouping of any importance.

The only o-stems are no-sc-o (and its compounds), fŏ-rem, etc. (imp. subj.) and fŏ-re (pres. inf.), and a few participles which have become adjectives in use.

[157] The modifications mentioned here, especially *nasalizing*, are sometimes by analogy carried also into the perfect-stem or simple-stem forms.

VERB-STEMS

simple stem. When not so, it is formed from the simple stem, —

(*a*) By reduplication.	158
(*b*) By lengthening the stem-vowel.	159
(*c*) By adding or inserting a nasal.	160
(*d*) By adding -sc, -esc, or -isc.	161
(*e*) By adding -a, -e, or -i.	162
The perfect stem is rarely like the simple stem. Usually it is formed from the simple stem, —	163

[158] Reduplication consists in repeating before the stem its initial consonant-sound with the following vowel, often with a weakening of the latter. Stems ending in a vowel lose the final vowel when reduplicated, and become consonant-stems.

Reduplication is found in the present stem in four cases; viz.: **bib-o** (ba-), **gign-o** (for *gigĕn-o*, gĕn-), **ser-o** (for *ses-o*, sa-), and **sist-o** (sta-). Sisto is peculiar in repeating only the initial s and the vowel (not st).

[159] *E.g.*, **dūc-o** (dūc-), **dic-o** (dīc-).

[160] *E.g.*, **sĭn-o** (sĭ-), **pung-o** (pŭg-), **find-o** (fĭd-).

[161] *E.g.*, **ac-esc-o** (ac-), **no-sc-o** (no-), **reviv-isc-o** (reviv-). When sc is added after a consonant, there is usually some obscurity of formation from euphonic loss.

Verbs which form the present stem in this way usually mean *to become* (so and so), *to begin to be* (so and so). They are often called, therefore, *inceptive* or *inchoative* verbs.

[162] A few present stems end in ll, which seems to have arisen from li; viz.: **cell-o**, **pell-o**, **toll-o**, also **sall-o** or **sallo** (*to salt*). But **sall-o** (*to leap*) and **sepell-o** do not change.

[163] Possibly all cases of likeness of form between the perfect stem and the simple stem are the result of loss. Stems in a close vowel often drop the v of the perfect stem; those in -u show the v only in old Latin. Others have lost a reduplication syllable, and possibly the stem-vowel is lengthened in others, where the syllable is long by position, and the real quantity of the vowel therefore not clear.

164		(*a*) By reduplication.
165		(*b*) By lengthening the stem-vowel.
166		(*c*) By adding -s.
167		(*d*) By adding -u or -v.

The "principal parts" of a verb are:—

168 ACTIVE
- The pres. ind. act., 1st sg. ⎫
- The pres. inf. act.   ⎬ which show the *present* stem.
- The perf. ind. act., 1st sg., which shows the *perfect* stem.
- The supine, which shows the *simple* stem.

169 PASSIVE
- The pres. ind. pass., 1st sg. ⎫
- The pres. inf. pass.   ⎬ which show the *present* stem.
- The perf. pass. participle, which shows the *simple* stem.

[164] In the perfect stem ă is regularly weakened to ĕ in the reduplication syllable, and to ĕ or ĭ in the stem syllable. **Bib-i (ba-)** seems to owe its form to the present **bib-o**; possibly **stit-i** has been affected in the same way by **sist-o**.

The stems which begin with two consonants (scid-, sta-, spond-) drop the initial s of the stem, after the reduplication syllable (making sci-cid-i, ste-t-i, spo-pond-i). For the loss of the final vowel of ba-, da-, and sta- in bib-i, ded-i, stet i or stit-i, see [158].

The reduplication of the perfect stem is usually dropped when the verb is compounded with a preposition. A few stems only retain it.

[165] *E.g.* lēg-i (lĕg-); pāv-i (păv-). The stem-vowel ă becomes ē when lengthened to form the perfect stem, except when followed by v (viz.: in cāv-i, fāv-i, lāv-i, păv-i) or b (in scāb-i). Thus, ēg-i (ăg-), pēg-i (păg-), etc.

[167] U is added after consonants, v after vowels, and the preceding vowel is regularly made long before the added -v.

[168] *E.g.*, am-o, amā-re, amāv-i, amā-tum, passive, am-or, amā-ri, amā-tus. These are the forms usually given in grammars and lexicons, and are based on a classification of verbs according to the ending of the pres. inf. as follows:—

First conjugation; inf. endings -ārĕ, -ārī, = a-stems.
Second   "   "   "   -ērĕ, -ērī, = e-stems.
Third   "   "   "   -ĕrĕ, -i,   = cons. u- and short i-stems.
Fourth   "   "   "   -īrĕ, -īrī, = long i-stems.

In most verbs the pres. inf. would be enough to identify the present stem, but short i-stems lose the i and become consonant-stems in this form. The pres. ind. is therefore added to identify such.

Verbal Suffixes.

170 The suffixes of the finite verb contain two elements, one of which shows the mood and tense (*mood-and-tense sign*), the other the person and number (*person-and-number suffix*).

171 The mood-and-tense signs are added to the stem as follows: —

172 Pres. ind., *none;* pres. imp., *none;* pres subj., ĭ in a-stems, ā elsewhere.
173 Imp. ind., ĕbā or ēbā; imp. subj., ĕrē.
174 Fut. ind., ĕb in open vowel-stems, ā and ē elsewhere.
175 Perf. ind. (ēs or īs? See 188); perf. subj., ĕrī.
176 Plup. ind., ĕrā; plup. subj., issē.
177 Fut. perf. ind., ĕr.

[170] The names "tense-and-mood sign," "person-and-number suffix," are used for convenience, without implying any theory of their origin, simply because they show to the eye or ear the tense and mood, person and number, and, incidentally, the voice of the verb. Grammarians are agreed that the suffixes of person and number are stunted forms of personal pronouns; and most of the signs of tense and mood are generally thought to be derived from the verbs "*be*" (stems -es, -fu) and "*go*" (stem -ī).

[171] Mood-and-tense signs are added, of course, to the present stem in the incomplete tenses, and to the perfect stem in the complete tenses.

[172] In the pres. subj. ĭ contracts with a preceding a to ē.

[173] The imp. ind. sign is -ēbā after a consonant or u, and almost always after i. ĕbā is used after open vowels, also in old Latin after i, but in both ēbā and ĕb the initial vowel is always absorbed. (See [178]).

[174] The fut. ind. sign ā is found in the first sg.; ē in the other forms. In old Latin, stems in i sometimes form the future with the sign ĕb.

[175] The perf. subj. sign is often -ĕrī, a result of confusion with the fut. perf. ind. which closely resembles it in form and use.

178 By adding the tense-and-mood signs to the stem, there is formed a stem or base for each tense. To this tense-base are added the suffixes of person and number, as follows: —

Indicative and subjunctive.

179 Act. 1. -ŏm 2. -ĭs 3. -ĭt 1. -ĭmŭs 2. -ĭtĭs 3. -unt
180 Pass. 1. -ŏr 2. -ĕrĭs 3. -ĭtŭr 1. -ĭmŭr 2. -ĭmĭnī 3. -untŭr

[178] The initial short vowel of the mood-and-tense signs is regularly absorbed by a preceding open vowel; *e.g.*, amā-bām (= ama-ĕba-m), monē-re-m (= mone-ĕre-m), etc. A preceding ĭ either absorbs it, *e.g.*, audī-re-m (st. audĭ-), or drops before it, leaving a consonant-stem, *e.g.*, cap-ĕre-m (st. capĭ-). The signs ĕbū, ĕb, ĕre-, therefore, appear in the forms bā, b, rē after stems ending in a, e, or ī. In the complete tenses the stem ends in a, e, or ī only when v is dropped. In such cases the initial vowel of the sign is regularly absorbed by a or e, very rarely by ī. See [215]. The long vowels ā, ē, ī are not absorbed, but ĭ contracts with a preceding a to ē, as stated in [172]. The loss of ĕ of the imp. subj. sign is a characteristic of certain irregular verbs. (See [220]).

The suffixes appear in the form given here after u or a consonant. After a, e, i, the initial vowel of the suffix is absorbed, making the preceding a, e, or i long. But o remains unabsorbed after stem-vowels, and itself absorbs the preceding a; and u remains unabsorbed after the stem-vowel i.

The initial vowel of the person-and-number suffixes, strictly speaking, is not a part of them. Its origin is a matter of dispute; some regard it as a simple insertion to attach the suffixes to the tense base (*connecting vowel*); others as an addition to the stem to fit it for the reception of the suffixes (*modal vowel* or *thematic vowel*). Its omission is one peculiarity of certain irregular verbs. (See [220]).

[179] m of -ŏm falls when ŏ is unabsorbed. -ŭm for -ŏm is found in sum. -ŭmus, an older form of -ĭmus, is found in sŭmus, quaesŭmus, volŭmus. -ĭnt for -unt is found in the fut. perf., evidently by confusion with the perf. subj. -īs, -īmŭs, -ītĭs, due, no doubt, to the same cause, are not unusual in the fut. perf. for -ĭs, -ĭmŭs, -ĭtĭs.

[180] -ĕrĕ for ĕrĭs is not unusual in poetry; rare in prose.

VERBAL SUFFIXES. 41

Imperative.

ACT.	2. -ĕ, -ĭtō	3. -ĭtō	2. -ĭtĕ, -ĭtōtĕ	3. -untō		181
PASS.	2. -ĕrĕ, -ĭtŏr	3. -ĭtŏr	2. -ĭmĭnī	3. -untŏr		182

The suffixes of the non-finite forms are:—

(*a*) From the present stem.

ACT. Pres. inf., -ĕrĕ; pres. part., -enti; gerund, -endo. **183**
PASS. Pres. inf., -ĕrī; pres. part., -endo. **184**

(*b*) From the perfect stem.

ACT. Perf. inf. (-sĕ ? see below, 190). **185**

(*c*) From the simple stem.

ACT. Fut. part., -tūro- (-sūro-); supine, -tu- (-su-). **186**
PASS. Perf. part., -to- (-so-). **187**

The perfect indicative active and perfect infinitive active have peculiar endings not easily resolved into sign and suffix. They are:— **188**

Perf. act. ind., -ī, -istī, -ĭt; -ĭmŭs, -istĭs, -ērunt. **189**
Perf. act. inf., -issĕ. **190**

[181] The imperative forms in -tō, -tōte, -ntō; -tŏr, -ntŏr are sometimes called future imperative. They are antiquated forms, retained in poetry and legal phraseology, rare elsewhere.

[183] For -endo, -undo is found; also for -enti, -unti in one verb (eo, "*go*").

[184] For -ĕrī, -ī is found in consonant and u-stems. An older suffix -ĕriĕr (in consonant and u-stems, -iĕr), is found in old Latin.

[186] -ĭtūro-, -ĭtu-, -ĭto-, are found in some cases. This may have been the form after vowel-stems, the ĭ disappearing by absorption. -sūro, -su, -so, are euphonic changes of -tūro, -tu, -to, used after certain letters. (See [209]).

[188] The perf. act. ind. and inf. seem to have -ĭs or -ēs as mood-and-tense sign, and to add the suffixes directly to the tense-base without the suffix-vowel. But some forms are quite irregular, and the second sg. ind. shows a suffix -tĭ, not found elsewhere in the Latin verb.

[189] For -ērunt, -ērĕ is found, also rarely -ĕrunt.

The Conjugations.

191 There are five forms of conjugation for the incomplete tenses, according to the form of the stem. They are: —

      1st. Stems in -a.
      2d. Stems in -e.
      3d. Stems in a consonant or in -u.
      4th. Stems in short -ĭ.
      5th. Stems in long -ī.

In the complete tenses there is but one form for all verbs.

192 The theme of the incomplete tenses is found by dropping the ending of the present infinitive.

193 The incomplete tenses are inflected by adding to the theme the following endings: —

---

[191] The final u of verb-stems does not contract with the vowel of the suffix, and there is therefore no difference between u-stems and consonant-stems in their inflection. Compare monosyllabic noun u-stems, 112. These different forms of inflection, like the different declensions, are simply variations resulting from contraction of stem-ending and suffix-vowel. The stems in short -ĭ and long -ī are so called for convenience of distinction, since the i appears as short in one and long in the other. But it seems probable that the final vowel of all verb-stems is properly short, and that its length in the incomplete tenses is the result of absorbing the suffix-vowel. The usual arrangement of conjugations (see [108]) places short I-stems with consonant and u-stems. As in i-stem nouns, the i of these verb-stems is lost in certain forms, leaving a consonant-stem.

Only one form of conjugation is found in the complete tenses, because the perfect stem always ends in u or a consonant, and consequently no variation of form from contraction takes place. The few cases in which the perfect stem is made to end in a, e, or i by the loss of v are too rare to make a difference of conjugation.

THE CONJUGATIONS.

A-STEMS.

194

	Present Active.				Present Passive.			
	Indic.	Subj.	Imper.	Non-finite.	Indic.	Subj.	Imper.	Non-finite.
Sg. 1	ŏ	ĕm		Inf. ārĕ	ŏr	ĕr		Inf. ārī
2	ās	ēs	ā, ātŏ̄		āris	ēris	ārĕ, ātŏr	
3	ăt	ĕt	ātŏ̄	Part. anti-	ātŭr	ētŭr	ātŏr	
Pl. 1	āmŭs	ēmŭs			āmŭr	ēmŭr		Part. ando-
2	ātis	ētis	ātĕ, ātōtĕ	Ger. ando-	āminī	ēminī	āminī	
3	ant	ent	antŏ̄		antŭr	entŭr	antŏr	

195

	Imperf. Active.		Imperf. Passive.		Fut. Act.	Fut. Pas.
	Indic.	Subj.	Indic.	Subj.	Indic.	Indic.
Sg. 1	ābăm	ārĕm	ābăr	ārĕr	ābŏ̄	ābŏr
2	ābās	ārēs	ābāris	ārēris	ābis	ābĕris
3	ābăt	ārĕt	ābātŭr	ārētŭr	ābit	ābitŭr
Pl. 1	ābāmŭs	ārēmŭs	ābāmŭr	ārēmŭr	ābimŭs	ābimŭr
2	ābātis	ārētis	ābāminī	ārēminī	ābitis	ābiminī
3	ābant	ārent	ābantŭr	ārentŭr	ābunt	ābuntŭr

EXAMPLE FOR PRACTICE.
Stem, āma-; theme, ăm-.

[194] ACTIVE
- ăm ŏ̄
- am ās
- am ăt
- etc.

- am ĕm
- am ēs
- am ĕt
- etc.

- am ā, am ātŏ̄
- am ātŏ̄
- etc.

- am ārĕ
- am āns, -ntis, etc.
- am andī, etc.

PASSIVE
- am ŏr
- am āris
- am ātŭr
- etc.

- am ŏr
- am ĕris
- am ētŭr
- etc.

- am ārĕ, am ātŏr
- am ātŏr
- etc.

- am ārī
- am andŭs, ā, ŭm

[195] ACTIVE
- am ābăm
- am ābās
- am ābăt
- etc.

- am ārĕm
- am ārēs
- am ārĕt
- etc.

- am ābŏ̄
- am ābis
- am ābit
- etc.

PASSIVE
- am ābăr
- am ābāris
- am ābātŭr
- etc.

- am ārĕr
- am ārēris
- am ārētŭr
- etc.

- am ābŏr
- am ābĕris
- am ābitŭr
- etc.

E-STEMS.

196

		Present Active.				Present Passive.			
		Indic.	Subj.	Imper.	Non-finite.	Indic.	Subj.	Imper.	Non-finite.
Sg.	1	eŏ	eăm		Inf. ērĕ	eŏr	eăr		Inf. ērī
	2	ēs	eās	ē, ētŏ̄		ēris	eāris	ērĕ, ētŏr	
	3	ĕt	eăt	ētŏ̄	Part. enti-	ētŭr	eātŭr	ētŏr	Part. endo-
Pl.	1	ēmŭs	eāmŭs			ēmŭr	eāmŭr		
	2	ētis	eātis	ētĕ, ētŏtĕ	Ger. endo-	ēminī	eāminī	ēminī	
	3	ent	eant	entŏ̄		entŭr	eantŭr	entŏr	

197

		Imperf. Active.		Imperf. Passive.		Fut. Act.	Fut. Pas.
		Indic.	Subj.	Indic.	Subj.	Indic.	Indic.
Sg.	1	ēbăm	ērĕm	ēbăr	ērĕr	ēbŏ̄	ēbŏr
	2	ēbās	ērēs	ēbāris	ērēris	ēbis	ēbĕris
	3	ēbăt	ērĕt	ēbātŭr	ērētŭr	ēbit	ēbitŭr
Pl.	1	ēbāmŭs	ērēmŭs	ēbāmŭr	ērēmŭr	ēbimŭs	ēbimŭr
	2	ēbātis	ērētis	ēbāminī	ērēminī	ēbitis	ēbiminī
	3	ēbant	ērent	ēbantŭr	ērentŭr	ēbunt	ēbuntŭr

EXAMPLE FOR PRACTICE.
Stem, mŏne-; theme, mŏn-.

[196] ACTIVE
{ mŏn eŏ / mon ēs / mon ĕt / etc. } { mon eăm / mon eās / mon eăt / etc. } mon ē, mon ētŏ̄ / mon ētŏ̄ / etc. mon ērĕ / mon ēns, -ntis, etc. / mon endī, etc.

PASSIVE
{ mon eŏr / mon ēris / mon ētŭr / etc. } { mon eăr / mon eāris / mon eātŭr / etc. } mon ērĕ, mon ētŏr / mon ētŏr / etc. mon ērī / mon endūs, ā, ŭm

[197] ACTIVE
{ mon ēbăm / mon ēbās / mon ēbăt / etc. } { mon ērĕm / mon ērēs / mon ērĕt / etc. }   mon ēbŏ̄ / mon ēbis / mon ēbit / etc.

PASSIVE
{ mon ēbăr / mon ēbāris / mon ēbātŭr / etc. } { mon ērĕr / mon ērēris / mon ērētŭr / etc. }   mon ēbŏr / mon ēbĕris / mon ēbitŭr / etc.

THE CONJUGATIONS.

CONSONANT-STEMS AND U-STEMS.

	Present Active.				Present Passive.				
	Indic.	Subj.	Imper.	Non-finite.	Indic.	Subj.	Imper.	Non-finite.	
Sg. 1	ŏ	ăm		Inf. ĕrĕ	ŏr	ăr		Inf. ī	**198**
2	ĭs	ās	ĕ, ĭtŏ̄		ĕris	āris	ĕrĕ, ĭtŏr		
3	ĭt	ăt	ĭtŏ̄	Part. enti-	ĭtŭr	ātŭr	ĭtŏr	Part. endo-	
Pl. 1	ĭmŭs	āmŭs		Ger. endo-	ĭmŭr	āmŭr			
2	ĭtis	ātis	ĭtĕ, ĭtŏtĕ		ĭmĭnī	āmĭnī	ĭmĭnī		
3	unt	ant	untŏ̄		untŭr	antŭr	untŏr		

	Imperf. Active.		Imperf. Passive.		Fut. Act.	Fut. Pas.	
	Indic.	Subj.	Indic.	Subj.	Indic.	Indic.	
Sg. 1	ēbăm	ĕrĕm	ēbăr	ĕrĕr	ăm	ăr	
2	ēbās	ĕrēs	ēbāris	ĕrēris	ēs	ēris	**199**
3	ēbăt	ĕrĕt	ēbātŭr	ĕrētŭr	ĕt	ētŭr	
Pl. 1	ēbāmŭs	ĕrēmŭs	ēbāmŭr	ĕrēmŭr	ēmŭs	ēmŭr	
2	ēbātis	ĕrētis	ēbāmĭnī	ĕrēmĭnī	ētis	ēmĭnī	
3	ēbant	ĕrent	ēbantŭr	ĕrentŭr	ent	entŭr	

EXAMPLE FOR PRACTICE.

Stem, rĕg-; theme, rĕg-.

[198] ACTIVE { reg ŏ̄ / reg ĭs / etc. }   reg ăm / reg ās / etc.   reg ĕ, reg ĭtŏ̄ / etc.   reg ĕrĕ / reg ĕns, -ntĭs, etc. / reg endī, etc.

PASSIVE { reg ŏr / reg ĕris / etc. }   reg ăr / reg āris / etc.   reg ĕrĕ, reg ĭtŏr / etc.   reg ī / reg endŭs, ă, ŭm

[199] ACTIVE { reg ēbăm / reg ēbās / etc. }   reg ĕrĕm / reg ĕrēs / etc.   reg ăm / reg ēs / etc.

PASSIVE { reg ēbăr / reg ēbāris / etc. }   reg ĕrĕr / reg ĕrēris / etc.   reg ăr / reg ēris / etc.

Stems in -u have the same endings as consonant-stems, the vowel being unabsorbed. *E.g.*, from the stem **trĭbu-** we have —

ACTIVE. trĭbu ŏ̄, etc.   trĭbu ăm, etc.   trĭbu ĕ, etc.   trĭbu ĕrĕ, trĭbu ĕns, trĭbu endī.
PASSIVE. trĭbu ŏr, etc.   trĭbu ăr, etc.   trĭbu ĕrĕ, etc.   trĭbu ī, trĭbu endŭs, ă, ŭm.
ACTIVE. trĭbu ēbăm, etc.   trĭbu ĕrĕm, etc.   trĭbu ăm, etc.
PASSIVE. trĭbu ēbăr, etc.   trĭbu ĕrĕr, etc.   trĭbu ăr, etc.

PART II.—FORMS.

200 There are two forms of inflection of verb-stems in -i. In one, i is short and falls before a short syllable, leaving a consonant-stem; in the other, i absorbs the vowel of a following short syllable, and is long. In both, i stands before long syllables.

SHORT *I*-STEMS.

201

	Present Active.				Present Passive.			
	Indic.	Subj.	Imper.	Non-finite.	Indic.	Subj.	Imper.	Non-finite.
Sg. 1	iŏ	iăm		Inf. ĕrĕ	iŏr	iăr		Inf. ī
2	ĭs	iās	ĕ, ĭtŏ		ĕrĭs	iārĭs	ĕrĕ, ĭtŏr	
3	ĭt	iăt	ĭtŏ	Part. ienti-	ĭtŭr	iātŭr	ĭtŏr	
Pl. 1	ĭmŭs	iāmŭs		Ger. iendo-	ĭmŭr	iāmŭr		Part. iendo-
2	ĭtĭs	iātĭs	ĭtĕ, ĭtōtĕ		ĭmĭnī	iāmĭnī	ĭmĭnī	
3	iunt	iant	iuntō		iuntŭr	iantŭr	iuntŏr	

202

	Imperf. Active.		Imperf. Passive.		Fut. Act.	Fut. Pas.
	Indic.	Subj.	Indic.	Subj.	Indic.	Indic.
Sg. 1	iēbăm	ĕrĕm	iēbăr	ĕrĕr	iăm	iăr
2	iēbās	ĕrēs	iēbārĭs	ĕrēris	iēs	iērĭs
3	iēbăt	ĕrĕt	iēbātŭr	ĕrētŭr	iĕt	iētŭr
Pl. 1	iēbāmŭs	ĕrēmŭs	iēbāmŭr	ĕrēmŭr	iēmŭs	iēmŭr
2	iēbātĭs	ĕrētĭs	iēbāmĭnī	ĕrēmĭnī	iētĭs	iēmĭnī
3	iēbant	ĕrent	iēbantŭr	ĕrentŭr	ient	ientŭr

[200] The i before the long vowel remains, though the vowel be shortened before final m, t, r, see [12] (*a*), and falls in the pres. inf. pass. where the proper ending -ĕrī has been shortened to -ĭ.

EXAMPLE FOR PRACTICE. Stem, căpĭ- or căp- (by dropping i); theme, căp-.

[201] ACTIVE { căpĭŏ / capĭs / capĭt / etc. } { capĭăm / capĭās / capĭăt / etc. } { capĕ, capĭtŏ / capĭtŏ / etc. } capĕrĕ / capiēns, -ntĭs, etc. / capiendī, etc.

PASSIVE { capĭŏr / capĕrĭs / capĭtŭr / etc. } { capĭăr / capiārĭs / capiātŭr / etc. } { capĕrĕ, capĭtŏr / capĭtŏr / etc. } capī / capiendŭs, ă, ŭm

THE CONJUGATIONS.

LONG I-STEMS.

	Present Active.				Present Passive.				
	Indic.	Subj.	Imper.	Non-finite.	Indic.	Subj.	Imper.	Non-finite.	
Sg.									
1	iō	iăm		Inf. irĕ	iŏr	iăr		Inf. īrī	203
2	īs	iās	ī, ītō		īris	iāris	irĕ, ītŏr		
3	it	iăt	ītō	Part. ienti-	ītŭr	iātŭr	ītŏr		
Pl.								Part. iendo-	
1	īmŭs	iāmŭs			īmŭr	iāmŭr			
2	ītis	iātis	ītĕ, ītōtĕ	Ger. iendo-	īminī	iāminī	īminī		
3	iunt	iant	iuntō		iuntŭr	iantŭr	iuntŏr		

	Imperf. Active.		Imperf. Passive.		Fut. Act.	Fut. Pas.	
	Indic.	Subj.	Indic.	Subj.	Indic.	Indic.	
Sg.							
1	iēbăm	īrĕm	iēbăr	īrĕr	iăm	iăr	
2	iēbās	īrēs	iēbāris	īrēris	iēs	iēris	204
3	iēbăt	īrĕt	iēbātŭr	īrētŭr	iĕt	iētŭr	
Pl.							
1	iēbāmŭs	īrēmŭs	iēbāmŭr	īrēmŭr	iēmŭs	iēmŭr	
2	iēbātis	īrētis	iēbāminī	īrēminī	iētis	iēminī	
3	iēbant	īrent	iēbantŭr	īrentŭr	ient	ientŭr	

[202] ACTIVE { cap iēbăm / cap iēbās / etc.   cap ĕrĕm / cap ĕrēs / etc.   cap iăm / cap iēs / etc.

PASSIVE { cap iēbăr / cap iēbāris / etc.   cap ĕrĕr / cap ĕrēris / etc.   cap iăr / cap iēris / etc.

EXAMPLE FOR PRACTICE. Stem, audi-; theme, aud-.

[203] ACTIVE { aud iō / aud īs / aud it / etc.   aud iăm / aud iās / aud iăt / etc.   aud I, aud ītō / aud ītō / etc.   aud īrŏ / aud iĕns, -ntis, etc. / aud iendī, etc.

PASSIVE { aud iŏr / aud īris / aud ītŭr / etc.   aud iăr / aud iāris / aud iātŭr / etc.   aud īre, aud ītŏr / aud ītŏr / etc.   aud īrī / aud iendŭs, ă, ŭm

[204] ACTIVE { aud iēbăm / aud iēbās / aud iēbăt / etc.   aud īrĕm / aud īrēs / aud īrĕt / etc.   aud iăm / aud iēs / aud iĕt / etc.

PASSIVE { aud iēbăr / aud iēbāris / aud iēbātŭr / etc.   aud īrĕr / aud īrēris / aud īrētur / etc.   aud iăr / aud iēris / aud iētŭr / etc.

PART II.—FORMS.

205 The theme of the complete tenses is found by dropping the ending of the perfect indicative active, first person singular.

The endings are the same for all verbs; viz.:—

206

		Perfect Active.			Pluperfect Active.		Fut. Perf. Active.
		Indic.	Subj.	Non-finite.	Indic.	Subj.	Indic.
Sg.	1	ī	ěrim		ěrăm	issěm	ěrō
	2	istī	ěrīs	Inf. issě	ěrās	issēs	ěrĭs
	3	it	ěrit		ěrăt	issět	ěrit
Pl.	1	imŭs	ěrĭmŭs		ěrāmŭs	issēmŭs	ěrĭmŭs
	2	istĭs	ěrĭtĭs		ěrātĭs	issētĭs	ěrĭtĭs
	3	ērunt	ěrint		ěrant	issent	ěrint

207 The lacking complete tenses of the passive voice are supplied, as in English, by the perfect passive participle and the verb "be."

---

[206] The theme of the complete tenses ends in u or a consonant, and the vowel of the endings therefore remains unabsorbed, except when brought after a vowel by the loss of v. See [215].

EXAMPLES FOR PRACTICE.

Stem						
ămāv-	ămāvī amāvistī etc.	amāvěrim amāvěrĭs etc.	amāvissě	amāvěrăm amāvěrās etc.	amāvissěm amāvissēs etc.	amāvěrō amāvěrĭs etc.
" mŏnu-	mŏnuī etc.	monuěrim etc.	monuissě	monuěrăm etc.	monuissěm etc.	monuěrō etc.
" rex-	rexī etc.	rexěrim etc.	rexissě	rexěrăm etc.	rexissěm etc.	rexěrō etc.
" trĭbu-	trĭbuī etc.	tribuěrim etc.	tribuissě	tribuěrăm etc.	tribuissěm etc.	tribuěrō etc.
" cēp-	cēpī etc.	cepěrim etc.	cepissě	cepěrăm etc.	cepissěm etc.	cepěrō etc.
" audīv-	audīvī etc.	audīvěrim etc.	audīvissě	audīvěrăm etc.	audīvissěm etc.	audīvěrō etc.

For the variation between **i** and **ī** in the perf. subj. and fut. perf. ind., see [175] and [179].

THE CONJUGATIONS. 49

208 The theme of the verb-forms from the simple stem may be found by dropping the ending of the supine or of the perfect passive participle.

The endings of the forms from the simple stem are:—

	Supine.	Future Active Participle.	Perf. Pass. Participle.
A-stems . . .	ātu-	ātūro-	āto-
E-stems . . .	ētu-	ētūro-	ēto-
I-stems	ītu-	ītūro-	īto-
O-stems . . .	ōtu-	ōtūro-	ōto-
U-stems . . .	ūtu-	ūtūro-	ūto-
Consonant-stems {	tu- (su-), *or* ītu-	tūro- (sūro-), *or* ītūro-	to- (so-), *or* īto-

209

[209] The endings -ītu-, -ītūro-, -īto-, though less common in consonant-stems, seem to be the usual form of the suffixes in vowel-stems,—the long vowel being due to the absorption of the ī of the suffix. In a few cases, however, vowel-stems show a short vowel in these endings, which may be explained by assuming that the suffix is appended directly to the stem without the vowel, as in most consonant stems. These cases number in all twelve; viz.: **dătus, rătus, sătus, stătus; cĭtus, ĭtus, lĭtus, qvĭtus, sĭtus; -clŭtus, fŭturus, rŭtus.**

Su-, sūro-, so-, are euphonic changes of **tu-, tūro-, to-**. They are used after stems ending in a dental-mute (except tend-, which has forms with both t and s, apparently by confusion with its kindred stem tĕn-) and after a few others, especially stems ending in two consonants with which an added t could not easily be pronounced. See [12]. The real form of the stem is often obscured before these suffixes by euphonic change.

ILLUSTRATIONS.

Stem	āmā-	amātum, amātū	amātūrus, a, um	amātus, a, um
"	dēle-	delētum, delētu	delētūrus, a, um	delētus, a, um
"	audī-	audītum, audītu	audītūrus, a, um	audītus, a, um
"	no-	nōtum, nōtu	nōtūrus, a, um	nōtus, a, um
"	trĭbu-	tribūtum, tribūtu	tribūtūrus, a, um	tribūtus, a, um
"	căp-	captum, captu	captūrus, a, um	captus, a, um
"	hăb-	habĭtum, habĭtu	habĭtūrus, a, um	habĭtus, a, um
"	lŭd-	lūsum, lūsū	lūsūrus, a, um	lūsus, a, um

210	The participles with the verb "be" are often used as in English with the force of finite verb-forms.
211	The present active participle is thus used only when it has become an adjective or noun in force and meaning.
212	The future active participle with the verb "be" makes the "first" or "active" periphrastic conjugation, and expresses an intended or destined action.
213	The present passive participle with the verb "be" makes the "second" or "passive" periphrastic conjugation, and expresses duty or necessity.
214	The perfect passive participle with the verb "be" supplies the lacking complete tenses of the passive voice.

[210] For the inflection of the verb "be," see [221].

[212] *E.g.*,

audītūrŭs sŭm, *I am going to hear; expect to hear; intend to hear*, etc.
audītūrŭs ĕrăm, *I was going to hear; expected to hear; intended to hear*, etc.

This form supplies the lacking subjunctive and infinitive of the future tense, when such forms are needed for precision.

[213] **audiendŭs sŭm**, *I must be heard; ought to be heard*, etc.
   audiendŭs ĕrăm, *I had to be heard; deserved to be heard*, etc.

[214]

Perf. pass. Ind.	amātŭs	sŭm	Perf. pass. subj.	amātŭs	sĭm
	"	ĕs		"	sīs
	"	est		"	sĭt
	amatī	sŭmŭs		amatī	sīmŭs
	"	estĭs		"	sītĭs
	"	sunt		"	sint
Plup. pass. Ind.	amātŭs	ĕrăm	Plup. pass. subj.	amātŭs	essĕm
	"	erās		"	essēs
	"	erăt		"	essĕt
	amatī	erāmŭs		amatī	essēmŭs
	"	erātĭs		"	essētĭs
	"	erant		"	essent
Fut. pf. pass. ind.	amātŭs	erŏ			
	"	erĭs			
	"	erĭt	Perf. pass. Inf.	amātŭs	essĕ
	amatī	erĭmŭs			
	"	erĭtĭs			
	"	erunt			

Irregular Verb-Forms.

215 The v used to form the perfect stem is sometimes dropped between vowels. See [12] (c).

216 The ending of the imperative active second singular is dropped in the verbs dīco, dūco, făcio, thus making dīc, dūc, făc.

Instead of the incomplete tenses of sŭm the complete tenses are sometimes used to make the perf., plup. and fut. perf. passive, with little or no difference of meaning; e.g., amatus fui = amatus sum; amatus fueram = amatus eram, etc. In all these periphrastic conjugations the participle is an adjective limiting the subject of the verb "be," and takes the same gender, number and case. See 255.

[215] An open vowel before v absorbs the following vowel after v falls; a close vowel does so rarely. Thus amāvistī becomes āmāstī; flēvistī becomes flēstī; nōveram becomes nōram, etc. But audīveram becomes audieram, etc.

A similar shortening in perfects formed with -s is rarer, — scripstī for scripsistī; dixe for dixisse, etc.

[216] The same loss of the imperative ending takes place also in the verbs sŭm, ĕdo, fĕro, vŏlo, but is part of a peculiar irregularity. (See 220.) In old Latin, and in compounds of făcio, the regular forms are found.

Other irregularities are rarer, and belong generally to the older language or to poetry. A list is given for reference: —

(a) In stems in -ĭ the imperf. and fut. ind. are sometimes formed with the signs ĕbā and ĕb; regularly so in eo, "go." See [227].

(b) An old fut. (or fut. perf.?) formed with the sign -s (or -ss), a subj. with the sign -sī (or -ssī), and an infin. with the ending -sere (or -ssere), are found in old writers.

(c) An old imper. pass. sg. ending -mǐno (corresponding to the pl. ending -mǐnī) is also found, and the active ending -to seems sometimes to have a passive sense.

(d) For the suffix -ĕrĕ = -ĕrĭs, see [180].

(e) For the perf. ind. act. ending -ērĕ = ērunt, see [189].

(f) For the ending -undī, etc., in the gerund, and -undus, -a, -um, in the pres. pass. part., see [183].

217 The verbs sŭm, ĕdo, fĕro, vŏlo, do, eo, queo, fīo, and their compounds, have special irregularities in the incomplete tenses, chiefly in: —

218 (*a*) Variation of the stem.

219 (*b*) Use of mood-and-tense signs unusual in stems of like form.

220 (*c*) Omission of the initial vowel of the mood-and-tense sign, or of the suffix. This occurs in sŭm, ĕdo, fĕro, vŏlo, which omit the initial vowel of the imperfect subjunctive sign, and the initial vowel of the suffix in the following forms; viz.: —
Present indicative, 2d and 3d sg. and 2d plural.
Present imperative, 2d and 3d sg. and 2d plural.
Present infinitive.

221 Sŭm (stem ĕs-) omits the vowel, uses ī as present subjunctive sign, loses initial e in certain forms, and retains older endings not found in the usual conjugations.

(*g*) Audeo, fīdo, gaudeo, soleo, have a passive form in the complete tenses, and are called semi-deponents.

(*h*) Morior, orior, potior, show a variation between long Ī-stem forms and short Ĭ-stem forms.

[220] The omission of the ĕ of the imperf. subj. sign -ĕrē causes it to take the form -sē in sum and ĕdo, and -lē in volo. Sē was, no doubt, the original form; lē arises by assimilation of -r to the preceding -l. The same change takes place in the pres. infin.

[221] Sŭm, esse, fŭi, fŭtūrŭs.

	Present.			Imperfect.		Future.
sŭm	sīm			ĕrăm	essĕm	ĕrō
ĕs	sīs	ĕs, esto	esse	erĭs	essēs	erĭs
est	sīt	esto		erĭt	essĕt	erĭt
sŭmŭs	sīmŭs		[-sens]	erĭmŭs	essēmŭs	erĭmŭs
estĭs	sītĭs	estŏ, estōtŏ		erātĭs	essētĭs	erĭtĭs
sunt	sint	sunto		erant	essent	erunt

IRREGULAR VERB-FORMS.

Compounds of **sŭm** are like **sŭm**, except **possŭm**, which contracts in certain forms. **222**

Edo (stem **ĕd-**) omits the vowel (with consequent euphonic change of **d** to **s**), and has present subjunctive sign **ī**. It has also the regular forms. **223**

For **sīm, sīs**, etc., an older form — **siem, sies**, etc. — is found. The 2d sg. pres. ind. **ĕs** stands for es-s (see [12] (*b*)), and is long in old Latin **ēs**, the result of the loss of the suffix. (See 362.) The pres. part. -sens is found only in the compounds, **ab-sens** and **prae-sens**.

The complete tenses are formed from a stem **fu-**, which appears as the simple stem also in **fŭ-tūrus**. From this stem is formed a pres. subj. **fuam**, etc.; and from another form of it, **fo-**, is formed an imperf. subj. **fŏrem**, etc., and an infin. **fŏre**. **Fŏre** has a future sense, as have also the old inceptive forms **escit, escunt** (= es-sc-it, es-sc-unt). For perfect stem the older language has also **fūv-**.

[222] **Possŭm, possĕ, pŏtui.**

PRESENT.			IMPERFECT.		FUTURE.
possŭm	possĭm		pŏtĕrăm	possĕm	pŏtĕrŏ
potĕs	possīs	possĕ	pŏtĕrās	possēs	poterĭs
potest	possĭt		etc.	possĕt	poterĭt
possŭmus	possīmus			etc.	poterĭmŭs
potestis	possītis				poterĭtĭs
possunt	possint				poterunt

Possiem, etc., is found for **possim**, etc.; also the uncontracted **potessem** for **possem**. **Possum** is for pot-sum by assimilation of t, which appears in its proper form before a vowel. The imperative and the participle are wanting.

Prosum is like **sum**, but the preposition **prō** keeps its original form, **prōd**, before those forms that begin with a vowel, — pro-sum, prod-ĕs, prod-est, pro-sŭmŭs, etc.

[223] **Edo, ĕdĕre, ēdi, ēsum.** The irregular forms are: —

PRESENT.				IMP. SUBJ.	
—	ĕdĭm			essĕm	
ĕs	ĕdĭs	ĕs, esto		essēs	PRES. PASS. IND.
est	etc.	esto	INFINITIVE.	essĕt	estŭr
—			essĕ	etc.	
estĭs		este, estōte			IMPERF. PASS. SUBJ.
—		—			essētŭr

Also regular **ĕdo, -ĭs, -ĭt**, etc., like **rego**. See [108].

PART II. — FORMS.

224 Fĕro (stem fĕr-) omits the vowel, and retains the original present passive infinitive suffix -rī, usually lost in consonant-stems.

225 Vŏlo (stem vŏl-) omits the vowel, has present subjunctive sign ī, and varies the stem to vul, vel, vil. Its compounds nōlo and mālo have the same irregularities, and suffer contraction in many forms.

[224] Fĕro, fĕrre, tŭlī, lātum.

	PRESENT.			IMPERFECT.		FUTURE.
ferō	ferăm		INF.	ferēbăm ferrĕm		ferăm
fers	ferās	fĕr, ferto	ferrĕ	ferēbās ferrēs		ferēs
fert	etc.	ferto	PART.	etc.	etc.	etc.
ferĭmus			ferens			
fertĭs		fertĕ, fertōtĕ	GER.			
ferunt		ferunto	ferendi			

Ferŏr, ferri, lātus.

	PRESENT.			IMPERFECT.		FUTURE.
ferŏr	ferăr			ferēbăr ferrĕr'		ferăr
ferrĭs	ferāris	ferrĕ, fertŏr	INF.	ferēbārĭs ferŏrĭs		ferēris
fertur	etc.	fertŏr	ferrī	etc.	etc.	etc.
ferĭmur			PART.			
ferĭmĭnī		ferĭmĭnī	ferendus			
feruntŏr		feruntŏr				

For perfect stem fĕro uses tŭl; for simple stem, lā (older tla). Both are variations of a stem seen also in tollo. Ferĭmĭnī (ind. and imper.) retains the vowel, but the 2d pl. pass. was originally a participial formation, not a finite form.

[225] Vŏlo, velle, vŏluī.

	PRESENT.			IMPERFECT.		FUTURE.
vŏlō	vŏlĭm		INF.	vŏlēbăm vellĕm		vŏlăm
vīs	vĕlĭs	(vel, used as a	vellĕ	volēbās vellēs		volēs
vult	vĕlĭt	conjunction)	PART.	etc.	etc.	etc.
vŏlŭmŭs	vellīmus		vŏlens			
vultĭs	etc.		GEN.			
vŏlunt			volendi			

Nōlo, nolle, nōluī.

	PRESENT.			IMPERFECT.		FUTURE.
nōlo	nōlĭm		INF.	nōlēbăm nollĕm		[nolam]
(nĕvīs)	nōlĭs	nōlī, nōlīto	nolle	nōlēbās nollĕs		nōlĕs
(nĕvult)	etc.	nolīto	PART.	etc.	etc.	etc.
nōlŭmŭs			nōlens			
[nevultis]		nolīte, nolītōtĕ	GEN.			
nōlunt		nolunto	nōlendi			

IRREGULAR VERB-FORMS.

226 Do (stem da-) omits the vowel of the suffix in the present tense and the vowel of the mood-and-tense sign in the imperfect and future, and consequently has short ă throughout, where a-stems usually have long ā. Most of its compounds lose this ă, and thus become consonant-stems.

227 Eo (stem i-) varies the stem to e before a vowel (except before o in the present active participle),

Nĕvīs, nĕvult, are old. The imperative (except 3d pl.) is from a stem nolī.

Mālo, malle, māluī.

	PRESENT.			IMPERFECT.		FUTURE.
mālo	mālim			mālēbam	mallem	[malam]
māvīs	mālīs		INF.	mālēbas	mallēs	mālēs
māvult	etc.	(Imperative	malle	etc.	etc.	mālet
mālŭmŭs		wanting.)	GER.			etc.
māvultīs			malendī			
mālŭnt						

Mavŏlo, mavĕllm, etc. (uncontracted), are old. The bracketed forms are lacking.

[226] Do, dărĕ, dĕdī, dătum. Its inflection is like that of amo, except that the final vowel of the stem is everywhere short. (The forms dās, dā, are lengthened by a general tendency to lengthen certain syllables. See 360, 361.) Only the form do has the suffix vowel. The quantity of the stem-vowel is seen, for example, in dămus, dăbit, dăbitur, dăbāmus, etc. Another form of the same stem, du-, gives a subjunctive duam, duas, etc.; or duim, duis, etc.

Do remains unchanged in circumdo, pessumdo, satisdo and venumdo. These are not full compounds, and are often written separately. In the future, the original form (e.g., red-dĭbo, etc.) is sometimes found in the consonant-stem compounds.

[227] Eo, īre, īvī, ĭtum.

	PRESENT.				IMPERFECT.		FUTURE.
eo	eam			INF.	Ibăm	Irĕm	Ibŏ
īs	eās	ī, īto		īre	ībās	īrēs	ībĭs
ĭt	eăt	īto		PART.	etc.	etc.	etc.
īmus	eāmus			iens, euntis, etc.			
ītĭs	eātĭs	ītĕ, ītōtĕ		GER.			
eunt	eant	eunto		iendī, etc.			

and forms the imperfect and future indicative with the signs ĕbā and ĕb, like a- and e-stems.

228 Qveo (stem qvi-) and its compound neqveo are like eo.

229 Fīo (stem fī-) keeps the vowel ĕ unabsorbed in the present infinitive and imperfect subjunctive. In all other forms the stem-vowel is long, even before a vowel. The present infinitive is passive in form.

Impersonal and Defective Verbs.

230 Impersonal verbs are such as do not take a personal subject. They are found only in the third person singular, and comprise: —

231 (a) Verbs referring to the state of the weather.

232 (b) A few verbs expressing feeling or emotion, the object of which denotes the person who experiences the feeling.

233 (c) Verbs which take a clause or an infinitive as subject. Many of these are also used personally.

---

[228] Qveo, qvīre, qvīvī, qvītum. So neqveo, neqvīre, etc. Only a few forms are in use.

[229] **Fīo, fĭĕrī,** [factus].

Present.				Imperfect.		Future.
fīo	fīăm			fīēbăm	fīĕrĕm	fīăm
fīs	fīās	fī		fīēbās	fīĕrēs	fīes
fīt	etc.		Infinitive.	etc.	etc.	etc.
fīmus			fĭĕrī			
fītis		fītĕ				
fīunt						

Fīo is passive in meaning, and is used as the passive of **făcio,** which supplies the lacking participle and the complete tenses. In old Latin fĭĕrĕm, etc., and fĭĕrī occur.

[231] *E.g.,* **pluit,** *it rains;* **ningit,** *it snows,* etc.

[232] *E.g.,* **pudet me,** (*it shames me, i.e.*) *I am ashamed,* etc.

[233] *E.g.,* **mihi ire licet,** (*to go is permitted to me*) *I am permitted to go,* etc.

IMPERSONAL AND DEFECTIVE VERBS.

(d) Many intransitive verbs, which may be used impersonally in the passive.	**234**
Some verbs are defective in Latin. Of these only ōdi and mĕmĭni need special mention. They lack the incomplete tenses, and the complete tenses have the time of the incomplete.	**235**

[234] *E.g.*, **pugnātur,** (*it is fought*) *there is fighting going on;* **invĭdētur mihi,** (*it is envied toward me*) *I am envied;* **ītur,** (*it is gone*) *people go,* etc.

[235] The forms of the most usual defective verbs are added for reference: —

1. ājo, āis, āit, ājunt. Imperf. ājēbam or āibam, etc.; subj. ājās, ājăt; part. ājens.
2. Imperat. ăve, ăvēto, ăvēte; inf. ăvēre.
3. fātur. Imperat. fāre; fut. fābor, fābĭtur; inf. fārī; sup. fātu; part. fans, fandus, fātus.
4. inqvam, inqvĭs, inqvĭt; inqvĭmus, inqvĭunt. Imperat. inqve, inqvĭto, inqvĭte; imperf. inqvĭēbat; fut. inqvĭēs, inqvĭĕt; perf. inqvii, inqvisti, inqvit.
5. mĕmĭni; the complete tenses, and an imperat. memento, mementōte. In compounds the incomplete tenses are found; *e.g.*, re-mĭn-isc-or, etc.
6. ōdi; only the complete tenses and part. ōsūrus.
7. Subj. ŏvet, ŏvāret; part. ŏvans, ŏvātus; ger. ŏvandi.
8. Imperat. salve, salvēte; inf. salvēre; fut. salvēbis.

Many verbs lack the forms from the simple stem or those from the perfect stem, and some lack both. Impersonal verbs lack all forms except the third personal singular; and intransitive verbs, except in the use mentioned above (234), of course lack the passive voice altogether. Such are not usually called defective, however, but the name is limited to those given here.

PART III. — WORD-FORMATION.

Roots and Stems.

236 A root is a simple sound, or combination of sounds, used in language to convey an idea without modification.

237 Roots are sometimes used in Latin as stems, and the suffixes of inflection joined to them directly. Usually, however, stems are formed from roots by vowel-change, or by the addition of a vowel, **a, e, i, o, u**; sometimes by both.

238 Stems formed from roots in either of these three

---

[237] Many verbs with consonant-stems, and a few with stems in -a, -e or -i, use an unmodified root as a stem. Most verbs with vowel-stems, however, use a primitive stem, or, far more often, a derivative stem as the verb-stem. The a, e or i added to form the present stem is, of course, no part of the verb-stem, but only a modification used in the incomplete tenses. The final a, e or i of the present stem belongs to the verb-stem only when it shows itself also in the perfect stem and in the simple stem.

Very few nouns and no adjectives have roots as stems.

[238] Final vowels of stems (except **u** sometimes) are dropped before suffixes beginning with a vowel, and are often weakened (and sometimes dropped) before those that begin with a consonant. Before some of the latter, however, the vowel is lengthened, perhaps by the absorption of an initial vowel, which generally appears when they are appended to consonant-stems. Compare the usage in the case of the verb-suffixes, 170-190.

Initial **t** of a suffix suffers the euphonic change to **s** after certain letters, as in the supine and participles of the verb.

ways are called primitive stems. From these, derivative stems are formed by adding suffixes of derivation. Both primitive and derivative stems, by the addition of suffixes of inflection, become words of the language, fitted for use in sentences.

Formation of Nouns.

Nouns are formed from other nouns with a variety of suffixes and meanings. **239**

Nouns formed from adjectives express the quality or condition denoted by the adjective. **240**

---

[239] The most common suffixes are these:—
-ātu (= Eng. *-ship*), name of office or condition of the primitive.
-ēto, -ārĭo, name of place where the primitive is found.
-tūt (= Eng. *-hood*), name of condition or quality of the primitive.
-ĭo, name of condition or quality of the primitive.
-lo, -la (= Eng. *-let*), diminutive nouns.
-cŭlo, -cŭla (= Eng. *-let*), diminutive nouns.

Illustrations are:—

consul-ātus, *consulship*;	from consul, *a consul*.
qverc-ētum, *oak forest*;	" qvercus, *an oak*.
vir-tus, *manhood*;	" vir, *a man*.
minister-ium, *service*;	" minister, *a servant*.
vicŭ-lus, *hamlet*;	" vicus, *a village*.
casŭ-la, *cottage*;	" casa, *a house*.
flos-cŭlus, *floweret*;	" flos, *a flower*.
securi-cŭla, *hatchet*;	" securis, *an axe*.

[240] The more usual suffixes are -tāt, -tūdĭn, -ĭa, -tĭa (= Eng. *-ness*).
Illustrations are:—

superb-ĭa, *pride*;	from superbus, *proud*.
soli-tūdo, *loneliness*;	" solus, *alone*.
boni-tas, *goodness*;	" bonus, *good*.
justi-tĭa, *justice*;	" justus, *just*.

241 Nouns from verbs denote the *doer, means, result, place, instrument,* etc., of the action, or the action itself.

Formation of Adjectives.

242 Adjectives formed from nouns are usually "possessive" adjectives, expressing "possessed of," "full of."

[241] The most usual suffixes are:—
-tŏr (sŏr), -trĭc (= Eng. *-er, -ster*), name of the doer.
-tu (-su), -tūra (-sūra), -tĭŏn (-sĭŏn), -ĭo, -ĭŏn, -ŏr, -mĭn, -mento, -cŭlo, name of the act, means, result.
-bŭlo, -tro, name of the place, means, instrument.

Illustrations are:—

audī-tor, *hearer;*	from audī-re, *to hear.*
lu-sor, *player;*	" lud-ere, *to play.*
al-trix, *nourisher;*	" al-ere, *to nourish.*
ic-tus, *blow;*	" ic-ere, *to strike.*
arā-tio, *ploughing;*	" ara-re, *to plough.*
effug-ium, *escape;*	" effug-ere, *to escape.*
suspic-io, *suspicion;*	" suspic-ere, *to suspect.*
am-or, *love;*	" ama-re, *to love.*
certā-men, *fight;*	" certa-re, *to fight.*
vesti-mentum, *clothing;*	" vesti-re, *to clothe.*
specta-cŭlum, *spectacle;*	" specta-re, *to view.*
sta-būlum, *stall;*	" sta-re, *to stand.*
ara-trum, *plough;*	" ara-re, *to plough.*

[242] Adjectives thus formed correspond to English derivative adjectives in *-ish, -y, -ed, -ful, -en,* etc. The suffixes used to form them are very numerous; the most common are -āto, -do, -no, -āno, -ino, -ŭli, -ili, -āri, -ūrio, -āti, -ensi, -ōso, -lento, -co, -io, -co, -acco.

Illustrations are:—

aur-atus, *gilded;*	from aurum, *gold.*
luctu-ōsus, *sorrowful;*	" luctus, *sorrow.*
Rom-ānus, *Roman;*	" Roma, *Rome.*
aur-eus, *golden;*	" aurum, *gold.*
ebur-nus, *ivory;*	" ebur, *ivory.*
mort-ālis, *mortal;*	" mors, *death.*
etc.	etc.

FORMATION OF VERBS.

"furnished with," "made of," "characterized by," "belonging to," and the like.

243 Adjectives from other adjectives are derivative numerals, comparatives and superlatives, and diminutives.

244 Adjectives from verbs are the regular participles, adjectives with the force of participles (usually active), and adjectives denoting capability (usually passive).

Formation of Verbs.

245 A few verbs are formed from noun- or adjective-stems by using the theme of the noun as a verb-stem.

---

[243] For the ordinal and distributive numerals, with their suffixes, see [118]; and for the comparative and superlative formations, see 119 ff. Diminutive adjectives have the suffixes -lo and -cŭlo, like diminutive nouns.

E.g., **albŭlus**, *whitish*, from **albus**, *white*.
fortĭcŭlus, *boldish, somewhat bold*, from **fortis**, *bold*.

[244] For the regular participles and their endings see 183–187. Adjectives with the general force of participles, but expressing a habit rather than a single act, are formed with the suffixes **-uo, -ivo, -tivo, -do, -bundo, -cundo, -aci**, etc. Illustrations are: —

contĭg-uus, *touching, adjacent;*	from **contĭng-ĕre**, *to touch.*
cad-īvus, *falling, fleeting;*	" **cad-ĕre**, *to fall.*
nomĭna-tivus, *nominative;*	" **nomĭna-re**, *to name.*
erra-bundus, *wandering, vagrant;*	" **erra-re**, *to wander.*

Adjectives denoting capability are formed with the suffixes **-li, -bĭli, -tĭli (-sĭli)**. Illustrations are: —

frag-ĭlis, *breakable, frail;*	from **frang-ĕre**, *to break.*
cred-ĭbĭlis, *credible;*	" **cred-ĕre**, *to believe.*
fer-tĭlis, *fertile, capable of producing;*	" **fer-re**, *to produce.*

[245] Thus, from **flor** (theme of **flos**, *a flower*) we have **flor-ēre**, *to flower;* from **arbŏr** (theme of **arbos**, *a tree*), **arbor-esc-ere**, *to become a tree;* from **dulc** (theme of **dulcis**, *sweet*), **dulc-esc-ere**, *to grow sweet*, etc. That the **e** of the present stem does not belong to the verb-stem, but is a formative addition, is shown by the form of the perfect stem, when one exists (*e.g.*, **flor-ui**). But most of these verbs have only the incomplete tenses.

In such verbs the present stem is formed by adding -e, or by adding -esc. In the former case the verb means "to be [so-and-so]"; in the latter, "to become [so-and-so]."

246 More often verb-stems are formed from noun- or adjective-stems by adding -a or -i to the theme. Verbs thus formed usually mean "to make [so-and-so]"; less often, "to be [so-and-so]."

247 Verbs formed from verbs are frequentatives, intensives, or desideratives.

[246] Thus, from **bellum,** *war,* **bellare,** *to war;* from **aeqvus,** *level,* **aeqvare,** *to level;* from **miles,** *soldier,* **militare,** *to be a soldier;* from **tenuis,** *thin,* **tenuare,** *to make thin;* from **insanus,** *mad,* **insanire,** *to be mad;* from **finis,** *end,* **finire,** *to end,* etc.

From stems in u, a-stem verbs are formed by adding a to the stem, not the theme; *e.g.,* **aestu-are** from **aestu-s.** But i is added to the theme in u-stems, as in others. See [238].

[247] Frequentatives denote a frequent or emphatic action. They are formed with the suffix -ta. Many verbs formed in this way, however, have lost the frequentative force. Illustrations are:—

  adven-tare, *to come often;*   from **adven-ire,** *to come.*
  rog-itare, *to ask eagerly;*   "   **rog-are,** *to ask.*
  dic-tare, *to say frequently;*   "   **dic-ere,** *to say.*
  dict-itare, *to say frequently;*   "   **dict-are,** *to say.*

Intensives denote an eager or earnest action. They are few in number, and are formed with the suffix -ess or -essi, the latter being used in the complete tenses and simple stem forms. Illustrations are:—

  fac-ess-ere, *to do eagerly;*   from **fac-ere,** *to do.*
  cap-ess-ere, *to take eagerly, to seize;*   "   **cap-ere,** *to take.*

Desideratives denote the desire to do an action. They are few in number, and are formed with the suffix -turi (-suri). Illustrations are:—

  cena-turire, *to wish to dine;*   from **cena-re,** *to dine.*
  emp-turire, *to wish to buy;*   "   **em-ere,** *to buy.*

Desideratives seem to be formed from the future active participle by the addition of i, as stated in 246, the u being shortened, probably by the change of accent.

Formation of Adverbs.

248 Many adverbs are case-forms of nouns and adjectives, often with obsolete endings. The locative, accusative and ablative are most frequent.

249 Adverbs of manner are formed from adjectives and verbs; adverbs of source from nouns; numeral adverbs from numeral adjectives.

Formation of Prepositions, Conjunctions, and Interjections.

250 The interjections proper are primitive sounds, but various nouns are used interjectionally in the nominative, accusative or vocative. So also are curt phrases.

251 The prepositions and conjunctions are in some cases case-forms or phrases, but most of them are not easily subjected to grammatical analysis, and may conveniently be regarded as primitive words.

---

[249] The most usual suffixes for adverbs of manner from adjectives are -ē and -tĕr; from verbs, -tim (-sim). Adverbs of source are formed from nouns with the suffix -tŭs. Illustrations are: —

    cert-e, *surely;*   from certus, *sure.*
    firmī-ter, *firmly;*   " firmus, *firm.*
    cau-tim, *cautiously;*   " cav-ēre, *to be cautious.*
    fundī-tus, *from the bottom;*   " fundus, *bottom.*

Adverbs of source are formed from adjectives also, and even from prepositions. For the numeral adverbs (ending -iens or -iēs) see [118].

[251] The manner of formation of prepositions and conjunctions is a subject for comparative grammar, and cannot be fully treated in an elementary book.

Composition.

252 Words are also formed by composition, *i.e.*, by combining two or more stems into one. The suffixes of inflection or derivation are then added to the last stem.

[252] The first stem usually modifies the second with the force of an adverb, an adjective, an oblique case, or a direct object; *e.g.*, —

>   **in-īqvus,** *unfair* (**in, aequus**).
>   **centi-manus,** *hundred-handed* (**centum, manus**).
>   **capri-cornus,** *goat-horned* (**caper, cornu**).
>   **partĭ-ceps,** *partaker* (**pars, capere**).
>   **sangui-sūga,** *bloodsucker, leech* (**sanguis, sugo**).
>   etc.   etc.

A few words are often written as compounds, though not really such; *e.g.*, **res publica,** *commonwealth;* **jus jurandum,** *oath;* **legis lator,** *legislator,* etc. The custom of writing them as single words has caused them to be looked on as compounds, and they are sometimes called "spurious compounds." Compare in English *instead* (i.e. *in stead*), *perchance, perhaps,* etc., where two words have grown into one.

PART IV.—SYNTAX.

Person, Number, Voice, Concord.

253 The modifications of person, number and voice have the same force in Latin as in English. Special rules are needed only for concord, for the use of the cases, tenses and moods, and for the non-finite verb-forms.

The rules of concord are:—

254 (*a*) The appositive or predicate noun agrees in *case* with the noun it limits.

255 (*b*) The adjective agrees in *gender, number* and *case* with the noun it limits.

---

[253] Except the reflexive use of the passive and the deponent verbs. See 154.

[254] The appositive and predicate noun are usually required by the sense to agree in number, and they agree in gender also, when possible.

Most nouns lack a separate form for the locative and vocative. Such nouns, when used as appositives to those cases, are put in other constructions to express the same idea; with the locative, in the ablative (or ablative with a preposition); with the vocative, in the nominative.

[255] An adjective may limit two or more nouns. In this case the predicate adjective is generally plural and masculine if the nouns denote persons; neuter, if they denote things. The attributive adjective, limiting two or more nouns, generally agrees with the nearest.

Two or more ordinal numerals may stand in the singular with a plural noun; *e.g.*, **prima et qvarta legiones,** *the first and fourth legions.*

256	(*c*) Pronouns agree with their antecedents in *gender*, *number* and *person*.
257	(*d*) The finite verb agrees with its subject in *number* and *person*.

The participles used to make the "periphrastic" verb-forms sometimes agree with an appositive or predicate noun rather than the subject, when it denotes the same thing.

The locative case is limited by no adjectives but possessives (except die in old Latin). A nominative used in direct address is in a few cases limited by an adjective in the vocative form. Nominatives so used are usually called vocatives. See [261].

A predicate noun or adjective after an infinitive without an expressed subject often agrees not with the omitted subject but with the same word expressed in the sentence in some other case; *e.g.*, **cupio esse bonus,** *I wish to be good;* **mihi licet esse bono,** *I am permitted to be good.* (In the former of these sentences **bonus** agrees with **ego,** expressed in the ending of the verb **cupio**; in the latter, **bono** agrees with **mihi**.) **Vobis necesse est fortibus viris esse,** *you must be brave men.*

[256] The rule applies, of course, only to substantive pronouns, and even these can show person only when they are used as subjects of finite verbs, which show by their ending the person of the subject. All adjective pronouns agree as adjectives. A few cases occur in poetry of an agreement of the relative pronoun in *case* also (attraction); and in a few instances the antecedent takes the case of the relative. A pronoun sometimes agrees with an appositive or predicate-noun of its antecedent. With more than one antecedent, pronouns follow the usage of adjectives in gender and number; that of verbs in person. See [255] and [257].

[257] With two or more subjects taken conjointly, the verb is plural. If the subjects differ in person the verb takes the first person in preference to the second, the second in preference to the third. But in such cases the verb often agrees with the nearest subject, especially if it precedes the subjects.

Occasional violations of the rules of agreement are found, the most common being an agreement according to sense rather than form. Thus, a feminine or neuter collective noun may take a plural adjective or verb referring to the implied individuals; two subjects, taken together, may take a singular verb if they express a single idea, etc.

Use of the Cases.

The NOMINATIVE is used —
  (*a*) As subject of a finite verb. | 258
  (*b*) In exclamations. | 259
  (*c*) To denote the person or thing spoken to. | 260

The VOCATIVE is used —
  (*a*) To denote the person or thing spoken to. | 261

The ACCUSATIVE is used —
  (*a*) As the direct object of an action. | 262

[258] The use of the *subject-nominative* is the same as in English.

[259] The *exclamatory nominative* may be considered the subject of a verb implied in the connection. It is usually accompanied by the interjection en or ecce. **en Priamus!** *Lo,* (*here is*) *Priam!* **En ego, vester Ascanius!** *Lo,* (*it is*) *I, your Ascanius!* **ecce tuae litterae!** *Now your letter* (*comes*)*!*

[260] The *nominative of direct address* is the regular usage in the plural number, where no vocative is found, but is rare in the singular, when a separate vocative form exists. It is usual to call nominatives vocatives when used in this way, if no separate vocative form is found. **audi tu, populus Albanus,** *hear, thou Alban nation.* **proice tela, sangvis meus,** *cast away thy weapons, my son.*

[261] **faciam, Laeli,** *I will do so, Laelius.* The vocative is the simple stem without a case-suffix. A vocative form is found in the singular in a-stems, masculine o-stems and semivowel-stems. In others the nominative is used as a vocative, and is usually called a vocative when so used. An adjective limiting such a nominative usually takes the vocative form, if it has a separate form for that case, but sometimes the nominative; *e.g.*, **sangvis meus,** above [260].

A form macte is called a vocative by some grammarians, an adverb by others. It is used as a simple exclamation, or with the imperative forms esto, este, as an exclamation of approval. **macte!** *good!* **macte virtute esto!** *bravo!*

[262] **omnem eqvitatum mittit,** *he sends all the cavalry.*
A special kind of direct object is the *cognate* accusative, which repeats the meaning of the verb in the form of a noun; *e.g.*, **vitam tutam vivere,**

263	(*b*) As subject of an infinitive.
264	(*c*) In exclamations.

to *live a safe life;* **servitutem servire,** *to slave slavery* (i.e., *undergo*). This form of direct object follows verbs which are otherwise intransitive.

Many verbs are transitive in Latin, while English verbs of like meaning are intransitive. In such cases a preposition is inserted in English; *e.g.*, **arma cano,** *I sing of arms;* **petit hostem,** *he aims at the foe,* etc. Other verbs, properly intransitive, sometimes take a direct object in poetical or figurative language; *e.g.*, **ardebat Alexin,** *he was hot for* (i.e., *loved*) *Alexis;* **redolere antiqvitatem,** *to smell of antiquity;* **saltare Cyclopa,** *to dance the Cyclops;* **resonant Amaryllida silvae,** *the groves echo* (*the name of*) *Amaryllis.* Many verbs also are made transitive by being compounded with prepositions.

In a few cases the action implied in a noun or adjective governs a direct object. The infinitives, participles and gerund, of course, retaining their verbal power, govern the same case as their verbs.

Factitive verbs (*i.e.*, verbs meaning *make, appoint, choose, name,* etc.) take two objects, as in English, denoting the same person or thing; *e.g.*, **populus Romanus Ciceronem creavit consulem,** *the Roman nation chose Cicero consul.*

Doceo (and compounds), **celo** and a few verbs of *demanding* and *questioning*, sometimes take two direct objects, — one denoting the person, the other the thing; *e.g.*, **non te celavi sermonem,** *I have not concealed from you the remark;* **te hoc rogo,** *I ask you this;* **Caesar Haeduos frumentum flagitare,** *Cæsar kept demanding corn from the Hæduans.* In the passive voice of these verbs the accusative of the person becomes the subject, and that of the thing remains. In many cases the accusative of the thing seems to be an accusative of specification, or to approach that meaning, and may be a development from it. See [267].

[263] This use is a development of (*a*), the subject of the infinitive being originally the object of the leading verb. It has been extended, however, to all uses of the infinitive except the historical infinitive, which is a finite verb-form in meaning. See [342]. **cum suos interfici viderent,** *when they saw that their men were being killed;* **necesse est legem haberi,** *it is needful that the law be kept;* **fama erat hostem advenire,** *there was a rumor that the foe was coming.*

[264] The *exclamatory accusative* is possibly the object of a verb implied in the connection, but in most cases none need be supplied in translation. An interjection often accompanies it. **heu, me miserum!**

USE OF THE CASES.

(*d*) To denote the place to which motion proceeds.	265
(*e*) To denote extent of time or space.	266
(*f*) With verbs or adjectives to define their application.	267
(*g*) With many prepositions.	268

Alas, unhappy me! hanc audaciam, the impudence! In old Latin the accusatives **cum, eam, illum, illam,** etc., are combined with the preceding en or ecce to **eccum, eccam, eccillam,** etc.

[265] *Accusative of limit.* This use is limited, in prose, to names of towns and small islands, and **domum, domos, foras, rus. Hennam profécti sunt,** *they went to Henna;* **ego rus ibo,** *I shall go to the country.* Other words require a preposition, except a few phrases with **eo,** "to go," or **do,** "to give," in which the freer use of early Latin is retained; *e.g.,* **pessum ire,** *to go to ruin;* **pessum dare,** [*to send to ruin,* i.e.] *to ruin;* **infitias ire, exseqvias ire, venum ire, venum dare.** Here belongs also the use of the accusative case of the supine. See 351.

[266] *Accusative of extent.* **paucos dies moratus,** *having waited a few days;* **millia passuum tria ab corum castris castra ponit,** *he pitches a camp three miles from their camp.* Extent of time or space is sometimes expressed by the ablative. See 302.

[267] *Accusative of specification.* This use is rare in prose, the ablative being the usual construction. The accusative is found, however, in neuter pronouns, **id, qvid,** etc., in **nihil**; in neuter adjectives, **pauca, multum,** etc.; and in a few idiomatic phrases. It is usually best translated by an adverb or an adverbial phrase; *e.g.,* **quid?** *why?* **maximam partem,** *chiefly;* **id temporis,** *then;* **istuc aetatis,** *at your age,* etc. In the phrases **id genus,** *of that sort;* **virile secus,** *of the male sex,* and the like, this accusative seems to qualify a noun, and is nearly equal in force to a genitive or ablative of description. Under this head come many so-called adverbs, **multum, plus, minus,** etc.

With **cingor,** *I bind on* (*myself*), and other passive forms used reflexively, an accusative is found, which is usually referred to this head. It is better treated, however, as direct object, since the verb is not properly passive. In poetical language many passive participles retain a direct object which may be explained in the same way.

[268] The accusative and ablative cases follow prepositions in Latin. A list of those that take the ablative is given in 308; all others take the accusative. Prepositions compounded with verbs sometimes retain their power of

| 269 | The DATIVE is used —
 (a) As indirect object of an action or feeling. |

governing an accusative. If the verb is transitive, it will then take two accusatives, — one a direct object, the other governed by the preposition. This use is rare, except with **trans**. **populos adit,** *he goes to* (i.e., *visits*) *the tribes;* **milites flumen transportabat,** *he was taking his troops over the river.*

Pridie, *the day before;* **postridie,** *the day after;* and the phrase **ante diem,** used in dates, are followed by an accusative, like prepositions. The construction seems to be elliptical.

The adjectives **propior, proximus,** and the corresponding adverbs **propius, proxime,** are followed by an accusative like their positive **prope,** which is both adverb and preposition. (Compare the similar prepositional use of *nearer, nearest,* in English.)

[269] The *dative of indirect object* denotes the person or thing *to* or *for which,* or *for whose advantage* anything is done or exists. Various prepositions are used to express the idea in English, *to* and *for* most often. Sometimes the English indirect objective will render it. **Himilconi respondit,** *he answered Himilco;* **mihi licet adire,** *I am allowed to come near* (*it is allowed to me*); **hostibus terrorem augere,** *to increase the fright of the enemy* (*increase fright for*); **pugnare hostibus,** *to fight with* (or *against*) *the foe.*

Sometimes, in poetry, the dative of the indirect object is found with verbs of motion, where a phrase expressing the *place to which* would be used in prose; *e.g.,* **it clamor caelo,** *the outcry goes to the sky.* This use arises from a poetical notion or conception, the rising of the shout being thought of not simply as going to the sky, but as affecting or having influence on the sky. So occasionally other verbs, the action being conceived of as done *to* the person or thing, though another construction would be used in prose; *e.g.,* **lateri abdidit ensem,** *buried the sword in his side.* So especially verbs meaning "*take away.*"

Many verbs are intransitive in Latin, though verbs of like meaning are transitive in English, and the indirect object with such becomes a direct object in translation. The most common are verbs meaning *help, please, trust, serve,* and the contrary; also *spare, pardon, envy, command, persuade,* and the like. If pains is taken to translate them by intransitive expressions, the dative will be seen to have its proper force. **non Herculi nocere voluit,** *she did not wish to do harm to Hercules* (= *injure*). **mundus deo paret,** *the world is subject to* (*obeys*) *a god.* Transitive verbs with the meanings given above govern an accusative, but may take a dative also, if

(*b*) To denote the possessor or apparent agent.	**270**
(*c*) With adjectives, to denote that to which the quality or feeling is directed.	**271**
(*d*) To denote purpose or end.	**272**

the meaning permits; and most of these verbs may take an accusative of the thing, especially a neuter pronoun, along with the dative of the person. **Hoc tibi impero,** *I give you this command* (*command this to you*). In the case of some of these verbs, usage is unsettled, and they take either a direct or an indirect object, with little or no difference of meaning.

The same remarks apply also to many verbs compounded with the prepositions **ad, ante, con, in, inter, ob, post, prae, pro, sub, super,** which take a dative, and if transitive an accusative also.

[270] The *dative of possessor* is simply an indirect object, denoting the person for whom, or for whose advantage or disadvantage something exists. It needs mention only on account of peculiarity of translation. **Gallis haec consuetudo est,** *the Gauls have this custom* (lit., *this custom exists for the Gauls*). The same is true of the *dative of apparent agent*, so named because translated "*by.*" It is found regularly with the present passive participle (rarely with the perfect passive participle or a verbal adjective in -bilis), and denotes the person who has the work to do. **multa mihi facienda sunt,** *much must be done by me, I have much to do* (lit., *the doing-of-much exists for me*). In poetry we sometimes find a dative of the real agent, or one which approaches that meaning.

[271] The *dative with adjectives* is also an indirect object, and denotes that toward which the implied feeling is exercised, or for which the implied quality exists. The adjectives most often limited by a dative are those kindred in meaning to the verbs that govern a dative, and those which mean *like, ready, friendly, easy, fit,* etc. **paucis carior fides quam pecunia fuit,** *to a few, truth was dearer than money;* **hoc luctuosum est parentibus,** *this is sad for parents.* **idem,** *same,* sometimes takes a dative (like adjectives of *likeness*).

In a few cases, a noun or adverb, derived from a verb or adjective which governs a dative, takes an indirect object like its primitive. **convenienter naturae,** *in agreement with nature.* Also, rarely, a dative is found with interjections. **vae victis!** *woe to the vanquished!* **vae mihi!** *ah me!*

[272] The *dative of purpose* is most frequent with the verb "*be.*" It is translated as a predicate-noun or an appositive with "*as,*" less often by "*for.*" **impedimento id fuit,** *this was a hindrance* (*served as a hindrance*);

	The LOCATIVE is used —
273	(*a*) To denote the place of an action.
274	(*b*) To denote price or value.

virtus non datur dono, *virtue is not given as a present;* **eqvitatum Caesari auxilio miserunt,** *they had sent cavalry as a help to Cæsar.* A second dative of the person to whom the action is of interest is often added, as in the last example. This use of the dative to express purpose is not common, except in the case of a few words. A few have become equivalent to adjectives, — **frugi bonae** = *honest*, **usui** = *useful*, **cordi** = *pleasing*, etc. In **operae est,** *it is worth while,* it is not clear whether **operae** is dative or genitive. **operae pretium est** also occurs, and the shorter expression may be derived from the latter.

On the border between the dative of indirect object and the dative of purpose stands its occurrence to denote the *use* to which a thing is put; *e.g.,* **domicilio locum delegerunt,** *they chose a place for a home;* **receptui signum,** *the "retreat-call," signal for retreat;* **esui olivae,** *eating-olives,* etc. This use of the dative is most common with the gerundive, in giving the duties of an officer or committee, and similar expressions; *e.g.,* **decemviri legibus scribendis,** *a committee of ten to compile the laws.* In such cases it seems to limit a noun, but the construction is probably elliptical.

[273] A separate form for the locative is found in Latin only in the singular of some names of towns and islands, and a few other words, **domi, humi, ruri** being the most frequent. (In other words, and in the plural, the ablative or a preposition is used to express "place where.") **cogitandum tibi erat Romaene et domi tuae, an Mitylenis aut Rhodi malles vivere,** *you had to consider whether you preferred to live at Rome and at your own home, or at Mitylenæ or Rhodes.* A locative **animi** occurs with verbs and adjectives of *feeling;* e.g., **aeger animi,** *sick at heart.*

In old Latin a locative **die** is found denoting the "time when"; *e.g.,* **qvinti die,** *on the fifth day;* **die crastini,** *to-morrow,* etc.

Several adverbs of place or time are locatives; *e.g.,* **hic,** *here;* **illic,** *there;* **postridie** (= **posteri die**), *on the following day;* **pridie,** *on the day before;* **qvotidie,** *daily,* etc.

In the case of plural names of towns, it is a matter of indifference whether the case used to denote place be called ablative or locative. The form is the same, and the use of the singular shows that either case may be used in this sense.

[274] A definite amount named as the price is expressed by the ablative. The locative is found in indefinite expressions of price or value; *e.g.,*

The genitive was originally the case of the *source* or (consequently) the *cause*. This idea can be seen in some of its uses; in others the idea of possession, developed from that of source, is more prominent.	275
The GENITIVE is used (as the case of *source* or *cause*) —	
(*a*) To denote the crime .	276
1. With verbs of *judicial action*.	277
2. With adjectives of *guilt* or *innocence*.	278
(*b*) To denote the person or thing that excites the feeling	279
1. With some verbs of *reminding, remembering, forgetting, pitying.*	280
2. With **miseret, paenitet, piget, pudet, taedet.**	281
3. With *adjectives* of like meaning.	282

magni aestimare, *to value highly;* **flocci non faciunt,** *they don't care a straw for* ——— ; **est mihi tanti,** *it is worth my while;* **aeqvi boni facere,** *to take in good part,* etc. In **homo nihili,** *a worthless fellow,* and the like, the locative seems to limit a noun, but the expression is perhaps elliptical.

The locative was not clear to the Romans themselves, and its similarity of form caused it to be confused, in the singular, with the genitive, and in a few cases genuine genitives were used with the force of locatives. Thus, **pluris** and **minoris** occur a few times to express value; a few other genitives occur once each. **mentis,** *in mind,* is found twice; it seems to have been formed after the analogy of **animi.**

[277] *i.e.,* verbs of *accusing, condemning, acquitting,* etc. **ambitus accusare,** *to accuse of bribery.*

[278] **insons culpae,** *innocent of fault;* **reus avaritiae,** *charged with avarice.*

[280] **admonebat cum egestatis,** *he reminded him of his poverty;* **veteris proverbii memini,** *I remember an old saw.*

[281] **cum libidinis infamiaeqve neqve pudet neqve taedet,** *he is neither ashamed of his licentiousness and ill-repute nor sick of them.* With **pudet** the person toward whom the sense of shame is felt is occasionally treated as the exciting object.

One or two other verbs of like meaning occasionally occur with a genitive, — **vereor,** *to feel awe;* **fastidio,** *to feel disgust.*

[282] **gloriae memor,** *mindful of glory;* **lassus militiae,** *sick of warfare.*

283	(*c*) To denote the whole, of which the word it limits denotes a part.
284	(*d*) To describe anything by denoting its qualities or its material.

[283] *Partitive genitive.* It may limit nouns, adjectives or adverbs, if they express a part. **pars militum,** *part of the soldiers;* **ubinam gentium sumus?** *where in the world are we?* (*in what place among nations?*) **omnium fluminum maximum,** *the largest of all rivers;* **genus eorum unum,** *one class of them.* Here belongs the genitive in various idiomatic phrases; *e.g.*, **id temporis,** *at that [point of] time;* **qvid novi?** *what news?* **id loci,** *that spot,* etc. As partitive genitives the personal pronoun forms **nostrum, vestrum** are used, not **nostri, vestri. ejus** is a partitive genitive in the phrase **qvod ejus,** = "*as far as*" (lit. *whatever of it*). **qvod ejus possis,** *as far as you can.* In older Latin, and in colloquial style, we find phrases like **scelus viri,** *a villain;* **qvid hominis?** *what sort of a fellow?* **monstrum hominis,** *a monster,* etc., which come under the head of partitives, as do also the phrases **compendi facere,** *to save;* **lucri facere,** *to gain,* and the like.

[284] *Descriptive genitive.* **res magni laboris,** *a task of great toil* (*very toilsome*); **murus pedum sedecim,** *a sixteen foot wall.* This genitive, when denoting a quality of the word it limits, regularly has an adjective with it, as in the examples given. (**bidui, tridui,** etc., have an adjective compounded with them.)

The descriptive genitive, when used to denote material, does not require a limiting adjective. This use is rare (an adjective is generally used to denote material), and in many cases seems to approach the idea of a partitive genitive. Examples are: **acervus frumenti,** *a heap of grain;* **talentum auri,** *a talent of gold.*

Other constructions occur instead of the genitive in all its uses to express source or cause. Thus, verbs of *accusing,* etc., verbs of *reminding,* etc., sometimes take a phrase with a preposition; verbs of *remembering,* etc., a direct object; **miseret,** etc., an infinitive; the various adjectives, also, are used with prepositional phrases instead of the genitive. The poets and later writers use the genitive more freely with adjectives to express cause; sometimes also to express specification, where an ablative or locative might be expected.

For a partitive genitive a phrase with a preposition is not unusual, oftenest with **de** or **ex.**

The GENITIVE is used (as a possessive case) —
(a) To denote the possessor. | **285**
(b) To define a noun more closely. | **286**
(c) To denote the subject of the implied action or feeling. | **287**
(d) To denote the object of the implied action or feeling. | **288**

The idea of *source* passes into that of *separation*, and in a few cases a genitive is found in poetry, where an ablative of separation would be the usual construction. Probably the habit of imitating Greek constructions (common in the Augustan poets) is the cause of this use.

[285] *Possessive genitive.* **membra hominis,** *a man's limbs;* **natura deorum,** *the nature of the gods.* Used with any noun denoting a thing capable of possession in the widest sense; also with adjectives used substantively; *e.g.,* **aeqvalis ejus,** *his equal in age;* **similis Caesaris,** *like Caesar* (*Caesar's like*), etc. This genitive is often put in the predicate, and mark, duty, or some such word supplied in translation; *e.g.,* **est hominis,** *'tis a man's duty;* **hominis est errare,** *it is characteristic of man to make mistakes.*

The genitive case of the personal pronouns is not used, in prose, as a possessive. The possessive pronouns are used instead.

A possessive genitive is found with **ergo, instar, tenus, pridie** and **postridie,** which were originally nouns, but have sunk to prepositions or adverbs.

[286] *Appositive genitive.* **urbs Romae,** (*Rome's city,* i.e.) *Rome;* **urbs Buthroti,** *the city of Buthrotum.* This is properly a possessive genitive. It is rarely found, an appositive being far more usual.

[287] *Subjective genitive.* **deorum factum,** *a deed of the gods.* The word it limits must imply, of course, an action or feeling. In some cases it is hard to draw the line between the subjective and the possessive use of the genitive, and the possessive pronouns are used for it as for a possessive genitive.

[288] *Objective genitive.* **usus membrorum,** *the use of the limbs;* **cura rerum alienarum,** *the care of others' interests.* The objective genitive limits nouns and adjectives that imply an action or feeling which may pass over to an object. **amans sui,** *fond of himself;* **capax urbis mag-**

	The genitive is used, further —
289	(*a*) To denote price or penalty.
290	(*b*) With a few verbs and adjectives of plenty and want.
291	(*c*) With **interest** and **rēfert**.

nae, *capable-of-holding a large city.* As objective genitives, **meī, tuī, suī, nostrī, vestrī** are used (**nostrum, vestrum** very rarely).

A phrase with a preposition (**in, erga**, etc.) may be used instead of the objective genitive. This use of the genitive, like that of the subjective genitive, is a development of the idea of possession, the action or feeling, whether done to one or by one, being thought of as something belonging to him.

[289] The genitive of price has been mentioned [274]. The genitive of penalty is found in **capitis damnare**, *to condemn to death*, and similar expressions. It seems to have arisen from confusion with the genitive of the crime, but possibly there may be an ellipsis of the word on which the genitive depends, the expression having been originally a legal phrase. Penalty is usually expressed by the ablative.

[290] With verbs and adjectives of *filling, fullness*, the genitive seems to come under the head of *source* or *cause;* but an ablative of means is more common. With other expressions the genitive is not common, except in the poets and later writers, who seem, in many cases, to use it in imitation of the Greek, to express not only *want* or *lack*, but often also *separation* or *specification*, ideas which are regularly expressed by the ablative. The verb **potior**, also, which usually takes an ablative, is found with a genitive. **domus erat plena ebriorum,** *the house was full of drunken men;* **temeritatis implere,** *to fill with rashness;* **exercitationis indiget,** *needs practice.*

[291] **nullius interest,** *it makes no difference to any one;* **illorum refert,** *it concerns them.* In this construction, the possessive pronoun forms **meū, tuū, suū, nostrā, vestrā** are used, instead of the genitive of a personal pronoun. The origin of this genitive is not clear, but **rēfert** is commonly thought to stand for **rem fert;** in which case the genitive is possessive, and **meū, tuū,** etc., stand for **meam, tuam,** etc. The genitive and possessive pronoun with **interest** may be explained as having arisen from the analogy of **rēfert**, which has the same meaning, and naturally takes the same construction.

USE OF THE CASES.

292 The ablative in Latin has taken on itself the functions of four different cases, the meaning and force of which are rudely given by the four prepositions most often used to translate it, — *from, by, in, with.*

1. FROM — The Ablative Proper.

The ABLATIVE PROPER is used —

293 (*a*) To denote the place from which motion proceeds.

294 (*b*) To denote separation, source and origin.

[292] The classification here given of the uses of the ablative is not meant to be absolute or scientific. The various uses shade into one another, and a sharp line of division is, in many cases, impossible. In doubtful cases, the clue offered by other constructions has been generally followed; thus *cause*, though often passing insensibly into *means*, has been put under "ablative proper" rather than "instrumental," because of the frequent use of a, de or ex to express cause; *price*, though in many cases "instrumental," has been put under "locative" because of the locative of price, etc. But analogy fails in many cases, — the name of a town used in dating letters is found not only in the ablative, but also in the locative and in the ablative with a. Should the ablative when so used be regarded as "place where" or "place from which"? Some of these doubtful cases are mentioned in the notes; if the teacher should choose to transfer any usage from one head to another, no harm will come of it, as the sole object of the classification is to render it easier to learn and keep in mind the various uses.

[293] This use is generally limited in prose to names of towns and small islands, and **domo, humo, rure**. (Other words usually take a preposition.) **Corintho fugit,** *fled from Corinth ;* **rure huc advenit,** *came hither from the country.*

[294] **hostem rapinis prohibere,** *to keep the foe from plunder ;* **Jove natus et Latonā,** *born of Jove and Latona;* **satus terrā,** *sprung from earth.* (A preposition is often used, however, to express separation or source.)

Under this head belongs the use of the ablative with verbs and adjectives denoting *want* and *lack; e.g.,* **vacuus curā,** *free from care;* **isto nomine caruit,** *it lacked that name.* (The genitive is also thus used; see 290.)

295	(*c*) To denote cause.
296	(*d*) To denote the standard of comparison.
	2. BY — The Instrumental Ablative.
	The INSTRUMENTAL ABLATIVE is used —
297	(*a*) To denote the means or instrument.

[295] The *ablative of cause* is used with a great variety of expressions, and rendered into English by various prepositions. **animi vitio id evenit,** *that came about from a fault of character.* So with **gaudere,** *to rejoice* (*in*); **niti,** *to depend* (*on*); **confidere,** *to trust* (*to*); **contentus,** *satisfied* (*with*); **laetus,** *glad* (*of*); etc.

[296] This ablative is translated "than." **nihil est viro dignius acqvitate,** *nothing is more worthy of a man than justice.* "Than" is also expressed by qvam, and the usage of Latin speech is roughly the following: —

(*a*) When the standard of comparison is a relative pronoun, the ablative is used.

(*b*) When the standard of comparison is subject, or an attribute of the subject, either the ablative or qvam may be used.

(*c*) When two adjectives are compared, qvam is used, and both adjectives take the same degree. **magis disertus qvam sapiens,** *more learned than wise;* **verior qvam gratior,** *more true than popular.*

(*d*) With adverbs the ablative is often used loosely in indefinite comparisons; *e.g.*, **dicto citius,** *sooner than said.* So **spe, opinione, justo,** etc.

(*e*) In expressions of *size, number, weight,* etc., after the adverbs **plus, minus, amplius, longius,** either the ablative or qvam may be used. But qvam is often omitted in such constructions, and the word denoting the standard of comparison left in the same case as if qvam were expressed; *e.g.*, **plus tria millia,** *more than three thousand.*

(*f*) In cases not included in the above qvam is used in prose, but the ablative is more freely used in poetry. So too with **alius,** *other* (*than*).

On the border between the ablative proper and the instrumental ablative stands its use to denote the material of which a thing consists; *e.g.*, **animo constamus et corpore,** *we are made up of soul and body.*

Here, too, may be placed the use of the ablative with **facio, fio** and **sum** in the peculiar idioms, **qvid facius . . . ?** *what can you do with . . . ?* and **qvid fiet . . . ?** *what will become of . . . ? e.g.*, **qvid hoc homine faciatis?** *what could you do with this fellow?*

[297] *Ablative of means.* **lacte et carne vivunt pellibusqve sunt**

USE OF THE CASES.

(*b*) To denote the amount of difference. **298**

3. IN — The Locative Ablative.

The LOCATIVE ABLATIVE is used —
(*a*) To denote the place where an action takes place. **299**

vestiti, *they live on milk and flesh and are clothed with skins;* **cum coronā donasti,** *you presented him with a crown.*

fruor, fungor, potior, utor, vescor are limited by an ablative of means, which is usually translated as a direct object. **lacte, caseo, carne vescor,** *I eat milk, cheese, flesh* (i.e., *feed myself with*); **Crassus aedilitate functus est,** *Crassus held (busied himself with) the aedileship.* In regard to the reflexive use of these deponents, see 154. (In old Latin they sometimes take a direct object, and a remnant of their transitive meaning is seen in their present passive participles, which are used with esse to make the "second periphrastic conjugation," like those of other transitive verbs. **potior** also takes a genitive; see [200].)

The ablative of means is used also with **opus** and **usus;** *e.g.,* **opus est pecuniā,** *(there is a work [to be done] with money,* i.e.*) there is need of money.* In this construction, instead of a noun denoting action we sometimes find the perfect passive participle, or the ablative of the supine; *e.g.,* **opus est properato,** *there is need of haste;* **opus est factu,** *there is need of action.*

The ablative may denote the road or route by which one goes. **Aureliā viā profectus est,** *he went by the Aurelian way;* **flumine adverso,** *up the river;* **recto litore,** *straight along the shore;* etc. This use may be considered either instrumental or locative, as the road is looked on as a *means* of travel or a *place* of travel.

[298] *Ablative of degree.* **paulo longius processit,** *he went on a little farther;* **decem annis ante Punicum bellum,** *ten years before the Punic war.* So with **abesse, distare,** etc., to express distance; *e.g.,* **qvinqve milibus ab urbe distat,** *is five miles from the city;* **a litore tridui navigatione,** *three days' sail from the coast.*

qvo ... eo and **qvanto ... tanto** occur often in correlative clauses, and are translated by *the ... the.* **qvo difficilius, eo praeclarius,** *the more difficult, the more glorious.*

[299] *Ablative of place.* This use is generally limited in prose to names of towns and islands, words which mean "place" (**loco, locis, parte,** etc.), words limited by **totus** or **medius,** and a few phrases. (Other words usually take a preposition. For the locative of "place where" see 273.) **Tamesis uno omnino loco transiri potest,** *the Thames can be crossed in*

300	(*b*) To define the application of the word it limits.
301	(*c*) To denote the time when or within which an action takes place.
302	(*d*) To denote extent of time or space.
303	(*e*) To denote price or penalty.

4. WITH—The Comitative Ablative.

The COMITATIVE ABLATIVE is used—

304	(*a*) To denote accompaniment.

one place only; **totis trepidatur castris**, *there is a panic in the whole camp.* So **Carthagine Novā**, *at New Carthage;* **Trallibus**, *at Tralles;* **terrā mariqve**, *by land and sea;* **dextrā**, *on the right*, etc. In the case of plural names of towns, it is indifferent whether the case be called ablative or locative.

[300] *Ablative of specification.* Translated *in, in respect to, in point of,* etc. **temporibus errasti**, *you were mistaken in the date;* **grandis natu**, *advanced in life;* **rex nomine, non potentiā**, *king in name, not in power.* Here belongs the ordinary use of the supine in the ablative; *e.g.*, **mirabile dictu**, *strange to tell;* possibly also the ablative with **dignus** and **indignus**; *e.g.*, **indignus est vitā**, *he is unworthy of life.* But see [303].

[301] *Ablative of time.* **tertiā vigiliā solvit**, *he set sail in the third watch;* **solis occasu**, *at sunset;* **decem diebus proximis**, *within the next ten days.* Some expressions of time contain at the same time a suggestion also of cause, means or specification; *e.g.*, **bello civili periit**, *he lost his life in the civil war;* **duobus his proeliis**, *in these two battles*, etc.

[302] *Ablative of extent.* **pugnatum est horis qvinqve**, *the fight lasted five hours.* An accusative is more often used to express extent of time or space. See 266.

[303] *Ablative of price.* **vendidit hic auro patriam**, *this man sold his country for gold.* *Ablative of penalty.* **tertiā parte agri damnati**, *fined a third part of their land;* **morte damnatus**, *condemned to death.* With verbs of *exchanging* either what is given or what is received may be treated as the price. With some verbs the ablative of price seems to be instrumental rather than locative. Price is also expressed by the locative, and penalty by the genitive. See 274 and 289.

An ablative is used with the adjectives **dignus** and **indignus**, and with the verb **dignor**, which seems to come under the head of price, but is not quite clear. See [300]. **haud me tali dignor honore**, *I do not think myself worthy of such honor.*

(*b*) To describe anything by expressing its qualities or appearance.	**305**
(*c*) To denote manner or attendant circumstances.	**306**
The ablative is used, further —	
(*a*) As the case absolute.	**307**

[304] *Ablative of accompaniment.* This use is limited in prose to military expressions, giving the troops or forces with which a movement is made. **Caesar subseqvebatur omnibus copiis,** *Cæsar followed with all his troops.* In other expressions the preposition **cum** is used.

[305] *Ablative of description.* In this use the ablative, like the descriptive genitive, requires a limiting adjective or a limiting genitive. **pari acclivitate collis,** *a hill of equal steepness;* **ore rubicundo homo,** *a red-faced fellow.* It is often best rendered by a compound adjective, as in the last example.

[306] The *ablative of manner* is generally limited in prose to words meaning "*manner*" (**modo, ratione,** etc.), and words which have a limiting adjective. **aeqvo animo mori,** *to die with resignation (an even mind);* **id summo studio a militibus administratur,** *this is performed by the soldiers with the greatest zeal.* Other words take regularly the preposition **cum,** except a few like **injuria,** *unjustly,* **silentio,** *silently,* which have become equivalent to adverbs in their use; and those which contain also the idea of *cause* or *means; e.g.,* **nox cantu aut clamore acta,** *the night was spent in singing and shouting;* **pedibus proeliari,** *to fight on foot;* **versibus scribere,** *to write in verse,* etc.

The *ablative of attendant circumstances* lies between the ablative of manner and the ablative absolute (which often expresses manner or circumstance), and cannot be separated by any distinct line from those uses. **In foro summa hominum frequentia exscribo,** *I am writing in the forum with a great crowd (around me).* So in various phrases: **injussu Caesaris,** *without Cæsar's orders;* **pace tua,** *by your leave;* **tuo periculo,** *at your own risk,* etc. Here seem to belong two or three cases of the gerundive (see 340), which are often regarded as ablative absolute. **nullis officii praeceptis tradendis,** *without giving rules of duty;* **accusandis Camillus dis hominibusqve senescebat,** *Camillus grew old accusing gods and men.*

[307] The *ablative absolute* may be referred to either division of the case, according to the modification it expresses. It denotes most often *time, cause, means, manner, concession* or an *accompanying event,* and should

308 | (*b*) With the prepositions a (ab, abs), absqve, de, coram, palam, cum, ex (e), sine, tenus, pro and prae; and sometimes with in, sub, subter, super.

be translated accordingly, usually by a modifying clause, but in the last case often by an independent clause, the proper connective (*and, but,* etc.) being supplied. **Germani, post tergum clamore audito, armis objectis, se ex castris ejecerunt,** *the Germans, when they heard the outcry in their rear, threw away their arms and burst out of the camp.* (Here **clamore audito** denotes time, and **armis objectis** an accompanying circumstance). **nostri omnes incolumes, perpaucis vulneratis,** *our men were all safe, though a few were wounded* (concession); **multis telis dejectis, defensores depellebant,** *they drove off the defenders by throwing many missiles* (means).

The ablative absolute consists regularly of a noun and a participle, the former being subject, the latter predicate of the implied statement. For predicate, however, a predicate-noun or adjective is often used, the lacking participle of the verb sum being supplied in translation. Rarely a clause or an infinitive is used as subject of the participle.

The ablative absolute is far more common than the English nominative absolute, to which it corresponds. Only seldom can the latter be used to translate it; the best rendering is usually by a modifying clause. The lack of a perfect active participle in Latin makes the construction far more frequent than it would otherwise be, and an English participial construction is often a good translation, if the voice of the Latin verb be changed; *e.g.*, **Caesar, obsidibus acceptis, exercitum in Bellovacos duxit,** *Cæsar, having received hostages, led his army,* etc.; **convocato consilio, eos incusavit,** *calling a council, he upbraided them.*

A few cases occur of the ablative absolute joined to the sentence it limits by a conjunction: **nisi munitis castris,** (*unless after the camp had been fortified*) *unless the camp had been* (*first*) *fortified*; **qvasi praedā sibi advectā,** *as if booty had been brought to him;* **tanqvam non transituris in Asiam Romanis,** *as if the Romans were not going to cross into Asia.*

In a few cases the participle stands alone as an ablative absolute, its subject being omitted. This corresponds to the impersonal use of a finite verb-form. **nihil festinato, nihil praeparato,** *without haste, and without preparation;* **diu certato,** *after a long fight* (lit. *it having been fought long*), like **diu certatum est,** (*it was fought long*) *there was a long fight.*

[308] The *ablative with prepositions* may be assigned to the divisions of the case as follows: —

Use of the Tenses.

309 The use of the tenses is, in general, the same as in English.

310 The perfect indicative, in its use, is either definite or indefinite. The perfect definite corresponds to

Ablative proper: **a, absqve, de, ex, sine.**
Locative ablative: **coram, palam, tenus, pro, prae, in, sub, subter, super.**
Comitative ablative: **cum.**

In and sub take the ablative with expressions implying rest, the accusative with expressions implying motion. Subter and super usually take the accusative; rarely the ablative, except super when it means "concerning."

A few words, commonly adverbs, are sometimes found with the ablative like prepositions; such are **procul, simul, clam.**

[309] The present indicative is often used, as in English, for a past tense (imperfect or perfect indefinite). In this use it is called "historical present." After the conjunction **dum,** "*while,*" the present is often used in the same way, though a past tense is necessary in English.

With adverbs meaning "*long*" (**jam, diu,** etc.), the present and imperfect, though they have their proper force, are usually rendered into English by the perfect and pluperfect. **jamdiu machinaris,** *you have long been plotting (and are plotting yet);* **diu comparabam,** *I had long been preparing (and was still doing so).*

The imperfect denotes a past action or state as continuing, repeated or customary, sometimes as attempted. **dicebat,** "*he said,*" "*he was saying,*" "*he used to say,*" or even "*he tried to say.*"

The future indicative is sometimes used, as in English, to express a command. Compare [315]. For the lacking future and future perfect subjunctive, the present and perfect subjunctive are commonly used; but when it is necessary to avoid ambiguity, the subjunctive of the first periphrastic conjugation may be used.

In letters, the imperfect and pluperfect tenses are sometimes found where the English would use the present and perfect; the time of the receipt of the letter, not the time of writing, being reckoned from.

Poets sometimes use the perfect indefinite, in imitation of Greek, to state a general truth.

[310] The perfect subjunctive is usually definite, except when it stands for an indefinite perfect indicative which has been changed to the subjunctive in a dependent statement, by 322.

the English "present perfect"; *e.g.*, **amavi**, *I have loved*. The perfect indefinite corresponds to the English "past"; *e.g.*, **amavi**, *I loved*.

311 The present, perfect definite, future and future perfect are primary tenses; the imperfect, perfect indefinite and pluperfect, secondary.

312 In most subordinate clauses the subjunctive takes a primary tense (present or perfect) when the verb on which it depends is primary, and a secondary tense (imperfect or pluperfect) when the verb on which it depends is secondary. This usage is called *sequence of tenses*.

Use of the Moods.

The INDICATIVE is used —

313 (*a*) To make a statement directly.
314 (*b*) To ask a question directly.

---

[311] The English "perfect with have" is usually the equivalent of the definite perfect, but rarely our idiom requires "have" as a translation of the indefinite perfect.

The historical present is sometimes secondary, following meaning rather than form.

[312] The rule of sequence is not a principle of grammar, but simply the statement of a somewhat unsettled usage. It is subject to violation whenever the sense requires; but this rarely happens, except in consecutive clauses, and conditions impliedly false. See 326 and 327.

[313] The use of the indicative is the same as in English.

[314] Questions answered by "yes" or "no" are not marked, as in English, by the order of the words, but by the interrogative particles -nĕ and num. -nĕ is appended to the prominent word of the sentence (usually the first word), and simply shows that the sentence is a question. **sentisne?** *do you perceive?* Rarely -nĕ is omitted.

The insertion of a negative word shows, as in English, that the answer "yes" is expected. In such a case, -nĕ is appended to the negative word. **nonne sentis?** *do you not perceive?*

USE OF THE MOODS.

The IMPERATIVE is used —	
(a) To give a command directly.	315
The SUBJUNCTIVE is used (in independent sentences) —	
(a) To make a statement doubtfully.	316
(b) To ask a question doubtfully.	317

num shows that the answer "no" is expected. num sentis? *you don't perceive, do you?*

Double (or alternative) questions take **utrum, num** or **-nĕ** in the first clause, and **an** or **-nĕ** in the second.

Exclamatory sentences are questions in form, are introduced by the same interrogative words, and take the same construction.

[315] The use of the imperative is the same as in English, but a prohibition is seldom expressed by the simple imperative. Instead of it we find (a) **nē** with the perfect subjunctive, (b) **nolī** (plural **nolīte**) with an infinitive, (c) **cavē** (plural **cavēte**) with the present subjunctive. "*Do not speak*" would be **ne dixeris, nolī dicere**, or **cave dicas**; seldom in prose, **ne dic**.

Rarely a future indicative is used in a command. **expectabis,** *you will wait*.

The imperative forms in **-to, -tote, -nto, -tor, -ntor** (often called future imperative), are old forms, usually found only in legal language (in laws, wills, etc.), and in poetry.

[316] *Potential* subjunctive. It corresponds to the English potential, and should be translated by *may, might, could, would, should,* etc., according to the sense of the passage. **velim,** *I should wish;* **vellem,** *I could wish;* **crederes,** *you would think;* **nemo istud concedat,** *no one would admit that.* Doubtful statements are most common with a conditional clause to limit them, and usually take the same form as the verb of the condition. Sometimes they are used where a conditional or concessive clause would have the same force.

The potential subjunctive may be used in dependent as well as independent sentences, where the indicative would make a positive statement, while the writer desires a doubtful one. This is especially the case in relative sentences, which, though dependent in form, are often practically equivalent to independent statements.

[317] There are two forms of questions in which the subjunctive is found. The first is simply the potential subjunctive of 316, when the statement is changed into a question; *e.g.,* **crederesne?** *would you think?* The

318	(c) To give a command doubtfully: —
319	1. In exhortations.
320	2. In wishes.
321	3. In requests or mild commands.

other use is the *dubitative* subjunctive. It is found in doubtful or rhetorical questions; *i.e.*, such as do not require an answer, but imply in themselves a negative answer. **qvid faciam?** *what can I do?* **qvid facerem?** *what was I to do?* **qvis dubitet?** *who doubts?* **qvis vellet?** *who could wish?* The implied answer in all these is "*nothing*," "*no one*." So **qviescerem et paterer?** *was I to keep quiet and suffer?* [*No.*] The subjunctive in such questions is really potential, but in English the indicative is often used, or the mood-verb *can*, while the subjunctive of 316 is more often rendered by *may, might* or *would*.

[319] *Hortatory* subjunctive. Used in the first person plural; *e.g.*, **moriamur!** *let us die!* **in arma ruamus!** *let us rush into the fight!*

[320] *Optative* subjunctive. **tibi di qvaecumqve precaris dent,** *may the gods give you all the blessings you pray for;* **moriar, ni puto,** *may I die, if I don't believe* ...! A particle of wishing (**O, uti, utinam,** etc.) often accompanies this use of the subjunctive. (**O si** is used in the same way, but is a conditional clause.) The secondary tenses imply that the wish cannot be realized, and sometimes approach the notion of a past obligation. **utinam viveret,** *would that he were alive!* **ne poposcisses,** *you ought not to have asked* (lit., *would that you had not asked*).

[321] *Jussive* subjunctive. Common in the third person, where the imperative is seldom used, but rare in prose in the second person, except in prohibitions (see [315]), and when the subject is indefinite (you = any one). **relinqvas,** *leave* (= *one may leave*). **hoc amet, hoc spernat,** *let him choose this and reject that.*

This subjunctive, beside the uses given, often occurs where other constructions are common in Latin, viz:

With **modo** or **tantum,** "*only*" as the equivalent of a condition.

With **ut, ne, qvamvis,** etc., "*however much,*" as the equivalent of a concessive clause.

E.g., **multa in eo admiranda sunt, eligere modo curae sit,** *there is much in him that is admirable, if one only takes pains in choosing* (lit., *only let it be your care to choose);* **velis tantummodo,** *if only you wish;* **qvamvis prudens sis, tamen** ..., *though you be wise, yet* ... (lit., *be as wise as you will*, **qvam vis**). At times, this subjunctive is so used without the adverbs mentioned; *e.g.*, **roges,** *you may ask* (i.e., *if you ask,* or *though you ask*).

The SUBJUNCTIVE is used (as the indirect mood) —
(*a*) In the subordinate clauses of dependent statements. | 322
(*b*) In dependent questions. | 323

[322] The subjunctive of 322, 323, and 324, is a substitute for the indicative and imperative of 313, 314, and 315, when direct statements, questions or commands are reported and made to depend on verbs of *saying* or *thinking, asking* or *answering, commanding* or *forbidding*.

Direct statements, when made dependent on verbs of *saying* or *thinking*, change the indicative of the principal clauses to the infinitive; that of the subordinate clauses to the subjunctive.

The potential subjunctive, in principal clauses, becomes the infinitive of the active periphrastic conjugation.

Occasionally subordinate clauses, especially relative clauses, take the infinitive, being equivalent to principal clauses in their meaning. A few cases occur of the use of the infinitive by a sort of attraction, even in conditional clauses and the like.

The same principle often causes the subjunctive to be used in relative and other subordinate clauses, that do not depend on verbs of saying or thinking, but limit a sentence whose verb implies the thought or statement of another person. **Paetus libros, qvos frater suus reliqvisset, mihi donavit,** *Paetus gave me the books which his brother (as he said) had left.* Sometimes, by a careless construction, the verb of saying is inserted, and put in the subjunctive instead of the verb of the sentence, which in this case depends on the inserted verb. **literas, qvas me misisse diceret, recitavit,** *he read a letter which he said I had written.* Causal clauses also take the subjunctive on this principle, when the cause is given not on the authority of the speaker or writer, but of some other person, and show the same irregular insertion of **dico.** Compare [328].

Subordinate clauses remain in the indicative, when they form no part of the reported statements, but are inserted by the narrator as explanations. Occasionally, also, though very rarely in good writers, other subordinate clauses are found in the indicative.

[323] Direct questions, when made dependent on a verb of *asking* or *answering*, change their verbs to the subjunctive. **qvis est?** *who is he?* (direct); **nescio qvis sit,** *I know not who he is* (indirect); **qvanto res sit in periculo, cognoscunt,** *they learn in how great danger the matter is.*

In old Latin dependent questions are often in the indicative.

In long passages of a formal, reported speech, dependent questions are

324   (*c*) In dependent commands.

The SUBJUNCTIVE is used (in dependent sentences)—

325   (*a*) In final clauses, and in substantive clauses developed from them.

---

sometimes in the infinitive. In such cases, the question is usually equivalent to a statement, and not asked for the sake of an answer. See 470, 477.

With **haud scio an, nescio an,** *I know not whether*, the verb often remains in the indicative, these phrases having become practically equivalent in force to adverbs, "*perhaps*," "*probably*."

[324] Direct commands, when made dependent on verbs of *commanding* or *forbidding*, change their verbs to the subjunctive. **patribus nuntia urbem muniant,** *tell the senate to fortify the city;* **jures postulo,** *I require you to swear;* **Ariovistus respondit, cum vellet, congrederetur,** *Ariovistus answered (telling him), to meet him when he pleased.* In many cases, however, **ut** or **ne** is inserted before the verb, thus making a purpose clause (see 325); and after **jubeo** and **veto,** less often after other verbs, the verb is changed to the infinitive, becoming an object. See 338.

[325] Final clauses denote purpose. In Latin they are relative clauses, and are introduced by relative pronouns or by relative adverbs. **legatos miserunt qvi dicerent,** *they sent envoys to say* . . . (lit. *who should say*).

Ut, *how*, is the most common to introduce a purpose clause. **Ne** is the negative of **ut,** and is used like a conjunction to introduce the purpose clause, **ut** being very rarely expressed before it. **ut iter faceret Genabum proficiscitur,** *he sets out to go to Genabus;* **postulavit ne qvem peditem Caesar adduceret,** *he demanded that Caesar should bring along no foot-soldier;* **veni ut te hortarem,** *I came to encourage you.*

Qvō is generally used instead of **ut** when the purpose clause contains a comparative. **qvo minus** (often written as one word) is the negative of **qvo,** and is found after verbs of *hindering, refusing,* etc. **qvo fiat facilius,** *that it may be done the more easily;* **me deterret hiems qvominus eam,** *the storm prevents me from going.*

Qvī (an old abl. = **qvo**) is common in the older language. **qvin** (= **qvi ne**) is the negative of **qvi.** It is often difficult to decide whether clauses with **qvin** and **qvominus** should be put under the head of purpose or result clauses. See [326].

Ut is often omitted after verbs of *willingness* and *permission*, and after **dic** and **fac;** seldom elsewhere. **fac sis,** *see that you be* . . . ; **dic veniat,** *tell him to come;* **volo facias,** *I wish you to do* . . . ; **licet eas,** *you may go*

(b) In consecutive clauses, and in substantive clauses developed from them. | 326

(lit., *it is allowed that you go*). **licet** with a following subjunctive often expresses a concession. **licet laudem fortunam, tamen ...**, *I may praise fortune, yet ...* (= *though I praise, yet ...*). **ne** is omitted after **cave, cavete**. **cave ignoscas**, *do not pardon* (compare [315] (c)). In many cases it is possible that these subjunctives might be classed as dependent commands; the verbs they depend on nearly all express *consent* or *command*.

The purpose clauses, **ut ita dicam**, "*so to speak*"; **ne longum sit**, "*to be brief*," and the like, are used parenthetically, as in English. The same is the case with **nedum**, "*much less*." **sumptus sufferre neqveo, nedum possis,** *I cannot stand the expense, much less can you.*

Purpose clauses easily pass into substantive clauses, and are often used in Latin where subject or object clauses are used in English, especially after verbs denoting an exercise of the will; e.g., *wishing, permitting, commanding,* etc. After verbs of *fearing* this difference of idiom compels us to translate **ne** by "*that*," and **ut** by "*that not*." **timeo ne veniat,** *I fear that he will come;* **timeo ut veniat,** *I fear that he will not come.*

[326] Consecutive clauses express a result. They are relative clauses in Latin, and are introduced by a relative pronoun, or by the relative adverbs **ut** or **qvin**. **tantus fuit terror ut Volusenus fidem non faceret,** *so great was the panic that Volusenus was not believed.* **qvin,** "*but that,*" is used after general negatives and after verbs of *hindering, doubting,* etc.; e.g., **non est dubium qvin,** *there is no doubt that ....*

Result clauses introduced by a relative pronoun express a characteristic, or a result of the nature or character of the antecedent; e.g., **non sum ille ferreus qvi non movear,** *I am not so callous as not to be moved.* They are most common after indefinite antecedents; e.g., **sunt qvi,** *there are (some) who;* **qvis est qvi,** *who is there that ...,* etc.; after **unus** and **solus**; and after general negatives **nemo, nullus, nihil.** In such clauses, **qvin** may be used for the nominative (rarely accusative) of the relative pronoun and a negative; e.g., **nemo est qvin putet,** *there is no one who does not think.*

Relative clauses of result may follow the adjectives **dignus, indignus, idoneus, aptus**. **dignus est qvi laudetur,** *he is worthy to be praised.* Here also belong the restrictive clause **qvod sciam,** *as far as I know,* and others like it.

Consecutive clauses, like final clauses, are very frequent in Latin where the English uses subject or object clauses, and it is often difficult to draw

327 (*c*) In conditions impliedly false.

The SUBJUNCTIVE *may* be used, further —

328 (*a*) In causal clauses.

the line between purpose and result. Clauses with **qvin**, in particular, often seem to be final rather than consecutive, and it is often a matter of indifference to which use such object-clauses should be referred.

Consecutive clauses easily pass into subject or object-clauses, and occur with a great variety of verbs. As subject they are found with verbs meaning "*it happens*," "*it remains*," etc.; as object they are most common with verbs meaning "*accomplish*," "*bring it about*"; **facio, efficio,** etc. In a few cases they pass into appositive clauses.

[327] Conditions impliedly false take the secondary tenses, — the imperfect for present time, the pluperfect for past time. **si tu hic esses,** *if you were in my place* (but you are not); **si adfuissem,** *if I had been there* (but I was not). Conditional clauses are introduced by **si,** *if,* and its compounds, or by a relative pronoun or adverb. Sometimes the conjunction **si** is omitted, as in English; *e.g.*, **fecisses,** *had you done* (= *if you had done*).

The primary tenses of the subjunctive are often used in conditions though the supposed case may be false, because the speaker or writer chooses to represent it as possible; *e.g.*, **tu si hic sis, aliter sentias,** *if you were I, you would feel differently* (more strictly, *if you should be in my case,* implying that such a thing is possible). Such are really future conditions in form, and come under 331.

Conjunctions meaning "*as if*" (**ac si, qvasi, qvamsi, tanqvam si, ut si, velut si, ceu,** also **tanqvam** and **velut** when **si** is omitted) are used with an ellipsis of the verb on which the condition depends. **ac si scripsisses,** *as (would be the case) if you had written;* **velut haud ulla mora futura esset,** *as if there were to be no delay.* Here too the primary tenses are often used, though the connection shows that the supposed case is untrue; *e.g.*, **tanqvam si claudus sim,** *as if I were lame* (i.e., *as would be the case if I should be lame*); **jacent tanqvam sine animo sint,** *they lie as if they were dead* (i.e., *as they would lie, if it should turn out that they are dead.* **essent** would imply that the speaker thinks that they are not dead).

[328] Causal clauses after a relative pronoun or **cum** take the subjunctive regularly, except in old Latin; after **qvoniam,** usually. After other causal conjunctions the indicative is used if the speaker or writer gives the cause on his own authority, the subjunctive if he gives it as the allegation of some one else. **qvae cum ita sint,** *since this is so;* **Panaetius laudat Africanum qvod fuerit abstinens,** *Panaetius praises Africanus because he*

(b) In concessive clauses.	**329**
(c) In temporal clauses.	**330**

was (as Panætius says) temperate. (Here Panætius is made responsible for the statement that Africanus was temperate; **qvod fuit** would make the statement the writer's.) The relative pronoun introducing a causal clause is often preceded by **ut, utpote, qvippe,** and the verb of the clause is sometimes, though rarely, in the indicative.

[329] Concessive clauses after **cum** are regularly in the subjunctive; after **qvamqvam,** in the indicative. Of the other conjunctions translated "*though,*" the compounds of **si** (ac si, etsi, etc., also **tanqvam, velut, sicut,** where **si** is omitted) introduce conditional clauses, and have the same construction; **qvamvis, ut** and **ne** take the subjunctive of doubtful command (see [321]); **licet** is a verb, and is followed by a final subjunctive with **ut** omitted (see [325]).

[330] Temporal clauses referring to past time usually take the indicative, except after **cum,** which takes the subjunctive of the secondary tenses; and, in later writers, after **anteqvam** and **priusqvam.**

Temporal clauses, however, in many cases express some other modification of the thought than simple time, and are therefore followed by the subjunctive. Thus:—

dum, dum modo take the subjunctive when they mean not simply "*as long as,*" but "*if,*" "*provided.*" **oderint dum metuant,** *let them hate as long as they fear* (i.e., *if they fear*).

dum, donec, quoad take the subjunctive when they imply purpose. **manebo, dum veniat,** *I shall wait for him to come* (*until he comes*).

ante qvam and **prius qvam** take the subjunctive of purpose, the clause expressing the act whose occurrence is to be prevented or anticipated, or, less often, a simple purpose, or something expected and counted on. **sic omne [opus] prius est perfectum qvam intellegeretur ab Afranio castra muniri,** *thus the whole work was finished before Afranius knew that the camp was being fortified* (i.e., *the work was done secretly, that Afranius might not know before it was done*); **anteqvam pronuntient, vocem sensim excitant,** *they excite the voice gradually, before they declaim* (i.e., *with the purpose or expectation of afterwards declaiming*).

The subjunctive is used in the same way with expressions that mean "*sooner than,*" "*rather than,*"—*e.g.,* **potius qvam, citius qvam, libentius qvam,**—though the idea of time has disappeared. **depugna, potius qvam servias,** *fight it out rather than be a slave* (i.e., *in order not to be a slave*). But **ut** is sometimes inserted after **qvam** in such clauses.

331   (*d*) In future conditions.
332   (*e*) In general conditions.
333   (*f*) In clauses dependent on a subjunctive.

Use of the Non-Finite Verb-Forms.

334   The infinitive is a verbal noun, originally in the dative case. It has become, however, in Latin, an indeclinable noun, and may replace any case in construction, but is restricted to certain uses.

Temporal clauses may take the subjunctive also, if they have the same force as conditional clauses which would take the subjunctive.

[331] A future condition is one, the truth or falsity of which will appear, if at all, in the future. The future (or future perfect) indicative may be used in such, or the present (or perfect) subjunctive. The latter has much the same force as in a doubtful statement, and leaves the hypothesis doubtful. It corresponds to the English "*should.*" **si veniat,** *if he should come;* **si probus sit,** *if he* (*should prove to*) *be honest.*

A relative or a temporal clause sometimes has the same force as a future condition, and takes the same construction.

[332] General conditions are such as refer to all time, and limit statements of general truths. **memoria minuitur, nisi eam exerceas,** *the memory weakens, unless one exercises it.* The indicative is more common in such, except when the subject is an indefinite person, as in the quotation.

In later writers the secondary tenses of the subjunctive are sometimes used in conditional clauses (and in relative or temporal clauses implying a condition) to express a repeated action. **ubi dixisset,** *whenever he had said . . . ;* **quocunque se intulisset,** *wherever he went . . . ,* etc.

[333] Clauses dependent on a subjunctive are attracted into the subjunctive if they contain an essential part of the thought, or give a modification of the verb they limit, which could not be omitted without an essential change of the idea. Restrictive clauses, for example, become subjunctive if dependent on a subjunctive, while those which are simply explanatory or parenthetical remain in the indicative. **non pugnabo quominus utrum velis eligas,** *I shall not oppose your taking which you will.* Here the speaker gives his opponent the privilege of taking either of two alternatives; (**vis** would imply that the opponent had in some way shown his

The INFINITIVE is used —	
(a) As an indirect object.	335
(b) To express purpose.	336
(c) As subject of a verb.	337
(d) As object of a verb.	338

choice, and that the speaker did not object to his taking *that one*, though he might not consent to his taking *the other*). The clause **utrum velis** is essential to the thought, because without it the speaker simply allows the taking of *one* alternative; with it, he allows the taking of *either one*.

In many cases, however, the subjunctive seems to be simply potential. See 316. Thus, **utrum velis** above, may be translated "*whichever you may wish.*" Whether the speaker shall use the indicative or the subjunctive in such clauses is to a great extent a matter of choice, as he may prefer to make the statement more or less positive in form.

[335] The infinitive of indirect object (also called *complementary* infinitive) follows intransitive verbs which require a second action of the same subject to make their sense complete, and the passive voice of verbs of *saying* and *thinking*, when they have a personal subject. **possum videre,** *I can see* (lit., *I am powerful for seeing*); **Caesar dicitur advenisse,** *Caesar is said to have arrived.* In some cases it is difficult to draw the line between the infinitive of indirect object and that of direct object. If the verb is transitive, the infinitive after it may be called direct object, but unless it takes a direct object in other constructions, the infinitive should be called indirect object. The English translation is no guide in such a case, as many verbs are transitive in English, while verbs of the same meaning are intransitive in Latin.

[336] This use is rare and poetical. It corresponds to the dative of purpose.

[337] The infinitive of subject or object is used as in English, but is far more common, being especially frequent with verbs of *saying* or *thinking*. It is thus used either with or without an expressed subject. **errare est humanum,** *to err is human;* **biennium sibi satis esse duxerunt,** *they thought that two years was enough for them.* For this infinitive the English often uses a subject or object clause with "*that,*" as in the example given.

[338] When the subject of an object infinitive is the same as that of the verb that governs it, this subject (se) is sometimes omitted. **quae**

339	(*e*) As an appositive or predicate noun.
340	(*f*) To limit nouns or adjectives as genitive, accusative or ablative.
341	(*g*) In exclamatory phrases.
342	(*h*) In vivid narration as a substitute for the indicative.

imperarentur, facere dixerunt, *they said that they were doing what was ordered.* (But **se facere** is more common.) In such cases, the predicate noun or adjective is usually attracted into the nominative. See [255].

[339] **Id nuntiatum est eos conari,** *this news was brought,* (*namely*) *that they were trying* .... An infinitive is frequent in apposition with **hoc, id, illud,** etc., used as subject or object, where the infinitive itself might stand as subject or object. (Compare, in English, "*it is human to err*," with "*to err is human.*") As a predicate-noun, the infinitive has nothing peculiar. **vivere est cogitare,** *living is thinking.*

[340] Rare and chiefly poetic. **tempus est cogitare,** *it is time to think;* **dignus amari,** *worthy to be loved;* **parati certare,** *ready to fight;* **certus ire,** *resolved to go.* The gerund or a derivative noun is generally used in such cases; **dignus amore, parati ad certandum, certus eundi.** In a few cases, it stands with a participle as ablative absolute, limiting the whole statement. See [307].

Many nouns and adjectives with the verb "be" have the force of verbs of saying or thinking, and take an infinitive which has the same force as an object infinitive. Thus, **auctor sum,** *I assert;* **sum dolore affectus,** *I am sorry,* etc. The infinitive after such seems to be object of the verbal notion implied, not depending directly on the noun or adjective, but governed by the verbal force of the phrase. It may be likened to the use of a direct object of a noun or adjective. See [202].

[341] The *exclamatory* infinitive may be compared with the nominative and accusative in exclamations. See 259 and 264. It is sometimes introduced by the interrogative particle -ne. **hoc non videre!** *not to see this!* **mene desistere!** *that I should cease!*

[342] Called *historical* infinitive. Occasionally found in rapid narration as a substitute for the present or imperfect indicative, and takes its subject in the nominative. **Caesar frumentum flagitare** (= **flagitabat**), *Caesar kept demanding the corn.*

USE OF THE NON-FINITE VERB-FORMS.

The PARTICIPLES are verbal adjectives, like the English participles. They are used —	343
(a) As simple adjectives, to limit nouns.	344
(b) As predicate adjectives with sum, to make the periphrastic conjugations.	345
(c) With the force of clauses.	346
The passive participles, when used as simple adjectives to limit nouns, often express a complex idea	347

[344] **furens regina,** *the raging queen;* **urbs mature peritura,** *a city destined soon to fall;* **fessi milites,** *wearied soldiers;* **hostis timendus,** *a fearful foe.* This use is most common with the present active and perfect passive participles. Some participles become adjectives altogether in force and construction.

The passive participles, in particular the present passive, when used as adjectives often have the force of the English verbal adjectives in *-able; e.g.,* **acceptus,** *acceptable;* **forma expetenda,** *desirable;* **sacra non adeunda,** *unapproachable;* **vix numeranda,** *almost innumerable.*

[345] This use is rare with the present active participle (where it makes a form equivalent to the present active of the verb; **amans est = amat**).

[346] This use is very common with the present active and perfect passive participles, especially in the construction of the ablative absolute, and the participle is predicate of the equivalent clause; the word it limits, subject. The participle thus used may have the force of a relative clause, modifying only the word it limits, but more frequently it modifies the whole statement and is equivalent to a temporal, causal, concessive, conditional, or (rarely) final clause; sometimes to an independent clause. **his rebus nunciatis,** *when this was reported;* **progressus in Nitiobriges,** *after he had advanced...;* **non audent, absente imperatore, egredi,** *they dare not go out, because the general is away;* **Cadurcus, in Rutenos missus,** *Cadurcus, who had been sent...;* **reluctante natura,** *if nature opposes;* **ut hos transductos necaret,** *to carry them over and kill them.* The present passive participle is rarely so used, however, being almost entirely restricted to uses (a) and (b); and the future active participle is not common in this use, though it is sometimes found with the force of a final clause, especially in later writers.

[347] **ab urbe condita,** *from the founding of the city;* **vos vitam ereptam negligetis?** *will you disregard the taking of life?* So always in

which is best rendered into English by a verbal or abstract noun containing the meaning of the participle, and an object or limiting phrase containing the meaning of the noun.

348 The GERUND is a verbal noun found in the oblique cases of the singular. It is declined and governed as a noun, but shows its verbal force in the fact that it is limited by adverbs, and may govern an object.

the gerundive construction. (See [349].) **consilia urbis delendae,** *plans for destroying the city;* **Platonis studiosus audiendi,** *desirous of hearing Plato.* So **ejecti reges,** *the expulsion of the kings;* **natus Augustus,** *the birth of Augustus,* etc. In **notum furens quid femina possit,** *the knowledge of what a mad woman can do,* the participle limits a clause.

[348] The name "nominative of the gerund" is often given to a construction, which most grammarians regard as an impersonal use of the passive periphrastic conjugation; *e.g.,* **mihi dormiendum est,** *I must sleep.* This construction resembles the passive periphrastic conjugation in conveying the notion of duty or propriety, but is sometimes like the gerund in being active and taking an object; *e.g.,* **via qvam nobis ingrediendum est,** *the road we must go;* **monendum te est mihi,** *I must warn you.* There seems to be no doubt that the gerund is a specialized use of the neuter of the present passive participle, at a period when the meaning and force of the form was not so definite as later. The gerund is often passive in force, — *e.g.,* **in res difficilis ad explicandum,** *a matter hard to be explained,* — and the passive participle is sometimes active, *e.g.,* **placenda dos est,** *the dower must please.* The "nominative of the gerund" seems to lie between the two.

The gerund in the genitive case, in a few instances, becomes so fully a noun that it takes an objective genitive instead of an object accusative, and takes the possessive pronoun adjective modifiers **mei, tui, sui, nostri, vestri,** instead of an object; *e.g.,* **exemplorum eligendi potestas,** *a chance to select examples;* **vestri adhortandi causa,** *for the sake of your encouragement* (i.e., *of encouraging you*). (In cases like this, however, the genitives **mei, vestri,** etc., may be considered objective genitives like **exemplorum** above.)

The gerund is limited in its use as follows: —

In the genitive it may be a possessive, an appositive, or an objective genitive. In the dative it may be an indirect object, or may limit adjec-

The gerund of transitive verbs is rare, and its place is usually supplied by the gerundive. This consists of a noun and the present passive participle in agreement with it (the two words expressing the complex idea spoken of in 347). | **349**

The SUPINE is a verbal noun, found only in the accusative and ablative singular. | **350**

The accusative of the supine is used with verbs of motion to express purpose. | **351**

tives. In the accusative it may follow a few prepositions (ad most often). In the ablative it may denote means or specification, rarely separation, manner or circumstance, and may also follow prepositions (in most often).

[349] The name gerundive is often used of the participle only, and the noun and participle taken together are then called the "gerundive construction."

The gerundive is less restricted in its use than the gerund. Besides the uses of the gerund it is used in the genitive (with causā omitted?) to express purpose; in the dative to express purpose, see [272]; in the accusative as direct object; in the ablative to express manner or the standard of comparison. A few illustrations of both gerund and gerundive are added:—

GENITIVE. **cupidus te videndi,** *desirous of seeing you;* **finem facit dicendi,** *he makes an end of speaking;* **sui muniendi non Galliae impugnandae causā,** *for the sake of defending himself, not of attacking Gaul.*

DATIVE. **scribendo dat operam,** *he gives attention to writing;* **rubens ferrum non est habile tundendo,** *not good for forging.* So in the phrase **non esse solvendo,** *to be unable to pay,* and the like.

ACCUSATIVE. **non vacuus sum ad narrandum,** *I have no leisure for story-telling;* **ad eum oppugnandum,** *to attack him;* **signum collocandum consules locaverunt,** *the consuls let out the (job of) setting up the statue;* **aedem habuit tuendam,** *he had the care of the temple.*

ABLATIVE. **in dando munificus,** *free in giving;* **alitur vitium tegendo,** *a vice is nourished by hiding it;* **de contemnenda morte,** *concerning contempt for death;* **de liberis educandis,** *of the training of children.* So, often in the titles of philosophical treatises.

[351] **venit auxilium postulatum,** *he came to ask help.* This is strictly an accusative of limit. (See 265.)

With **ire,** "*go,*" the accusative of the supine make a construction nearly the same in force as the future tense; *e.g.*, **imusne sessum?** (*are we going*

352. The ablative of the supine is used as an ablative of specification. (See 300.)

to sit?) *shall we take a seat?* By putting the infinitive **ire** in the passive, a form is obtained to supply the lacking future infinitive passive; *e.g.*, **putat se visum iri,** *he thinks he will be seen.*

[352] **horribile visu!** *fearful to see!* **mirabile dictu!** *strange to tell!* In some of its uses the ablative of the supine seems to approach the meaning of a dative, and may be so called if one prefers. The form may be in either case.

With **opus** the ablative of the supine seems to come under the head of means rather than specification. See [297].

PART V.

THE LAWS OF VERSE IN LATIN.

Quantity.

353 Latin versification is based on a regular succession of long and short syllables. Quantity is therefore usually treated in connection with versification.

354 General rules of quantity are such as apply to all syllables. (They have been given, 14–18.)

355 Special rules of quantity are such as apply only to particular syllables. In Latin we have special rules of quantity for final vowels of stems and for suffix-vowels.

356 The original quantity of final vowels of stems and of suffix-vowels has been changed in many instances by certain tendencies affecting final syllables; viz.:—

---

[353] The system of versification described here was borrowed with slight modifications from the Greek poets, and was in use during and after the classical period. An older system, called Saturnian, is found in fragments of the older Latin, in epitaphs, etc., but is not found in literature.

[354] The rules for syllables, long or short by position, do not always apply in the comedies; syllables are treated as short in many cases, though their vowels are followed by two consonants. This is especially the case before final -s, which had but a slight sound in old Latin.

In older Latin also, many of the special rules of quantity which follow are not applicable, as the tendencies spoken of had not taken effect so fully as later. In most cases the difference consists in the use of a vowel as long which is shortened in the later language. In a few cases the later poets have followed the older quantity, in imitation of the older writers.

[356] These are called tendencies, and not rules, because they do not act systematically but affect certain words and leave others untouched.

357	1. A tendency to shorten final open vowels.
358	2. A tendency to shorten vowels before final -m, -r and -t.
359	3. A tendency to lengthen final close vowels.
360	4. A tendency to lengthen open vowels before final -s.
361	5. A tendency to lengthen accented monosyllables.
362	6. A tendency to lengthen the vowel of a final syllable if an inflectional letter has been dropped.
363	These tendencies seem to be allowed freer play, or to be restricted in their effect, when for metrical convenience it is desirable to use a long syllable or a short one instead of the reverse.

It is probable that some old law of accent is at the bottom of most of them. Their influence is more often negative than positive, *i.e.*, they act as a restraint on certain syllables that would otherwise be more liable to change.

[360] When an open vowel is brought before final -s by the loss of t or d, the tendency to lengthen seldom shows itself.

[361] This tendency would explain dūs, dū, vās, pēs, grūs, sūs, vīs (from volo), vīs (noun), various particles, and perhaps sūl, sōl, lār, pūr, mās, though these fall also under No. 6. But it is difficult to see why the neuters, měl, fěl, ŏs, etc., should be left short, or why certain unaccented prepositions and conjunctions should be made long; *e.g.*, why the preposition ăb should be short while the same preposition ā should be long. It is clear that accent does not explain the difference; and we may regard this tendency as doubtful, or greatly restricted.

[362] The inflectional letters most often lost are the nominative singular suffix -s of masculine and feminine semivowel-stems, and the suffix -m of the first singular active of verbs. The loss of a stem-letter does not seem to affect the preceding vowel. vīs (= vīl-s) seems to come under No. 5.

[363] Thus ăbiēs, ăriēs, păriēs, perhaps to prevent the concurrence of so many short syllables, are brought under the influence of No. 4, though usually such words remain unaffected. See [300]. A final syl-

The special rules for quantity are the following:—	364
I. In open vowel noun- and adjective-stems	
The vowel after the theme is short in the nom., acc. and voc. sg.; long elsewhere,	365
Except -ēs in the nom. sg. of e-stems. (4)	366
Except -ă in the nom. and acc. pl. of neuter o-stems. (1)	367
II. In close vowel noun- and adjective-stems	
The vowel after the theme is short in the nom. and acc. sg., and in the dat. and abl. pl.; long elsewhere,	368
Except -ēs in the nom. sg. of i-stems. (4)	369
Except -ū in the nom. and acc. sg. of neuter u-stems. (3)	370
III. The vowels of suffixes of nouns and adjectives, when not contracted with the stem-vowel, are short,	371
Except -ī final in the gen. and dat. sg. (3)	372
Except -ēs in the nom. and acc. pl. (4)	373
VI. The pronouns in general follow the rules of quantity for noun- and adjective-stems of like form.	374

lable may be subject to more than one tendency, acting in the same or in contrary directions; in the latter case a common syllable is sometimes the result. For example, ō, in the present indicative active first singular of the verb, comes under 6 and 1.

[364] The numbers following the exceptions refer to the tendencies that explain them.

[365] o is short in duŏ; sometimes in ambŏ. These rules, I. and II., are rules for final stem-vowels, but the expression "vowel after the theme" is used, because the stem-vowel often disappears by contraction with the vowel of the suffix.

[368] I-stems, when they lose i and become consonant-stems, of course come under rule III.

For grūs, sūs and vīs, see [301]. Bōs is contracted.

[374] O of ĕgŏ is short; quī (nom.) is long. (5).

In the forms unlike those of nouns and adjectives, it should be noticed that we find the vowel after the theme long in

375   The nom. neuter forms in -c,   (6)
376   The personal pronouns, except the dat. sg.; and common in
377   The gen. sg. ending -ĭus.

We find the suffix vowel

378   Common in the dat. sg., -bĭ, -hĭ.   (3)
379   Long in the dat. and abl. pl., -bīs.

380   **V.** In the nominative singular of consonant-stems the quantity of the last syllable of the stem is retained, except in

381   Nominatives in -ŏ from stems in -ōn and -ĭn. (1, 6)
382   Nominatives in -ŏr from stems in ōr.   (2)
383   arbōs, Cerēs, pubēs; abiēs, ariēs, pariēs, pēs. (4)
384   sāl, lār, pār; mās.   (5 or 6)

385   **VI.** In the verb the final vowel of vowel-stems is long
386   Except before final -m or -t.   (2)

387   **VII.** In the mood-and-tense signs the initial vowel before -r is short when unabsorbed; the other vowels are long
388   Except before final -m, -r and -t.   (2)

---

[378] The same suffix **bĭ** is found in **ĭbĭ** and **ŭbĭ**, old case-forms of **ĭs** and **qvi**.

[385] The length of the final vowel of verb-stems is due to the absorption of the initial vowel of the sign or suffix. It is short, therefore, in those verb-forms that omit this vowel; viz., the verb **do**, throughout [except **dās, dā** (5)] and in the subjunctive **fŏrem**, etc., infinitive **fŏre**, and the twelve non-finite stem-forms given in [209].

In the imperative active second singular, the stem-vowel e is occasionally shortened in a few forms that are often used interjectionally; *e.g.*, **vĭdĕ**, *see!* **tăcĕ**, *hush!* **căvĕ**, *beware!*

VIII. The vowels of verb-suffixes are short | **389**
  Except final -ī. (3) | **390**
  Except -ŏ of the ind., when unabsorbed. (1, 5) | **391**
  Except -ō in the imper. endings -ĭtō, -ĭtōtĕ, -untō. | **392**
  Except -ū in the fut. act. part. ending -tūro. | **393**

IX. The reduplication-prefix is short. | **394**

X. Uninflected monosyllables are long, if they end in a vowel; short, if they end in a consonant. | **395**

XI. In uninflected polysyllables the tendencies mentioned above have fuller effect, and become rules, | **396**
  Except final -ă. | **397**

Versification.

Syllables, in Latin verse, are either long or short, a long syllable being in most cases the equivalent of two short ones. | **398**

---

[387] E is usually long in the perfect active ending **-ērunt** (rarely **-ĕrunt**); i is short in the perfect active ending **-imus**. The occasional shortening of i in the perfect subjunctive sign is due to confusion with the future perfect indicative. See [175].

[389] For ī in the future perfect active suffixes, see [179].

[390] The final ī of **-imini** is properly a nominative plural ending of an old participial form, and therefore long by rule III.

[395] **Crās** and **ēn** are long; also **nōn** (contracted). **Cūr, hīc, hūc, qvīn, sīc, sīn,** contain old case-forms.
Qvĕ, nĕ, vĕ, cĕ, ptĕ, are always attached to other words, and are therefore not monosyllabic in their use. **Rĕ-** is usually short (standing for an older form **rĕd-**).

[396] Final **ē** and **ō** in adverbs from o-stems are only apparent exceptions; such adverbs are old case-forms. But a few of these are shortened (by 1), giving **benĕ, malĕ, infernĕ, supernĕ; citŏ, modŏ, illicŏ, profectŏ;** rarely other words. **ōhē** should, perhaps, be two words.

[397] Final a is shortened in **ejă, ită, pută, quiă** (an old accusative plural). Note as an exception also **penĕs**.

PART V.— THE LAWS OF VERSE IN LATIN.

399 A foot is a combination of two or more syllables, used as the element of a verse.

400 The fundamental feet in Latin verse are the following: —

401 The Dactyl (*one long, two short*), $-\smile\smile$.

402 The Anapest (*two short, one long*), $\smile\smile-$.

403 The Trochee (*one long, one short*), $-\smile$.

404 The Iambus (*one short, one long*), $\smile-$.

405 By substituting a long syllable for the two short ones in the dactyl or anapest we get a spondee, $--$; and by resolving the long syllable of the trochee or iambus into two short ones, we get a tribrach, $\smile\smile\smile$. These are not used as the fundamental foot of a verse, but are often substituted for it, and may therefore be called "substitute" feet.

[401] It will be noticed that the dactyl and anapest, being equivalent to four short syllables, correspond to quadruple time in music, while the trochee and iambus correspond in like manner to triple time. They may be represented in musical notation as follows: —

The accent given above shows the metrical stress. Substitute feet take the metrical accent of the feet they replace, and when a long syllable is resolved into two short ones, the metrical stress falls on the first of the two short.

In lyric and dramatic writers are found other feet also; viz.: the Pyrrhic, $\smile\smile$; the Bacchīus, $\smile--$; the Cretic, $-\smile-$. By combining the fundamental feet and their substitutes are formed various compound feet; e.g., Diiambus, $\smile-\smile-$; Ditrochee, $-\smile-\smile$; Dispondee, $----$; Choriambus, $-\smile\smile-$; Greater Ionic, $--\smile\smile$; Lesser Ionic, $\smile\smile--$; etc.

406 The trochee and iambus are not used singly to form verses, but in pairs, called *dipodies*.

407 A verse is a set of feet or dipodies, recurring regularly, and forming a "line" of poetry.

408 Verses are named from their fundamental foot, and from the number of feet or dipodies they contain.

409 The most common kinds of verse are the following: —

410 (*a*) Dactylic Hexameter, — six dactyls or equivalent spondees. Its scale is

$$- \cup \cup \mid - \cup \cup \mid - \cup \cup \mid - \cup \cup \mid - \cup \cup \mid - \underset{\smile}{\times}$$
$$- - \mid - - \mid - - \mid - - \mid (- -)$$

411 The spondee is regular in the sixth foot, but rare in the fifth.

412 (*b*) Dactylic Pentameter, — two parts, each of two dactyls and a half. Its scale is

$$- \cup \cup \mid - \cup \cup \mid - \quad \Big| \quad - \cup \cup \mid - \cup \cup \mid \underset{\smile}{\times}$$
$$- - \mid - -.$$

413 The spondee is allowed in the first part, not in the second.

---

[408] Dactylic, trochaic, iambic, etc., from the kind of foot; monometer, dimeter, trimeter, etc., from the number of feet or dipodies.

[410] The cæsura (see 420) usually falls in the third foot; less often in the fourth, or second.

[411] A trochee often replaces the final spondee. See 419.

[412] The dactylic pentameter is the same as the hexameter, with the loss of the second half of the third and sixth feet. This loss is analogous to a rest in music. The pentameter is not used alone, but alternately with the hexameter to form the "elegiac couplet." The following verses give illustrations of this use, and show the character of each kind of verse: —

ille ĕgŏ qvī fŭĕrim, ‖ tĕnĕrōrum lūsŏr ămōrum,
qvem lĕgis, ut nōris, ‖ accĭpĕ postĕrĭtās.
Sulmo mihi patria est, ‖ gĕlĭdis ūbĕrrĭmus undīs,
mīlĭă qvī nŏvĭēs ‖ distăt ăb urbĕ dĕcĕm.

414 Iambic and trochaic verses are composed of dipodies, and verses of various length occur, either complete or catalectic (*i.e.*, lacking the last syllable).

415 The first foot of any iambic dipody, and the second foot of any trochaic dipody may be replaced by a spondee, or, rarely, by the equivalent of an iambus, trochee or spondee.

416 In comedy the spondee, and the equivalents of the spondee, the trochee, or the iambus may stand in any foot except the last.

417 In order to understand the structure of Latin verse, the following facts of usage must be noted: —

418 (*a*) A final vowel, or final -m with the foregoing vowel, is regularly dropped when the next word begins with a vowel or h.

419 (*b*) The last syllable of a verse may be either long or short at the option of the writer.

ēdĭtŭs hinc ĕgŏ sum, ǁ nec nōn ūt tempŏră nōrĭs,
    cum cecĭdĭt fātō ǁ consŭl ŭterqvĕ părī:
sī qvĭd ĭd est, usqve ā prŏăvīs ǁ vĕtŭs ordĭnĭs hērēs,
    non mŏdŏ fortūnae ǁ mūnĕrĕ factŭs ĕqvĕs.

(For the loss of a final vowel in verse before an initial vowel, see 418.)

[414] The most common iambic verse is the trimeter, consisting of three dipodies; the most common trochaic verse is the tetrameter catalectic; four dipodies, but lacking the last syllable. The cæsura of the former occurs in the second dipody, usually in the first foot; the latter is divided uniformly by a diæresis after the second dipody.

[416] Various kinds of verses, besides those mentioned here, are found in the lyric poets, and the editions of their writings generally contain schedules of the metres used. It has not seemed necessary, therefore, to insert any description of them here.

[418] Called *elision*. It occurs very rarely at the end of a verse. Rarely, also, a vowel remains unelided within a verse. Such cases are called *hiatus*.

[419] *I.e.*, a short syllable may be used though the meter calls for a long one, and *vice versa*.

VERSIFICATION.

420 (c) Long verses are regularly divided into two nearly equal parts by a metrical pause, which usually coincides with a pause in the sense. This pause is called *cæsura* when it occurs within a foot, and *diæresis* when it falls between feet.

421 (d) Metrical irregularities occur at times, as in English poetry. A short syllable is found now and then where the metre calls for a long one, or a long one where the metre requires a short one. Two syllables are sometimes run into one. Such irregularities are very rare in good poets.

---

[420] A *cæsura* occurs whenever a foot is divided between two words, but the name is usually given only to the *chief cæsura* as here. The dactylic pentameter gives a good illustration of diæresis.

SUPPLEMENT TO SYNTAX.

[*A few peculiarities of usage, belonging rather to the lexicon, or to a manual of Latin composition, than to a grammar, are added here for convenience of reference.*]

A. Negative Particles.

422 The usual negative is **nōn**.

423 An older negative is **haud**. It survives in a few phrases.

424 **Nē** is used in commands and in final sentences, also in **nē ... quidem**, *not even*.

425 **nĕqvĕ** (or **nĕc**) is equivalent to **et nōn**; **nēvĕ** (or **neu**) to **et nē**.

B. Interrogative Particles.

426 Questions answered by *yes* or *no* are not indicated, as in English, by the order of the words, but by the use of the interrogative particles **-nĕ** and **num**.

427 **-nĕ** appended to the prominent word of the sentence shows that it is a question, but gives no indication what answer is expected.

428 The insertion of a negative word shows, as in English, that the answer *yes* is expected. In such cases **-nĕ** is appended to the negative as the prominent word.

429 **num** shows that the answer *no* is expected.

aderasne? *were you present?* **dixitne?** *did he speak?*
nonne aderas? *were you not present?* **nunqvamne dicet?** *will he never speak?*
num aderas? *you were not present, were you?*

430 The interrogative particle is sometimes omitted.

431 Questions are usually answered by repeating some of the words of the question, but sometimes **non** is used for *no*, and **etiam**, **vero**, or some other adverb of emphasis, for *yes*.

Alternative or double questions generally take **utrum** or **-ne** in the first member, and **an** in the second. **432**
 utrum aderas an aberas? *were you present or absent?*
If the second member is simply a negative, "*or not*," it is expressed by **an non** or **necne**. **433**
 utrum aderas necne? *were you present or not?*
The first member of an alternative question is sometimes omitted, and **an** seems to introduce a single question. In such cases the question expresses some surprise, and **an** is nearly equivalent to **num**. **434**
 an aderas? [*am I mistaken or*] *were you present?*

C. Use of the Pronouns.

The use of the pronouns is, in general, as follows: —
 Ego and **tu** are used as in English, but are regularly omitted in the nominative case, except when emphatic, as the personal endings of the verb express them. **435**
 nos is sometimes used for a single person (= **ego**); **vos** is never so used for **tu**. **436**
 sui is used for *him, her, them, their,* when these words refer to the subject of the clause in which they stand. In a dependent clause **sui** refers to the subject of the principal clause, if the subordinate clause expresses the purpose or thought of that subject. (For a pronoun of the third person not referring to the subject, a demonstrative is used. See below.) **437**
 se and **suus** are sometimes used, however, referring to some other word than the subject, if no ambiguity is caused by doing so. **438**
 The possessive pronouns are used as in English. **Suus**, like **sui**, is reflexive. (For a third person possessive, not reflexive, the genitive of a demonstrative, **ejus, illius**, etc., is used.) **439**
 Hic means *this,* **ille,** *that;* **iste,** *that (of yours),* and from its frequent use in addressing an opponent, often has a contemptuous meaning. **is** is a weaker *this* or *that,* and is the usual third personal pronoun not reflexive. As antecedent of a relative, **is qvi** means "*he who,*" "*any one who*"; **ille qvi** means "*that (man yonder) who.*" **440**

441 Ipse, when used as a substantive, is an emphatic "*he*," "*he himself.*" As an adjective, it emphasizes the word it limits; **homo ipse**, "*the man himself*," "*the very man*"; **ego ipse**, "*I myself,*" etc. The genitive is used to emphasize the possessive idea of the possessive pronouns; **mea ipsius sententia**, *my own opinion*.

442 When subject and object are the same, the Latin regularly emphasizes the former. **me ipse diligo**, *I love myself* (not **me ipsum**).

443 The relative **qvi** has the same force as the English *who, which,* or *that*, but is used more freely, often where the English uses a separate independent statement, so that **qvi** has the same force as **et is, et ille**, or **is autem, ille vero**, etc.

444 The indefinite pronouns in general mean *some, any, one,* etc. **qvidam** means "*a certain*"; **qvis** and **qvispiam**, "*one*," "*any one*"; **aliqvis**, "*some one.*" **qvivis** and **qvilibet** mean "*any one you please*"; **qvisqvam** and **ullus**, "*any whatever,*" and are usually used in negative sentences, so that with the negative they mean "*none at all.*"

445 Many other words are used to express the indefinite idea of *some, any, a few,* etc. Their force and meaning must be learned from the lexicon and by practice in reading and writing the language.

D. Forms of Conditional Sentences.

446 Conditional clauses are regularly introduced by **si**, *if*, or a compound of **si**, and the verb of such a clause usually takes the mood of the verb on which it depends. The dependent condition is often called a *protasis*, the conclusion on which it depends an *apodosis*.

447 There are three well-marked forms of conditional sentences,—(*a*) with the indicative; (*b*) with a primary tense of the subjunctive; (*c*) with a secondary tense of the subjunctive:—

448 (*a*) The indicative in conditions has its usual force and needs no special explanation. It regularly limits an indicative, but may depend on an imperative or a subjunctive of command. It implies nothing as to the truth or falsehood of the supposed case.

FORMS OF CONDITIONAL SENTENCES.

si deus es, tribuere mortalibus beneficia debes, *if you are a god, you ought to give benefits to men.*

sin autem homo es, semper cogita... etc., *but if you are a man, always consider*... etc.

inteream, si novi! *may I perish if I know!*

449 (*b*) The primary tenses of the subjunctive denote the nonexistence of the supposed state, but imply its possibility, and refer therefore to the future. They usually limit a present or perfect potential subjunctive, but are also used to limit verbs whose meaning is such as to express a potential or hypothetical idea; *e.g.*, **debeo, possum, volo,** etc., or the periphrastic conjugation forms. See 331.

si negem, mentiar, *if I should deny it, I should lie.*

defendat patrem, si arguatur, *he would defend his father, if he should be accused.*

450 (The perfect tense is rare, and differs from the present only in laying stress on the completion of the action.)

451 (*c*) The secondary tenses of the subjunctive express the nonreality of the supposed case, and refer therefore to the present or past, the imperfect being used for present time, the pluperfect for past. They regularly limit an imperfect or pluperfect potential subjunctive. See 327.

pacem non peterem nisi utilem crederem, *I should not ask for peace, if I did not think it advantageous.*

te necassem, nisi iratus essem, *I should have killed you had I not been angry.*

452 The second person singular of the present and imperfect subjunctive is used, moreover, in a general condition, to limit a present or imperfect indicative which states a general truth. See 332.

mens et animus, nisi oleum instilles extingvuntur senectute, *mind and soul are extinguished by age, unless one pours in oil.*

si attenderes acrius, strepitus vinculorum reddebatur, *if one listened more attentively, the rattling of chains was heard.*

453. The conditional particle **si** is sometimes omitted. The verb is then usually put first, as in English.

roges me, nihil respondeam, *should you ask me, I should make no answer;* **dedisses,** *had you given,* etc.

454. So **absqve te esset,** *were it not for you,* and like expressions in the comic poets.

455. The real conclusion is often omitted, or only implied in an epithet or exclamation. In such cases a conditional subjunctive often seems to limit an indicative, but the sense of the passage usually suggests the proper conclusion. Here belong expressions of wishing with **O si** (see 320); clauses expressing a comparison after **qvasi,** etc. (see [327]), subjunctives depending on **debeo, possum,** etc. (see 449), and various cases where the writer prefers to put a direct statement in place of a doubtful one suggested by the form of the thought.

456. Relative and temporal clauses sometimes imply a condition, and take the same construction as the implied condition would take, if formally expressed.

E. Reported Speech.

457. Reports of speeches or thoughts of others may be made by quoting the exact words uttered or thought, or with the form changed by making the words or thoughts dependent on some verb of saying or thinking, etc. In the latter case, the language is called "oratio obliqua," or "indirect discourse." *E.g.*, "*He said that he had made a mistake,*" is indirect discourse corresponding to the direct form ("oratio recta"), "*I have made a mistake.*"

458. When the words of a speaker or writer are quoted in the indirect form, the following changes take place:—

459. (*a*) The pronouns will change in person, as in English, according to the circumstances and requirements of the sense (ordinarily all becoming of the third person).

460. (*b*) The tenses only change as required by the rule of sequence, 312. But the imperfect and pluperfect subjunctive in a condition impliedly false remains after primary tenses, to prevent confusion of meaning with future or possible conditions, and the primary tenses are often retained after a secondary tense for vividness or exactness.

461 (c) When indicatives of those tenses which have no subjunctive (viz., *future* and *future perfect*) are changed to the subjunctive, or when indicatives of those tenses that have no infinitive (viz., *imperfect, pluperfect, future,* and *future perfect*) are changed to the infinitive, they take the tense nearest them in time. Thus the —

Future ind.	becomes	pres. subj. (or imperfect by sequence).	**462**
Fut. pf. ind.	"	perf. subj. (or pluperfect by sequence).	**463**
Imperf. ind.	"	perfect infinitive.	**464**
Plupf. ind.	"	perfect infinitive.	**465**
Future ind.	"	present inf. of active periphrastic conj.	**466**
Fut. pf. ind.	"	present inf. of active periphrastic conj.	**467**

(d) The moods change as follows: —

In *principal* sentences,

Statements	in ind. (313)	become	infinitive.	**468**
	in sub. (316)	"	inf. of active periph. conj. (usually perf., rarely pres.)	**469**
Questions	in ind. (314) 1st & 3d pers.	"	infinitive.	**470**
	in ind. (314) 2d person	"	subjunctive.	**471**
	in sub. (317)	"	subjunctive.	**472**
Commands	in imp. (315)	"	subjunctive.	**473**
	in sub. (318)	"	subjunctive.	**474**

In *subordinate* sentences,

All verbs	in ind. in sub.	"	subjunctive.	**475**

476 As the first periphrastic conjugation has only an active meaning, when a subj. of statement is passive, it is expressed in the oratio obliqua by **futurum fuisse ut** (less often **futurum esse** or **fore**), followed by a passive verb.

477 (e) Relative clauses, though subordinate in form, are in many cases equivalent to principal clauses, and statements contained in such are sometimes treated as principal statements and are put in the infinitive instead of the subjunctive. In a few cases other subordinate clauses are treated in the same way, if the meaning would not be changed by making them independent in the direct form. The same principle is the cause of the use of the infinitive in reported questions of the first or third person, these questions being usually equivalent to statements, and put in the form of questions only for rhetorical effect.

478 (*f*) The indicative is used in explanatory clauses inserted by the narrator, and not belonging, therefore, to the reported speech. Rarely, also, the indicative is found in other subordinate clauses.

F. Order of Words and Clauses.

479 In a normal prose sentence the subject comes first and is followed by its modifiers; the verb stands last, preceded by its modifiers.

480 Modifiers of nouns may either follow or precede their nouns; modifiers of other parts of speech more often precede.

481 Demonstrative pronouns usually precede, and relative and interrogative pronouns regularly stand at the beginning of their clauses.

482 Modifying clauses are subject to the same general rules of order as words and phrases; those which limit nouns more often follow; those which limit verbs more often precede.

483 Few sentences of any length, however, show the normal order, as the usual position of words and clauses is constantly varied for the sake of rhythm or emphasis.

484 No definite statement of the influence of rhythm on the order of words can be given, but a dislike of a monosyllable (other than **est** or **sunt**) at the end of a sentence or of a line of poetry is noticeable in good Latin writers.

485 Any word may be emphasized by putting it out of its usual position. The beginning and end of a sentence are the specially emphatic positions.

486 In poetry the order of words is fixed to a great extent by the requirements of metre.

G. Dates.

487 The year is expressed in Latin by giving the names of the consuls for that year in the ablative absolute, or by the number of years from the founding of the city; *e.g.*:—

> L. *Pisone, A. Gabinio consulibus*
> *anno urbis conditae* DCXCVI } = 58 B.C.
> *anno ab urbe condita* DCXCVI

488 These expressions are seldom written in full. For *consulibus* we find *coss.*; for *anno urbis conditae, a. u. c.*

489 The month is expressed by *mense* with the proper month-name added as an adjective; *e.g.*, *mense Junio*, in June; *exeunte mense Aprili*, at the end of April, etc.

490 The day of the month was reckoned backward from three fixed dates, the Kalends, Nones, and Ides (*Kalendae, Nonae, Idus*); the first being originally the day of the new moon, the last, that of the full moon. The Kalends was the first day of the month; the Nones was usually the fifth, but in March, May, July, and October, the seventh; the Ides was the eighth day after the Nones, and, therefore, the thirteenth or fifteenth.

491 Dates falling on the Kalends, Nones or Ides were expressed by *Kalendis, Nonis* or *Idibus*, with the name of the month added as an adjective; *e.g.*, *Kalendis Juniis* (June 1), *Nonis Aprilibus* (April 5), *Idibus Decembribus* (Dec. 13), etc.

492 Dates falling between the Kalends and Nones are reckoned backward from the Nones. The day before the Nones was called *pridie Nonas* (see [268]); the second day before was expressed by *tertio die ante Nonas*, or *ante diem tertium Nonas*, as the Romans counted in the day reckoned from. In like manner the third day before was called *fourth*, etc.

493 Dates falling between the Nones and Ides were expressed in the same way, *pridie Idus Aprilis, ante diem sextum Idus Martias*, etc. So, too, dates falling between the Ides and Kalends, the adjective added being, of course, the name of the following month.

494 These expressions are seldom written in full, the usual contraction being of the form *prid. Kal. Mart., IV. Non. Apr., VI. Id. Sept.*, etc.; or *a. d. iv Non. Apr.*, etc.

495 In leap-year the 24th of February was counted twice, so that both the 24th and 25th of the month were called *VI. Kal. Mart.*

SUPPLEMENT TO SYNTAX.

496. The days of the months are given in the following schedule:—

Day of Month.	January (also August and December).	February.		March (also May, July, and October).	April (also June, Sept., and November).
1	Kal. Jan.	Kal. Feb.		Kal. Mart.	Kal. Apr.
2	IV Non. Jan.	IV Non. Feb.		VI Non. Mart.	IV Non. Apr.
3	III " "	III " "		V " "	III " "
4	prid. " "	prid. " "		IV " "	prid. " "
5	Non. Jan.	Non. Feb.		III " "	Non. Apr.
6	VIII Id. Jan.	VIII Id. Feb.		prid. " "	VIII Id. Apr.
7	VII " "	VII " "		Non. Mart.	VII " "
8	VI " "	VI " "		VIII Id. Mart.	VI " "
9	V " "	V " "		VII " "	V " "
10	IV " "	IV " "		VI " "	IV " "
11	III " "	III " "		V " "	III " "
12	prid. " "	prid. " "		IV " "	prid. " "
13	Id. Jan.	Id. Feb.		III " "	Id. Apr.
14	XIX Kal. Feb.	XVI Kal. Mart.		prid. " "	XVIII Kal. Maias.
15	XVIII " "	XV " "		Id. Mart.	XVII " "
16	XVII " "	XIV " "		XVII Kal. Apr.	XVI " "
17	XVI " "	XIII " "		XVI " "	XV " "
18	XV " "	XII " "		XV " "	XIV " "
19	XIV " "	XI " "		XIV " "	XIII " "
20	XIII " "	X " "		XIII " "	XII " "
21	XII " "	IX " "		XII " "	XI " "
22	XI " "	VIII " "	In leap year.	XI " "	X " "
23	X " "	VII " "		X " "	IX " "
24	IX " "	VI " "	VI Kal. M.	IX " "	VIII " "
25	VIII " "	V " "	VI " "	VIII " "	VII " "
26	VII " "	IV " "	V " "	VII " "	VI " "
27	VI " "	III " "	IV " "	VI " "	V " "
28	V " "	prid. " "	III " "	V " "	IV " "
29	IV " "		prid." "	IV " "	III " "
30	III " "			III " "	prid. " "
31	prid. " "			prid. " "	

497. The schedule here given was in use after Cæsar's reform of the calendar, B.C. 45. Before that date the Roman year had only 355 days, and an extra month was inserted every other year after Feb. 23.

APPENDIX.

498. List of Verbs

[*Compiled from Roby's Latin Grammar.*]

[This list contains all the verbs of the Latin language, with the following exceptions, viz.: —

1. Stems in -a or -i, which use the simple stem as present stem and form the perfect stem by adding -v. Most of them are derived from nouns or adjectives, and form their principal parts after the models here given: —

| dŏno | donāre | donāvi | donātum | dōna- |
| fīnio | finīre | finīvi | finītum | fīni- |

2. Consonant-stems which form the present stem by adding -e, and the perfect stem by adding -u; and lack the forms from the simple stem. Most of them are derived from nouns or adjectives, and form their principal parts after the model here given: —

| flŏreo | florēre | florui | | flŏr- |

3. Verbs which form the present stem by adding -sc, -esc or -isc, and have only the incomplete tenses, or form the perfect stem, when one is found, by adding -u. Examples are: —

gemmasco	gemmascĕre		gemma-
rŏresco	rorescĕre		rŏr-
ingĕmisco	ingemiscĕre	ingemui	in-gĕm-

4. Compounds which do not differ from the simple verb, or differ only in the usual weakening of the stem vowel, or in being defective. Weakening of diphthongs is mentioned, however.

The supine form is given, though but few verbs have a supine in use, whenever a future active or perfect passive participle is found to decide what the form of the supine would be.

Forms preceded by a hyphen (*e.g.*, -lictus) are found only in compounds.]

APPENDIX.

Pres. Ind.	Pres. Inf.	Perf. Ind.	Sup. or Part.		Stem.

Accerso (another spelling of **arcesso**).

ăcuo	acuĕre	acui	acūtum	sharpen	ăcu-
aegreo	aegrēre			be sick	aegr-?
ădŏlesco (see -oleo)				grow	ăd-ŏle-
agnosco (see nosco)				know	ad-gno-
ăgo	agĕre	ēgi	actum	drive	ăg-
ājo (defective. See [235].)				say	āg-?
albeo	albēre			be white	alb-?
algeo	algēre	alsi		be cold	alg-
ălo	alĕre	alui	altum	nourish	ăl-

  alĭtum also in later writers.

ămĭcio	amicīre	amici	amictum	clothe	ămĭc-

  amicui, amixi are mentioned as perf.

ango	angĕre			throttle, vex	ang-
ăpiscor	apisci		aptus	get	ăp-
arceo	arcēre	arcui	{ arctus { artus	inclose	arc-

  In compounds, ex-ercĭtus, co-ercĭtus.

arcesso	arcessĕre	arcessīvi	arcessītum	summon	arcess-i-
ardeo	ardēre	arsi	arsum	be on fire	ard-
arguo	arguĕre	argui	argūtum	charge	argu-

  arguĭturus, once.

audeo	audēre		ausum	dare	aud-

  For perf. **ausus sum** is used. See [216] (g).

ăve (defective. See [235].)				hail!	
ăveo	avēre			long	ăv-?
augeo	augēre	auxi	auctum	increase	aug-

Bātuo	batuĕre	batui		beat	bātu-
bĭbo	bibĕre	bĭbi		drink	bĭb-

  The stem is properly **ba**, but becomes **bĭb-** by reduplication and loss of the final vowel. See [158].

-būro	-burĕre	-bussi	-bustum	burn	būs-

LIST OF VERBS.

Pres. Ind.	Pres. Inf.	Perf. Ind.	Sup. or Part.		Stem.
cădo	cadĕre	cĕcĭdi	cāsum	*fall*	căd-
caecūtio	caecutīre			*be blind*	caecūti?
caedo	caedĕre	cĕcīdi	caesum	*fell, kill*	caed-

Compounds weaken ae to ī.

căleo	calēre	calui	calĭtum	*be hot*	căl-
calveo	calvēre			*be bald*	calv-?
calvor	calvi			*play tricks*	calv-
căneo	canēre			*be gray*	căn-?
căno	canĕre	cĕcĭni	(-cantum)	*sing*	căn-

In compounds, the perfect is -cĭnui (oc-cĕcĭni once).

căpesso	capessĕre	capessīvi	capessītum	*seize*	căpess-i-
căpio	capĕre	cēpi	captum	*take*	căp-
căreo	carēre	carui	carĭtum	*be in want*	căr-
căro	carēre			*card*	căr-
carpo	carpĕre	carpsi	carptum	*pluck*	carp-
căveo	cavēre	cāvi	cautum	*beware*	căv-

cavītum, rare.

cēdo	cedĕre	cessi	cessum	*yield*	cēd-

cĕdo (imperative) plur. cette, no other forms. *give* cĕd-?

-cello	-cellere	-cŭli	-culsum	*strike?*	cĕl-

Also ex-cellui. celsus, excelsus, praecelsus are adjectives.

-cendo	-cendĕre	-cendi	-censum	*set on fire*	cend-
censeo	censēre	censui	censum	*count*	cens-
cerno	cernĕre	crēvi	crētum	*decide*	cĕr-, cre-

certus is used as an adjective.

cieo / cio	ciēre / cīre	cīvi	cĭtum	*stir up*	ci-

In compounds also -cĭtus sometimes.

cingo	cingĕre	cinxi	cinctum	*gird*	cing-
clango	clangĕre			*clang*	clang-
claudo	claudĕre	clausi	clausum	*close*	claud-

Compounds weaken the stem to -clūd.

clĕpo	clepĕre	clepsi	cleptum	*steal*	clĕp-
clueo	cluĕre		-clŭtum	*be called*	clu-
coenātŭrio	coenaturīre			*wish to dine*	coenātŭri-?

Pres. Ind.	Pres. Inf.	Perf. Ind.	Sup. or Part.		Stem.
cognosco	(see nosco)			know	co-gno-
cōgo	cogĕre	coēgi	coactum	compel	co-ăg-
cŏlo	colĕre	colui	cultum	cultivate	cŏl-
coepio	coepĕre	coepi	coeptum	begin	co-ăp-
cōmo	comĕre	compsi	comptum	comb	cōm-
comperco	compercĕre	compersi		save	com-parc-
comperio	(see pario)			find out	com-păr-
compesco	(see pasco)			curb	com-păss-
concino	(see cano)			sing	con-căn-
consŭlo	consulĕre	consului	consultum	consult	consŭl-
cŏqvo	coqvĕre	coxi	coctum	cook	cŏqv-
crēdo	credĕre	credĭdi	credĭtum	believe	crē-d-
crĕpo	crepāre	crepui	crepĭtum	rattle	crĕp-
cresco	crescĕre	crēvi	crētum	grow	cre-
{ cŭbo { -cumbo	{ cubāre { -cumbere	cubui	cubĭtum	lie	cŭb-

cubāvi, rare.

cūdo	cudĕre	cūdi	cūsum	hammer	cūd-
cŭpio	cupĕre	cupīvi	cupītum	desire	cŭp-i

Imperfect subjunctive cupīret once.

curro	currĕre	cŭcurri	cursum	run	curr-

Compounds sometimes retain the reduplication.

-cŭtio (see qvătio).

Dēbeo	debēre	debui	debĭtum	owe	dēb-
dēgo	degĕre			pass time	dēg-
dēleo	delēre	delēvi	delētum	destroy	dē-le-
dēmentio	dementīre			be mad	dēmenti-?
dēmo	demĕre	dempsi	demptum	remove	dēm-
depso	depsĕre	depsui	depstum	knead	deps-
dīco	dicĕre	dixi	dictum	say	dīc-
dīlego	(see lĕgo).				
disco	discere	dĭdĭci		learn	dīc-

Compounds keep the reduplication.

dīvĭdo	dividĕre	divīsi	divīsum	divide	dī-vĭd-
do (see 226)	dăre	dĕdi	dătum	give	da-

Compounds retain the reduplication (except abscon-di).

LIST OF VERBS.

Pres. Ind.	Pres. Inf.	Perf. Ind.	Sup. or Part.		Stem.
dŏceo	docēre	docui	doctum	*teach*	dŏc-
dŏleo	dolēre	dolui	dolĭtum	*grieve*	dŏl-
dŏmo	domāre	domui	domĭtum	*tame*	dŏm-
dūco.	ducĕre	duxi	ductum	*lead*	dūc-

Ĕdo (see 223)	edĕre	ēdi	ēsum	*eat*	ĕd-
essum and estum, rare.					
ĕmo	emĕre	ēmi	emptum	*take, buy*	ĕm-
emptŭrio	empturīre			*wish to buy*	emptŭri-?
eo (see 227)	īre	īvi	ĭtum	*go*	i-
Perfect -ii in compounds.					
excello (see cello)				*excel*	ex-cel-
expergiscor	expergisci		experrectum	*arouse*	ex-pĕr-rĕg-
expergĭtum, old.					
exuo	exuĕre	exui	exūtum	*strip off*	exu-

Făcesso	facessĕre	facessīvi	facessītum	*make*	făcess-i-
făcio	facĕre	fēci	factum	*make*	făc-
fallo	fallĕre	fĕfelli	falsum	*deceive*	fall-
farcio	farcīre	farsi	fartum	*stuff*	farc-
făteor	fatēri		fassus	*confess*	făt-
fătisco	fatiscĕre		-fessum	*gape*	făt-
Also deponent.					
făveo	favēre	fāvi	fautum	*favor*	făv-
-fendo	-fendere	-fendi	-fensum	*strike*	fend-
fĕrio	ferīre			*strike*	fĕri-?
fĕro	ferre	(tŭli)	(lātum)	*carry*	fĕr-
tŭli and lātum are borrowed from tollo. tĕtŭli is old.					
{ ferveo { fervo	{ fervēre { fervĕre	fervi, ferbui		*boil*	ferv-
fīdo	fidĕre		fīsum	*trust*	fīd-
fīsus sum is used as perfect. See [216], (g).					
fīgo	figĕre	fixi	fixum	*fix*	fīg-
fictus, rare.					
fīo (see 229)	fĭĕri		(factus)	*become*	fī-
findo	findĕre	fīdi	fissum	*cleave*	fĭd-

Pres. Ind.	Pres. Inf.	Perf. Ind.	Sup. or Part.		Stem.
fingo	fingĕre	finxi	fictum	*form*	fĭg-
flaveo	flavēre			*be yellow*	flav-?
fleo	flēre	flēvi	flētum	*weep*	fle-
flecto	flectĕre	flexi	flexum	*bend*	flect-
-flīgo	-flīgĕre	-flixi	-flictum	*strike*	flīg-
fluo	fluĕre	fluxi	fluxum	*flow*	flŭgv-
fŏdio	fodĕre	fŏdi	fossum	*dig*	fŏd-
fodīri old.					
foeteo	foetēre			*be fetid*	foet-?
[for] see [235]	fāri		fātum	*speak*	fa-
fŏveo	fovēre	fōvi	fōtum	*cherish*	fŏv-
frango	frangere	frēgi	fractum	*break*	frăg-
frĕmo	fremĕre	fremui	fremĭtum	*roar*	frĕm-
frendo	frendĕre		fressum	*gnash*	frend-
Also frēsum.					
frĭco	frĭcāre	fricui	frictum	*rub*	frĭc-
Also fricātum.					
frĭgeo	frigēre	frixi		*be cold*	frĭg-
frīgo	frigĕre		frictum	*roast*	frīg-
frondeo	frondēre			*leaf*	frond-?
fruor	frui		fructum	*enjoy*	fru-, frug-?
fruĭtus once, fruĭtūrus once.					
fŭgio	fugĕre	fŭgi	fugĭtum	*flee*	fŭg-
fulcio	fulcīre	fulsi	fultum	*prop*	fulc-
⎰ fulgeo	⎰ fulgēre	fulsi		*shine*	fulg-
⎱ fulgo	⎱ fulgĕre				
fundo	fundĕre	fūdi	fūsum	*pour*	fŭd-
fungor	fungi		functus	*discharge*	fung-
[fuo] (see sum)		fui	fŭtūrus	*be*	fu-
fŭro	furĕre			*rage*	fŭr-
Gaudeo	gaudēre		gāvīsum	*be glad*	gāvĭd-
gavīsus sum is used as perfect. See [216], (*g*).					
gĕmo	gemĕre	gemui	gemĭtum	*groan*	gĕm-
gĕro	gerĕre	gessi	gestum	*carry*	gĕs-
gigno	gignĕre	gĕnui	genĭtum	*beget*	gĕn-
gigno for gigĕno. gĕno is old.					

LIST OF VERBS.

Pres. Ind.	Pres. Inf.	Perf. Ind.	Sup. or Part.		Stem.
glisco	gliscĕre			swell	gli-
glōcio	glocīre			cluck	gloci-?
glūbo	glubĕre		gluptum	peel	glūb-
grădior	gradi		gressus	step	grăd-

In compounds -gredīri is found.

-gruo	-gruĕre	-grui		?	gru-
Hăbeo	habēre	habui	habĭtum	have	hăb-
haereo	haerēre	haesi	haesum	stick	haes-
haurio	haurīre	hausi	haustum	drain	haus-
hĕbeo	hebēre	_		be blunt	hĕb-?
hisco	hiscĕre			yawn	hi-
hūmeo	humēre			be moist	hum-?

-icio (for jacio in compounds).

Ico?	icĕre	īci	ictum	strike	Ic-
imbuo	imbuĕre	imbui	imbūtum	imbue	imbu-
incesso	incessĕre	incessīvi		attack	incess-i-
indulgeo	indulgēre	indulsi		yield	indulg-

indultum, late.

induo	induĕre	indui	indūtum	put on	indu-
ĭneptio	ineptīre			trifle	ĭnepti-?
infīt (no other form)				begins	?
inqvam (see [235])		inqvii		quoth	inqvi-?
intellĕgo (see lego)				understand	intel-lĕg-
īrascor	irasci		irātus	be angry	ira-

Jăceo	jacēre	jacui	jacĭtum	lie	jăc-
jăcio	jacĕre	jēci	jactum	throw	jăc-
jŭbeo	jubēre	jussi	jussum	bid	jŭb-
jungo	jungĕre	junxi	junctum	yoke	jung-
jŭvo	juvāre	jūvi	jūtum	aid	jŭv-

Also juvātūrus.

Lābor	labi		.lapsus	slip	lāb-
lăcesso	lacessĕre	lacessīvi	lacessĭtum	provoke	lacess-i-
lacteo	lactēre			suck	lact-?
laedo	laedĕre	laesi	laesum	hurt	laed-

Compounds weaken ae to ī.

PRES. IND.	PRES. INF.	PERF. IND.	SUP. OR PART.		STEM.
lambo	lambĕre	lambi		lick	lamb-
langveo	langvēre	langvi		be faint	langv-
lăvo / lăvo	lavĕre / lavāre	lāvi	lotum / lautum	wash	lăv-

Also lavātum.

lĕgo	legĕre	lēgi	lectum	choose	lĕg-

Perf. -lexi in dī-lĕgo, intel-lĕgo, neg-lĕgo.
-leo (see dēleo).

lībet	libēre	libuit	libĭtum	it pleases	lĭb-

Also spelled lŭbet.

lĭceo	licēre	licui	licĭtum	be on sale	lĭc-
lĭceor	licēri		licĭtus	bid for	lĭc-
lĭcet	licēre	licuit	licĭtum	it is allowed	lĭc-
-lĭcio	-licĕre	-lexi, -licui	-licĭtum	entice	lăc-
lingo	lingĕre		linctum	lick	ling-
lĭno	linĕre	lēvi, līvi	lĭtum	smear	li-
linqvo	linqvĕre	līqvi	-lictum	leave	līqv-
līqveo	liqvēre	licui		be clear	līqv-
līqvor	liqvi			melt	līqv-
līveo	livēre			be livid	līv-?
lŏqvor	loqvi		locūtus	speak	lŏqv-
lūceo	lucēre	luxi		beam	lūc-
lūdo	ludĕre	lūsi	lūsum	sport	lūd-
lūgeo	lugēre	luxi		mourn	lūg-
luo	luĕre	lui	-lūtum	pay	lu-
Măceo	macēre			be lean	măc-?
maereo	maerēre			grieve	maer-?
mălo	malle	malui (see 225)		prefer	ma-vŏl-
mando	mandĕre	maudi	mansum	chew	mand-
măneo	manēre	mansi	mansum	wait	măn-

ē-minui also in perfect.

mĕdeor	medēri			cure	mĕd-
mĕmĭni (see [235])				remember	măn-
mĕreo	merēre	merui	merĭtum	earn	mĕr-
mergo	mergĕre	mersi	mersum	sink	merg-
mētior	metīri		mensus	measure	met-?
mĕto	metĕre	messui	messum	mow	mĕt-

LIST OF VERBS.

Pres. Ind.	Pres. Inf.	Perf. Ind.	Sup. or Part.		Stem.
mĕtuo	metuĕre	metui	metūtus (once)	*fear*	metu-
mĭco	micāre	micui		*glitter*	mĭc-

-micāvi, -micātum in compounds.

-mĭniscor	-minisci		-mentus	*call to mind*	măn-
mingo	mingĕre	minxi	mictum		mĭg-

Pres. also mējo (for mĕg-i-o).

mĭnuo	minuĕre	minui	minūtum	*lessen*	mĭnu-
misceo	miscēre	miscui	mixtum, mistum	*mix*	misc-
mĭsĕreor	miserēri		miserĭtus	*pity*	mĭsĕr-

misertus, rare, also rarely an active form misereo.

mĭsĕret	miserēre	miseruit	miserĭtum	*it pities*	mĭsĕr-
mitto	mittĕre	mīsi	missum	*send*	mitt-
mŏlo	molĕre	molui	molĭtum	*grind*	mŏl-
mŏueo	monēre	monui	monĭtum	*warn*	mŏn-
mordeo	mordēre	mŏmordi	morsum	*bite*	mord-
mŏrior	mori See [216] (*h*)		(moritūrus)	*die*	mŏr-

mortuus sum is used as perfect. morīri is old.

mŏveo	movēre	mōvi	mōtum	*move*	mŏv-
mūceo	mucēre			*be moldy*	mūc-?
mulceo	mulcēre	mulsi	mulsum	*soothe*	mulc-

Also per-mulctus.

mulgeo	mulgēre	mulsi		*milk*	mulg-
-mungo	-mungĕre	-munxi	-munctum	*wipe*	mung-

Nanciscor	nancisci		nactus, nanctus	*gain*	năc-
nascor	nasci		nātus	*be born*	na-·

The full stem gna- appears in some compounds.

nĕco	necāre	{ necāvi { nĕcui	{ necātum { -nectum	*kill*	nĕc-
necto	nectĕre	nexi	nexum	*join*	nect-
neglĕgo (see lego).					
neo	nēre	nēvi	nētum	*spin*	ne-
nĕqveo (see qveo)				*can not*	nĕ-qvi-
nexo	nexĕre	nexui		*tie*	nex-
{ ningit { ningvit	ningĕre	ninxit		*it snows*	{ ning- { ningv-
nītor	niti		nixus, nīsus	*lean*	nict-

126   APPENDIX.

Pres. Ind.	Pres. Inf.	Perf. Ind.	Sup. or Part.		Stem.
-nīveo	-nivēre	-nīvi, -nixi		wink	nigv-
nŏceo	nocēre	nocui	nocĭtum	harm	nŏc-
nōlo	nolle	nolui	See 225	be unwilling	nĕ-vŏl-
nosco	noscere	nōvi	nōtum	learn	no-

The full stem gno- appears in some compounds. -gnĭtum is found in a-gnitum, co-gnitum.

nūbo	nubĕre	nupsi	nuptum	marry	nūb-
-nuo	-nuĕre	-nui		nod	-nu-
ab-nuĭturus once.					

Oblīviscor	oblivisci		oblītus	forget	ob-līv-?
occŭlo	occulĕre	occului	occultum	conceal	oc-cŭl-
odi (sec 235).					
{ -ŏleo	{ -olĕre	{ -olĕvi	{ -olētum	grow	ŏl-? ŏle-?
{ -ŏlesco	{ -olescĕre	{ -olui	{ -olĭtum		
ădolesco has ad-ultus.					

{ ŏleo	{ olĕre	olui		smell	ŏl-
{ ŏlo	{ olĕre				
ŏportet	oportēre	oportuit		it is proper	ŏpòrt-
ordior	ordīri		orsus	commence	ord-
ŏrior	orīri See [216] (h)		ortus	rise	ŏr-
Also orĭtūrus.					

[ŏvo] defective. See [235].

Păciscor	pacisci	pĕpĭgi	pactum	bargain	păc-, păg-
paenĭtet	paenitēre	paenituit		it repents	paenĭt-
paenĭtūrum is mentioned by grammarians.					
pando	pandĕre	pandi	pansum, passum	open	pand-
pango	pangĕre	pēgi	pactum, panctum	fasten	păg-
parco	parcĕre	{ pĕperci { parsi	parsum	spare	parc-
păreo	parēre	parui	parĭtum	appear	păr-
părio	parēre	pĕpĕri	partum	bring forth	păr-
Also parĭtūrus. Compounds have -perīre.					
partŭrio	parturīre			be in labor	partŭri-
pasco	pascĕre	pāvi	pastum	feed	păs-
-pescui in compesco and dispesco.					

LIST OF VERBS.

Pres. Ind.	Pres. Inf.	Perf. Ind.	Sup. or Part.		Stem.
pătior	pati		passus	be or	păt-
păveo	pavēre	pāvi		fear	păv-
pecto	pectĕre	pexi	pexum	comb	pect-
pĕdo	pedĕre	pĕpĕdi			pĕd-
pello	pellĕre	pĕpŭli	pulsum	drive	pĕl-
pendeo	pendēre	pĕpendi	pensum	hang	pend-
pendo	pendĕre	pĕpendi	pensum	weigh	pend-
pergo	pergĕre	perrexi	perrectum	continue	pĕr-rĕg-
-pĕrio	-perīre	-perui	-pertum		pĕr-

perītus as an adjective, and in opperītus.

pĕto	petĕre	petīvi	petītum	seek	pĕt-i-
pĭget	pigēre	piguit	pigĭtum	it vexes	pĭg-
pingo	pingĕre	pinxi	pictum	paint	pĭg-
{ pinso { pīso	{ pinsĕre { pisĕre	{ pinsui { pinsi	{ pinsitum { pistum	pound	pīs-

pisi once, pinsībant once.

plăceo	placēre	placui	placĭtum	please	plăc-
plango	plangĕre	planxi	planctum	beat	plang-
plaudo	plaudere	plausi	plausum	clap	plaud-

Most compounds weaken au to ō.

plecto	plectĕre			strike	plect-
-plector	-plecti		-plexus	twine	plect-
-pleo	-plēre	-plēvi	-plētum	fill	ple-
plĭco	plicāre	{ -plĭcui, { -plicāvi	{ -plicĭtum, { plicātum	fold	plĭc-
pluo	pluĕre	pluit		rain	plu-

pluvit often in Livy.

polleo	pollēre			be strong	pŏll-?
pollŭceo	pollucĕre		polluctum	offer	pollūc-
pōno	ponĕre	pŏsui	posĭtum	place	pŏ-s-

pono is for po-sino; see sino. posīvi and posi are found, and in poetry postus.

posco	poscĕre	pŏposci			posc-

Compounds retain reduplication.

possum	posse	pŏtui	See 222	can	pŏt-ĕs-
pŏtior	potīri	See [216] (h)	potītum	be master	pŏti-
pŏto	potāre	potāvi	pōtum, potātum	drink	pōta-

pōtum seems to belong to a simpler stem, po-.

APPENDIX.

Pres. Ind.	Pres. Inf.	Perf. Ind.	Sup. or Part.		Stem.
praebeo	praebēre	praebui	praebĭtum	*furnish*	praeb-
prandeo	prandēre	prandi	pransum	*dine*	prand-
{ prehendo	prehendēre	prehendi	prehensum	*seize*	{ prehend-
{ prendo	prendēre	prendi	prensum		{ prend-
prĕmo	premĕre	pressi	pressum	*press*	prĕm-
prŏfīciscor	proficisci		profectus	*advance*	prŏ-făc-
prŏmo	promĕre	prompsi	promptum	*bring out*	prŏm-
prŭrio	prurīre			*itch*	prŭri-?
psallo	psallĕre	psalli		*play*	psall-
pŭdet	pudēre	puduit	pudĭtum	*it shames*	pŭd-
pungo	pungĕre	pŭpŭgi	punctum	*prick*	pŭg-

Compounds have -punxi.

| Qvaero | qvaerĕre | qvaesīvi | qvaesītum | *seek* | qvaes-i- |

qvaeso and qvaesumus are old colloquial forms. Compounds weaken ae to ī.

| qvătio | qvatĕre | | qvassum | *shake* | qvăt- |

Perfect -cussi in compounds. See -cutio.

qveo (228)	qvīre	qvīvi	qvītum	*can*	qvi-
qvĕror	qveri		qvestus	*complain*	qvĕs-
qviesco	qviescĕre	qviĕvi	qviētum	*rest*	qvie-
-qvĭnisco	-qviniscĕre	-qvexi		*defile*	qvĭc-

Răbo	rabĕre			*rave*	răb-
rādo	radĕre	rāsi	rāsum	*scrape*	rād-
răpio	rapĕre	rapui	raptum	*seize*	răp-
răvio		(-rausi)	(rausurus)	*be hoarse*	răv-
rĕfert	rĕferre	rĕtŭlit		*it concerns*	rĕ-fĕr-
rĕgo	regĕre	rexi	rectum	*rule*	rĕg-
rĕnīdeo	renidēre			*glitter*	rĕ-nīd-
reor	rĕri		rătus	*think*	ra-
rĕpĕrio	reperīre	reppĕri	repertum	*discover*	rĕ-păr-
rĕpo	repĕre	repsi	reptum	*creep*	rĕp-
rĕsĭpisco	see săpio				rĕ-săp-
rīdeo	ridēre	rīsi	rīsum	*laugh*	rīd-
ringor	ringi			*grin*	rĭg-
rōdo	rodĕre	rōsi	rōsum	*gnaw*	rōd-

LIST OF VERBS.

Pres. Ind.	Pres. Inf.	Perf. Ind.	Sup. or Part.		Stem.
rŭdo	rudĕre	rudīvi	*in. rŭs.*	bray	rŭd-i-
rumpo	rumpĕre	rūpi	ruptum	break	rŭp-
ruo	ruĕre	rui	rŭtum	dash	ru-
ruĭturus, late.					
Saepio	saepīre	saepsi	saeptum	hedge	saep-
⎰ salio	⎰ (salīre ?)		⎰ salitum	salt	sal-
⎱ sallo	⎱ sallĕre		⎱ salsum		
sălio	salīre	salui		.	săl-
Also salīvi, rare.					
salve, see [235].					
sancio	sancīre	sanxi	sanctum	hallow	sanc-
sancītum, rare.					
săpio	sapĕre	sapīvi		be wise	săp-
Also perfect re-sipui-.					
sarcio	sarcīre	sarsi	sartum	patch	sarc-
sărio	sarīre	sarui, sarīvi	sarītum	hoe	săr-, sări-?
sarpo	sarpĕre		sarptum	trim	sarp-
sătăgo (= săt ăgo, see ăgo).					
scăbo	scabĕre	scābi		scratch	scăb-
scalpo	scalpĕre	scalpsi	scalptum	scrape	scalp-
scando	scandĕre	scandi	scansum	climb	scand-
scăteo	scatĕre			bubble	scăt-?
scindo	scindĕre	scĭdi	scissum	cut	scĭd-
scīcĭdi is old.					
scisco	sciscĕre	scīvi	scītum	enact	sci-
scrībo	scribĕre	scripsi	scriptum	write	scrīb-
sculpo	sculpĕre	sculpsi	sculptum	carve	sculp-
sĕco	secāre	secui	sectum	cut	sĕc-
secāturus, once.					
sĕdeo	sedēre	sēdi	sessum	sit	sĕd-
sentio	sentīre	sensi	sensum	think	sent-
sĕpĕlio	sepelīre	sepelīvi	sepultum	bury	sepĕl-
sĕqvor	seqvi		secūtus	follow	sĕqv-
sĕro	serĕre	sēvi	sătum	sow	sa-
sĕro	serĕre	-serui	-sertum	put in rows	sĕr-
serpo	serpĕre	serpsi	serptum	crawl	serp-

130   APPENDIX.

Pres. Ind.	Pres. Inf.	Perf. Ind.	Sup. or Part.		Stem.
sīdo	sidĕre	sīdi		settle	sīd-
sēdi and sessum (borrowed from sĕdeo) are also found.					
singultio	singultīre			sob	singulti-?
sĭno	sinĕre	sīvi	sĭtum	permit	si-
sisto	sistĕre	stĭti	stătum	set	sta-
Compounds keep the reduplication.					
sŏleo	solēre		solĭtus	be wont	sŏl-
solitus sum is used as perfect; see [216] (g).					
solvo	solvĕre	solvi	solūtum	loose	solv-
sŏno / sŏno	sonāre / sonĕre	sonui	sonĭtum	sound	sŏn-
sonāturus, once.					
sorbeo	sorbĕre	sorbui		swallow	sorb-
Perfect -sorpsi, late and rare.					
spargo	spargĕre	sparsi	sparsum	scatter	sparg-
sperno	spernĕre	sprēvi	sprētum	despise	spĕr-, spre-
-spĭcio	-spicĕre	-spexi	-spectum	look	spĕc-
splendeo	splendēre			shine	splend-?
spondeo	spondēre	spŏpondi	sponsum	promise	spond-
de-spŏpondi, old.					
spuo	spuĕre	spui	spūtum	spit	spu-
sqvāleo	sqvalēre			be rough	sqvăl-?
stătuo	statuĕre	statui	statūtum	set up	stătu-
sterno	sternĕre	strāvi	strātum	strew	stĕr-, stra-
sternuo	sternuĕre	sternui		sneeze	sternu-
sterto	stertĕre	stertui		snore	stert-
stingvo	stingvĕre	-stinxi	-stinctum	extinguish	stingv-
sto	stāre	stĕti	stătum	stand	sta-
Also stăturus, rare.					
strĕpo	strepĕre	strepui	strepĭtum	make a noise	strĕp-
strīdeo / strīdo	stridēre / stridĕre	strīdi		hiss	strīd-
stringo	stringĕre	strinxi	strictum	graze	strĭg-
struo	struĕre	struxi	structum	build	strŭgv-
sūgo	sugĕre	suxi	suctum	suck	sūg-
sum see 212	esse	(fui)	(futurus)	be	ĕs-
Complete tenses and future participle borrowed from [fuo].					

LIST OF VERBS.

Pres. Ind.	Pres. Inf.	Perf. Ind.	Sup. or Part.		Stem.
sūmo	sumĕre	sumpsi	sumptum	*take*	sūm-
suo	suĕre	sui	sūtum .	*sew*	su-
surgo	surgĕre	surrexi	surrectum	*rise*	sur-rĕg-
svādeo	svadēre	svāsi	svāsum	*persuade*	svād-
svesco	svescĕre	svēvi	svētum	*get wont*	sve-

Tābeo	tabēre			*waste*	tāb- ?
tăceo	tacēre	tacui	tacĭtum	*be silent*	tăc-
taedet			taesum	*it wearies*	taed-

tăgo (old form of tango).

tango	tangĕre	tĕtĭgi	tactum	*touch*	tăg-
tĕgo	tegĕre	texi	tectum	*cover*	· tĕg-
temno	temnĕre	tempsi	temptum	*despise*	tem-
tendo	tendĕre	tĕtendi	tentum, tensum	*stretch*	tend-
tĕneo	tenēre	tenui	tentum	*hold*	tĕn-

tĕtĭni is quoted.

terreo	terrēre	terrui	terrĭtum	*frighten*	terr-
{ tergeo { tergo	{ tergēre { tergĕre	tersi	tersum	*wipe*	terg-
tĕro	terēre	trīvi	trītum	*rub*	tĕr-, tri-

at-terui, once.

texo	texĕre	texui	textum	*weave*	tex-
{ tingo { tingvo	{ tingĕre { tingvēre	tinxi	tinctum	*dye*	tingv-
tollo	tollere	(sustŭli)	(sublātum)	*lift*	tŏl-, tla-

The simple tŭli and lātum have the sense of fĕro, and the compound forms given are used in the sense of tollo.

| tondeo | tondēre | tŏtondi | tonsum | *shear* | tond- |
| tŏno | tonāre | tonui | tonĭtum | *thunder* | tŏn- |

in-tonātus, once.

torqveo	torqvēre	torsi	tortum	*twist*	torqv-
torreo	torrēre	torrui	tostum	*roast*	tors-
traho	trahĕre	traxi	tractum	*drag*	trăh-
trĕmo	tremĕre	tremui		*tremble*	trĕm-
trĭbuo	tribuĕre	tribui	tribūtum	*assign*	trĭbu-
trūdo	trudĕre	trūsi	trūsum	*thrust*	trūd-

APPENDIX.

Pres. Ind.	Pres. Inf.	Perf. Ind.	Sup. or Part.		Stem.
{ tueor { tuor	{ tuēri { tui	.	tūtus, tuĭtus	*look at*	tu-
tundo	tundĕre	tŭtŭdi	tūsum, tunsum	*thump*	tŭd-
Also perfect re-tundi.					
tūrgeo	turgĕre	tursi		*swell*	turg-
Ulciscor	ulcisci		ultus	*avenge*	ulc-
{ ungo { ungvo	{ ungĕre { ungvĕre	unxi	unctum	*anoint*	ungv-
urgeo	urgĕre	ursi		*urge*	urg-
ūro	urĕre	ussi	ustum	*burn*	ūs-
ūtor	uti		ūsus	*use*	ūt-
Vādo	vadĕre	-vāsi	-vāsum	*go*	vād-
văleo	valēre	valui	valĭtum	*be strong*	văl-
vĕgeo	vegēre			*arouse*	vĕg-?
veho	vehĕre	vexi	vectum	*carry*	vĕh-
vello	vellĕre	velli	vulsum	*pluck*	vĕl-
Perfect also vulsi, late.					
vendo	vendĕre	vendĭdi	vendĭtum	*sell*	ven-d-
vĕneo	venīre	venīvi		*to be sold*	vĕn-i-
vĕnio	venīre	vĕni	ventum	*come*	vĕn-
vĕreor	verēri		verĭtus	*fear*	vĕr-
vergo	vergĕre			*incline*	verg-
verro	verrĕre	verri	versum	*brush*	verr-
verto	vertĕre	verti	versum	*turn*	vert-
vescor	vesci			*eat*	vesc-?
vĕto	vetāre	vetui	vetĭtum	*forbid*	vĕt-
Also vetāvi, rare.					
vĭdeo	vidēre	vīdi	vīsum	*see*	vĭd-
-vĭdo, see dīvĭdo.					
vieo	viēre		viētum	*plait*	vie-
Also viĕtus.					

LIST OF VERBS.

Pres. Ind.	Pres. Inf.	Perf. Ind.	Sup. or Part.		Stem.
vincio	vincīre	vinxi	vinctum	*bind*	vinc-
vinco	vincĕre	vīci	victum ·	*conquer*	vĭc-
vīso	visĕre	vīsi		*visit*	vīs-
vīvo	vivĕre	vixi	victum	*live*	vĭgv-
vŏlo	velle	volui	see 225	*wish*	vŏl-
volvo	volvĕre	volvi	volūtum	*roll*	volv-
vŏmo	vomĕre	vomui	vomĭtum	*vomit*	vŏm-
vŏveo	vovēre	vŏvi	vōtum	*vow*	vŏv-

499. INDEX OF TOPICS.

Ablative case, use of......292–308
Ablative proper..........293–296
Accent.....................19, 20
Accusative case, use of....262–268
a-declension...............52–56
Adjectives, a- and o-stems....70–72
  agreement of........255
  consonant-stems..91–93
  formation of...242–244
  i-stems........106–108
Adverbs, formation of.....248–249
Alphabet.......................1
Appositives, agreement of.....254
-ātes, decl. of adjs. in........[108]

Calendar.....................496
Case-endings, a-stems.......... 54
  consonant-stems 74, 75
  e-stems...........58
  i-stems......99, 101
  o-stems........62, 63
  u-stems.....110, 111
Cases......................42–49
  use of.............258–308
Cognate accusative.:........ [262]
Comitative ablative.......304–306
Comparatives, decl. of........[92]
  formation of....119
Comparison..............119–123
Complete tenses..............144
  of pass.[207], [214]
Composition 252
Concord, rules of.........254–257

Conditional sentences, forms of
                      446–456
Conjugations.............191–193
Conjunctions, formation of....251
Consonants, classification of....12
  euphony of......[12]
  sounds of........6–11
Consonant declension.......73–93

Dates 487–497
Dative case, use of........269–272
Declensions................50, 51
Defective nouns ....[117]
Defective verbs...............235
Demanding, verbs of........[262]
Demonstrative pronouns...127–137
Deponent verbs 154
-dicus, comp. of adjs. in........122
Diphthongs 4, 5
Distributive numerals........[118]

e-declension 57–60
Endings defined 28, 29
  a-stem nouns..........54
  a-stem verbs.....194–195
  complete tenses.......206
  consonant-stem nouns
                  74, 75
  consonant-stem verbs
                  198, 199
  e-stem nouns 58
  e-stem verbs......196, 197
  i-stem nouns.......99, 101

INDEX OF TOPICS.

Endings long *i*-stem verbs..203, 204
    o-stem nouns.......62, 63
    short *i*-stem verbs.200, 202
    simple-stem forms 200
    u-stem nouns.....110, 111
    u-stem verbs.....198, 199
-*er*, stems in, decl. of............80
    comp. of..........121
-*eri*, stems in, decl. of...........102
    comp. of 121
-*ero*, stems in, decl. of............66
    comp. of 121
Exclamatory sentences ......[314]

Factitive verbs, constr........[202]
-*ficus*, compar. of adj. in.......122
Finite verb.....148, agreement 257
Future in -*so*................[216]
    imperative..........[181]

Gender 30-40
    grammatical and natural 31
    natural, rules of.....32-40
    a-stem nouns...........56
    consonant-stem nouns 82-90
    e-stem nouns........59, 60
    i-stem nouns......103-105
    o-stem nouns...........69
    u-stem nouns 113
Genitive case, use of......275-291
Gerund.....................150
    use of...........348, 349
Gerundive, use of.............349

-*i*, dat. ending.................71
Imperative, use of............315
Impersonal verbs..........230-234
Inceptive verbs.............[161]
Inchoative verbs............[161]
Incomplete tenses.............143
Indefinite pronouns.......140, 141
Indicative, use of........313, 314

Infinitive 149
    use of..........335-342
Inflection 21-26
Instrumental ablative 297, 298
Interjections, formation of.....250
Interrogative particles.....426-434
    pronouns 139
-*io*, stems in, decl. of............67
Irregular declension.......114-117
    verbs 215-220
i-declension 94-108
i-stem adjectives..........106-108
-*ites*, decl. of adjs. in ....[108]
-*ius*, gen. ending................71

Locative ablative 299-303
Locative case, *a*-stems..........55
    consonant-stems..77
    e-stems ....[58]
    o-stems......... 65
    use of......273, 274
    u-stems.......[110]

-*mino*, imperative ending.....[216]
Mood-and-tense signs......171-178
Moods..................145-147
    use of............313-333

Nasalizing 160
Negative particles.........422-425
Nominative case, use of....258-260
Non-finite verb-forms, use of 334-352
Nouns, formation of 239-241
Number 41, 253
Numerals 118

o-declension 61-69
Open vowels....................3
Order of words and clauses.479-486

Participles 152
    use of........343-347

INDEX OF TOPICS.

Passive voice............153, 154
Passive voice, complete tenses..153
Perf. act. endings.........189, 190
Perfect stem of verbs.....163-167
Periphrastic conjugations..212, 213
Person....................41, 253
Person-and-number suffixes 179-182
Personal pronouns........124, 125
-plex, decl. of adjs. in........[108]
Possessive pronouns...........126
Predicate noun, agreement of..254
Prepositions, formation of 251
    use of.......268, 308
Present stem of verbs.....157-162
Principal parts of verbs...168, 169
Pronouns 124-141
   agreement of........256
   use of..........435-445

Quantity, gen. rules.........14-18
   sp. rules........364-397
Questioning, verbs of........[262]

Reduplication, pres. stem......158
   perf. stem......164
Reflexive meaning of passive...154
Relative pronouns............138
Reported speech. 457-478
Roots 236

Semi-vowel stems, decl. of ...78, 79
Sequence of tenses............312
Stem, defined...................27

Stems, formation of.......237, 238
Subjunctive, use of.......316-333
Suffixes, defined 27
  verbal..........179-187
Superlative 120
Supine 151
  use of.............350-352
-tat, stems in, decl. of ....[81]
Tendencies affecting quantity
      356-363
Tenses, use of............309-312
Theme, defined............28, 29
-trix, decl. of adjs. in.........[108]
Two objects, vbs. with ....[262]

u-declension 100-113

v dropped....................215
Verb-forms 142-235
Verb-stems 155, 167
Verbal suffixes...........170-190
Verbs, formation of.......245-247
  list of................498
Verse, laws of............353-421
Versification 398-421
Vocative case, o-stems..........64
  use of...............261
Voice 253
volus, comp. of compounds of..122
Vowels, sound of................2
  euphony of...........[2]

Weakening of vowels.......[2], 76
Word-formation 236-252

500. INDEX OF WORDS.

[*This list contains all words mentioned in the book because of any peculiarity of form or construction.*]

ABBREVIATIONS.

abl. .... *ablative.*	indic. .... *indicative.*
acc. .... *accusative.*	inflect. .... *inflection.*
assim. .... *assimilation.*	irreg. .... *irregular.*
comp. .... *comparison.*	loc. .... *locative.*
constr. .... *construction.*	pron. .... *pronoun.*
cmpds. .... *compounds.*	quant. .... *quantity.*
dat. .... *dative.*	redupl. .... *reduplication.*
decl. .... *declension.*	semi-dep. .... *semi-deponent.*
def. .... *defective.*	subj. .... *subjunctive.*
gen. .... *genitive.*	vb. .... *verb.*
gend. .... *gender.*	w. .... *with.*

---

ab .... assim. [12]	ambŏ .... decl. [72], quant. [365]
abies .... quant. 383	amni .... abl. [99]
absens .... [221]	amplius .... constr. [296]
accipiter .... decl. [80]	amussim .... acc. [99]
acies .... decl. [58]	angvi .... abl. [99]
acus .... gend. [113]	animi .... loc. [273]
ad .... assim. [12]	ante ...... in cmpds. w. dat. [269]
ad .... in cmpds. w. dat. [269]	ante diem .... w. acc. [268]
adeps .... gend. [82]	antes .... gend. [103]
aedili .... abl. [99]	Aprili .... abl. [99]
agger .... gend. [89]	Arar .... decl. [102]
ajo .... def. vb. [235]	Arari .... abl. [99]
aliqvi } .... decl. 141	Ararim .... acc. [99]
aliqvis }	arbŏs .... gend. [89], quant. 383
alius .... decl. 71, w. abl. [206]	arcus ..... decl. [110], gend. [113]
alter .... decl. 71	aries .... quant. 383
alvus .... gend. [69]	artus .... decl. [110]

INDEX OF WORDS.

as .... decl. [98]
assis .... decl. [98]
asser .... gend. [80]
audeo .... semi-dep. [216]
ave .... def. vb. [235]
avi .... abl. [99]
axi .... abl. [99]

balneum .... decl. [115]
bene .... quant. [396]
bibi .... redupl. [164]
bibo .... redupl. [158]
bidui .... constr. [284]
bonus .... comp. [123]
bōs ...... decl. [112], quant. [368]
burim .... acc. [99]
buris .... gend. [103]

caelum .... decl. [116]
calix .... gend. [82]
callis .... gend. [103]
canis .... decl. [96]
caput .... gend. [82]
carbasus .... gend. [69], decl. [110]
carcer .... gend. [80]
cardo .... gend. [80]
caro .... decl. [115]
caulis .... gend. [103]
cave .... w. subj. [315]
-ce .... [19], quant. [395]
celer .... decl. [93], [108]
cello .... [102]
celo .... w. two acc. [262]
Cerēs .... quant. 383
cinis .... gend. [80]
citerior .... comp. [123]
citimus .... comp. [123]
citŏ .... quant. [396]
cītus .... quant. [200]
civi .... abl. [99]
clam .... w. abl. [308]
classi .... abl. [99]

classis .... gend. [103]
clunis ....,......... gend. [103]
-clūtus .... quant. [209]
cohors .... gend. [105]
colli .... abl. [99]
collis .... gend. [103]
colus .... gend. [69], [113]
com .... assim. [12]
complures .... decl. [92]
con .... in cmpds. w. dat. [269]
cor .... gend. [82], decl. [98]
corbi .... abl. [99]
corbis .... gend. [103]
cortex .... gend. [83]
cos .... decl. [98]
crās .... quant. [395]
cratim .... acc. [99]
cravim .... acc. [99]
cucumi .... abl. [99]
cucumim .... acc. [99]
cucumis .... gend. [80], [103]
cujus .... decl. [139]
-cum .... [19]
cupido .... gend. [84]
cūr .... quant. [395]

dă .... quant. [361], [385]
dās .... quant. [361], [385]
dătus .... quant. [209]
dea .... decl. [50]
dens .... gend. [105]
deus .... decl. 68
Dīana .... quant. [17]
dic 216
dic .... loc. [58], [273]
dies .... gend. 60
difficilis .... comp. 121
dignor .... w. abl. [303]
dignus .... w. abl. [300], [303]
dissimilis .... comp. 121
dīus .... quant. [17]
do ...... irreg. vb. 226, quant. [385]

INDEX OF WORDS.

doceo .... w. two acc. [202]
domi....:............... loc. [273]
domo .... constr. [293]
domos .... constr. [265]
domui .... loc. [110]
domum .... constr. [265]
domus ...... gend. [113], decl. [115]
dos .... decl. [98]
duam .... subj. [226]
duc 216
duim .... subj. [226]
dum .... w. pres. [309]
-dum .... [10]
duŏ .... decl. [72], quant. [365]

campse .... [132]
capse .... [132]
eāpse .... [132]
ebur .... [76]
ceqvi ⎫
ceqvis ⎭ .... decl. 141
edim .... subj. [223]
edo .... irreg. vb. 223
effigies .... decl. [58]
egŏ .... decl. 125, quant. [374]
ĕheu .... quant. [17]
ejă .... quant. [307]
eluvies .... decl. [58]
ĕn .... quant. [395]
eo .... irreg. vb. 227
copse .... [132]
epulum .... decl. [115]
ergo .... w. gen. [285]
escit .... [221]
escunt .... [221]
eumpse .... [132]
exseqvias ire .... [265]
exterus .... comp. [123]
extimus .... comp. [123]
extremus .... comp. [123]

fac 216

facies .... decl. [58]
facilis .... comp. 121
faex .... decl. [98]
fames .... decl. [115]
familia .... decl. [54]
fascis .... gend. [103]
febri .... abl. [99]
febrim .... acc. [99]
fel .... gend. [88]
femur .... [76], decl. [115]
fero .... irreg. vb. 224
fides .... decl. [58]
fido .... semi-dep. [216]
filia .... decl. [54]
fini .... abl. [99]
finis .... gend. [103]
fio ...... quant. [17], irreg. vb. 229
follis .... gend. [103]
fons .... gend. [105]
[for] .... def. vb. [285]
foras .... constr. [265]
fŏre ⎫
fŏrem ⎭ [155], [221], quant. [385]
forceps .... gend. [82]
forfex .... gend. [83]
fornix .... gend. [82]
frater .... decl. [80]
fraus .... decl. [98]
frenum .... decl. [110]
fruor .... w. abl. [297]
fuam, etc. .... subj. [221]
fungor .... w. abl. [297]
fusti .... abl. [99]
fustis .... gend. [103]
fŭturus .... [221], quant. [200]

gaudeo .... semi-dep. [216]
gigno .... redupl. [158]
glacies .... decl. [58]
glis .... decl. [98]
gracilis .... comp. 121
grex .... gend. [82]

grūs ..... decl. [112], quant. [361]

Hadria .... gend. [33]
haud scio an .... w. indic. [323]
hebes .... decl. [93], [108]
hic .... decl. 134
hīc .... quant. [395]
hiems ...... decl. [78], gend. [81]
hūc .... quant. [395]
humilis .... comp. 121
humi .... loc. [273]
humo .... constr. [293]
humus .... gend. [69]

ibĭ .... quant. [378]
id genus .... [267]
id temporis .... [267]
idem ...... decl. 136, w. dat. [271]
idus .... gend. [113]
igni .... abl. [99]
ilicŏ .... quant. [396]
ille .... decl. 131
illic .... decl. [135]
imber ..... decl. [102], gend. [103]
imbrex .... gend. [83]
imbri .... abl. [99]
imus .... comp. [123]
in .... assim. [12]
in .... in cmpds. w. dat. [269]
-inde .... [19]
indignus .... w. abl. [300], [303]
infernĕ .... quant. [396]
inferus .... comp. [123]
infimus .... comp. [123]
infitias ire .... [203]
inqvam .... def. vb. [235]
instar .... w. gen. [285]
inter .... in cmpds. w. dat. [269]
interest .... w. gen. [291]
interior .... comp. [123]
intimus .... comp. [123]
ipse .... decl. 132

ipsus .... [132]
is .... decl. 129
iste .... decl. 130
istic .... decl. [135]
istuc aetatis .... [267]
istus .... [130]
ită .... quant. [397]
iter .... decl. [115]
Ytus .... quant. [209]

jecur .... [76], decl. [115]
jocus .... decl. [116]
jugerum .... decl. [115]
junior .... comp. [123]
Jupiter .... decl. [112]
juvenis .... decl. [96], comp. [123]

lac .... gend. [105]
lacti .... abl. [101]
lacus .... decl. [110]
lapis .... gend. [82]
lār .... quant. 384
larix .... gend. [82]
later .... gend. [80]
lentim .... acc. [99]
Liger .... decl. [102]
Ligeri .... abl. [99]
Ligerim .... acc. [99]
linter ..... decl. [102], gend. [103]
lis .... decl. [98]
lītus .... quant. [209]
locus .... decl. [116]
longius .... constr. [290]
lues .... decl. [112]
lux .... decl. [98]

macte .... [201]
magis .... comp. with, 123
magnus .... comp. [123]
major .... comp. [123]
malĕ .... quant. [396]
malo .... irreg. vb. 225

INDEX OF WORDS. 143

malus .... comp. [123]
manus .... gend. [113]
margo .... gend. [84]
mās .... decl. [98], quant. 384
mater .... decl. [80]
maturus .... comp. [121]
maxime .... comp. with 123
maximus .... comp. [123]
maximus natu .... [123]
mel .... gend. [88]
melior .... comp. [123]
memini .... def. vb. [235]
mentis .... [274]
meridies .... gend. 60
messim .... acc. [99]
messis .... gend. [103]
-met .... [10]
meus .... decl. 126
mille .... decl. [118]
minimus .... comp. [123]
minimus natu .... [123]
minor .... comp. [123]
minoris .... [274]
minus ... comp. [123], constr. [296]
miseret .... w. gen. 281
modŏ .... quant. [396]
mons .... gend. [105]
morior .... inflect. [216]
multus .... comp. [123]
mus .... decl. [98]

navi .... abl. [99]
navim .... acc. [99]
-nĕ .... [19], [314], quant. [395]
neqveo .... irreg. vb. 228
nescio an .... w. indic. [323]
neuter .... decl. 71
ningvis .... decl. [98]
nix .... decl. [98]
nolo .... irreg. vb. 225
nōn .... quant. [395]
nosco .... an *o*-stem, [155]

nullus .... decl. 71
num .... [314]

ob .... assim. [12]
ob .... in cmpds. w. dat. [269]
obex .... gend. [83]
odi .... def. vb. 235
ŏhĕ .... quant. [17], [396]
olle .... [130]
operae est .... [272]
optimus .... comp. [123]
opus .... w. abl. [297]
orbi .... abl. [99]
orbis .... gend. [103]
ordo .... gend. [84]
'orior .... inflect. [216]
os .... gend. [89]
[ovo] .... def. vb. [235]

paenitet .... w. gen. 281
pār .... quant. 384
pār .... decl. [93], [102], [108]
paries ...... gend. [82], quant. 383
parti .... abl. [99]
partim .... acc. [99]
partus .... decl. [110]
parvus, ... comp. [123]
pater .... decl. [80]
pax .... decl. [98]
pecten .... gend. [87]
pejor .... comp. [123]
pelagus .... decl. [115]
pello .... [102]
pelvi .... abl. [99]
pelvim .... acc. [99]
penĕs .... quant. [307]
penus .... gend. [112]
pēs ... gend. [82], quant. [361], 383
pessimus .... comp. [123]
pessum dare .... [265]
pessum ire .... [265]
piget .... w. gen. 281

plebes................decl. [58]
plebes................decl. [98]
plebs.................decl. [98]
plurimus.............comp. [123]
pluris................[274]
plus..decl. [92], comp. [123],
    constr. [290]
pons..................gend. [105]
porticus..............gend. [113]
portus................decl. [110]
possiem, etc..........subj. [222]
possum...............irreg. vb. 222
post.......in cmpds. w. dat. [269]
posterus.............comp. [123]
posti.................abl. [99]
postis................gend. [103]
postremus............comp. [123]
postridie.w. acc. [268], w. gen. [285]
postumus............comp. [123]
potessem, etc.........[222]
potior................w. gen. [290]
potior..inflect. [216], w. abl. [298]
prae.......in cmpds. w. dat. [269]
praecox..........decl. [93], [108]
praesens..............[221]
praesepim.............acc. [99]
pridie...w. acc. [268], w. gen. [285]
primus................comp. [123]
prior.................comp. [123]
pro........in cmpds. w. dat. [269]
procul................w. abl. [308]
profectŏ..............quant. [390]
propior..comp. [123], w. acc. [268]
propius...............w. acc. [268]
prosum...............irreg. vb. [222]
proxime...............w. acc. [268]
proximus..comp. [123],w. acc. [268]
-ptĕ............[19], quant. [395]
pubēs................quant. 383
pudet.................w. gen. 281
pulvis................gend. [89]
puppi.................abl. [99]

puppim...............acc. [99]
pută..................quant. [397]

qvaesumus............[179]
-qvando...............[19]
qvanto ... tanto.......[290]
-qvĕ............[19], quant. [395]
qveo..................irreg. vb. 228
qvi........decl. 138, quant. [374]
qviă..................quant. [397]
qvid facias, etc........w. abl. [297]
qvid fies, etc.........w. abl. [297]
qvīn..................quant. [395]
qvinam................[139]
qvinqvatrus...........gend. [113]
Qvintili..............abl. [99]
qvis..................decl. 139
qvisnam...............[139]
qvĭtus...............quant. [209]
qvo ... co.............[290]

rastrum...............decl. [116]
rătus.................quant. [209]
ravi..................abl. [99]
ravim.................acc. [99]
rĕ-...................quant. [395]
rēfert.................w. gen. 201
res...................decl. [58]
restim................acc. [99]
Rhēa..................quant. [17]
robur.................[76]
rumex.................gend. [83]
rumi..................abl. [99]
rure..................constr. [293]
ruri..................loc. [273]
rus...................constr. [265]
rŭtus.................quant. [209]

săl.....*....gend. [88], quant. 384
sallo.................[102]
salve.................def. vb. [235]
sam...................pron. [128]

INDEX OF WORDS.

sangvis.....gend. [87], decl. [115]
sas..................pron. [128]
satur.................decl. [71]
sătus...............quant. [209]
scrobis.....decl. [98], gend. [103]
scrobs................decl. [98]
securi..................abl. [99]
securim................acc. [99]
sedes..................decl. [96]
sementim..............acc. [99]
senex.....decl. [115], comp. [123]
sentis................gend. [103]
series.................decl. [58]
sero...............redupl. [158]
Sextili.................abl. [99]
sīc..................quant. [395]
siem, etc..............subj. [221]
silex.................gend. [83]
similis................comp. 121
simul...............w. abl. [308]
sīn..................quant. [395]
sisto...............redupl. [158]
siti....................abl. [99]
sitim..................acc. [99]
sītus........ ....quant. [209]
sodali..................abl. [99]
solco.............semi-dep. [216]
solus..................decl. 71
sorti...................abl. [99]
species................decl. [58]
specus.....decl. [110], gend. [112]
spes...................decl. [58]
stătus...............quant. [209]
stiti...............redupl. [164]
strigili.................abl. [99]
sub...................assim. [12]
sub.........in cmpds. w. dat. [269]
sui....................decl. 125
sum...............irreg. vb. 221
sum..................pron. [128]
summus... ....comp. [123]
sumus...................[179]

sūs......decl. [112], quant. [361]
supellex..............decl. [115]
super......in cmpds. w. dat. [269]
supernē:............quant. [396]
superus.............comp. [123]
supremus...........comp. [123]

taedet...............w. gen. 281
tellus.................gend. [80]
tenus .'.............w. gen. [285]
teres..........decl. [93], [108]
Tiberi.................abl. [99]
Tiberim................acc. [99]
tollo......................[162]
torqvis..............gend. [103]
torris................gend. [103]
totus...................decl. 71
trabes................decl. [98]
trabs.................decl. [98]
tres.................decl. [118]
tribus.....decl. [110], gend. [113]
tridui...............constr. [284]
tu.....................decl. 125
turbo.................gend. [86]
turri...................abl. [99]
turrim..................acc. [99]
tussi...................abl. [99]
tussim.................acc. [99]
tussis................gend. [103]

ubī.................quant. [378]
ullus..................decl. 71
ulterior..............comp. [123]
ultimus..............comp. [123]
ungvi..................abl. [99]
ungvis..............gend. [103]
unus...................decl. 71
usus...............w. abl. [207]
uter..............(pron.) decl. 71
uter......decl. [102], gend. [103]
utor................w. abl. [298]

vannus ....gend. [69]	veterrimus ....comp. [123]
varix................gend. [82]	vetus ....comp. [123]
vas ....decl. [115]	vi....................abl. [99]
vates ....decl. [96]	vim ....acc. [99]
-vĕ............[19], quant. [395]	vir....................decl. [66]
vectis ....gend. [103]	virile secus................[267]
venum dare ....[265]	virus ....decl. [115]
venum ire................[265]	vīs......decl. [115], quant. [361]
venter.....decl. [102], gend. [103]	volo..............irreg. vb. 225
veru.................decl. [110]	volumus ....[179]
vescor..............w. abl. [208]	vomer................gend. [89]
vesper......gend. [89], decl. [115]	vulgus ....decl. [115]

LATIN EXERCISES

INTRODUCTORY TO

CÆSAR'S GALLIC WAR,

TO ACCOMPANY THE STUDY OF

BLACKBURN'S "ESSENTIALS OF LATIN GRAMMAR."

BOSTON:
GINN, HEATH, AND COMPANY.
1883.

Entered, according to Act of Congress, in the year 1883,
BY F. A. BLACKBURN,
In the Office of the Librarian of Congress at Washington.

J. S. CUSHING & CO., PRINTERS, BOSTON.

PREFACE.

THESE exercises have been prepared as a necessary supplement to my "Essentials of Latin Grammar" to furnish the needed illustration and drill for the beginner. They do not essentially differ from other collections of the same plan and aim, but in compiling them I have kept in view the following objects : —

1. To provide the means for studying the Grammar systematically from the beginning. Most exercise-books for beginners in Latin are so arranged as to use the Grammar as a reference-book only, giving the pupil detached principles to hold in memory until he begins the study of his first Latin author. In this, on the contrary, the Grammar is taken in its own order, and the few verb-forms and principles of syntax necessary to make sentences are put in the vocabularies and notes; nothing is anticipated, and the use of the Grammar as a book of reference is limited to portions already mastered, until the pupil reaches the exercises on syntax.

2. To make the earlier lessons very simple, so as to require as little labor as possible in translation and leave a broad margin of time for the thorough mastery of forms. If my experience is of any value, poor scholar-

ship in Latin is far more often the result of lack of training in the inflections than in the syntax. The latter is comparatively easy when the forms are perfectly familiar and the general force of flectional syllables understood and felt. The earlier sentences, therefore, are very easy; exercise in translation will come later.

3. To make the pupil familiar, so far as it can be done in a book of this kind, with the vocabulary and style of Cæsar's Commentaries, and thus render easier the hardest step in the study of Latin,— the transition from the exercise-book to a Latin author. To this end all the words are taken from the first book of the Gallic War, and the sentences are from the same source with the necessary changes, omissions, and variations. The Gallic War has been chosen because it is usually the first Latin author put into the pupil's hands, and these exercises are meant to be, as they are entitled, "introductory" to it.

In the matter of orthography I have followed, though with reluctance, the usual custom of distinguishing *j* from *i* and *u* from *v* (except after *q*, *g*, and *s*), believing that the slight inconsistency of usage between the Grammar and Exercise-book would be less trouble to a beginner than the difficulty of unlearning a system after once becoming familiar with it. Marks of quantity have been added in the vocabularies and indices, but in the exercises they have been used only as an aid to pronunciation and accent, and this aid is gradually withdrawn.

No consistent plan of noting quantity has been followed; the marks have been added to those syllables which as experience shows, are most often mispronounced. In a few instances also the quantity mark has been used to give the pupil a hint of the case used; *e.g.*, the ablative singular of *a*-stems or accusative plural of *i*-stems.

References to the Grammar are added in both vocabularies and indices to all words in the form or syntax of which there is anything irregular or peculiar. The notes are intended to cover all cases where the pupil, if left without help, would be likely to go astray, and the hints and directions for the use of the book are meant for such teachers as from lack of experience in teaching elementary Latin may feel the need of them.

Corrections and suggestions will be welcome.

F. A. BLACKBURN.

SAN FRANCISCO, CAL.,
July 27, 1883.

ABBREVIATIONS.

abl.	ablative.
acc.	accusative.
act.	active.
adv.	adverb.
(c.)	common (gender).
conj.	conjunction.
(f.)	feminine.
ind.	indicative.
inf.	infinitive.
(m.)	masculine.
(n.)	neuter.
pl.	plural.
prep.	preposition.
pres.	present.
sing.	singular.
w.	with.

Gr., *Blackburn's " Essentials of Latin Grammar."*

A small figure added to a word refers to the notes which follow the exercises.

CONTENTS.

EXERCISES ON FORMS.

I. PRELIMINARY 9
II. The a-declension; present indicative of sum; subject nominative; agreement of the finite verb; agreement of the predicate-noun 9
III. The e-declension; imperfect indicative of sum . . 10
IV. The o-declension; questions 11
V. Adjectives of the a- and o-declensions; agreement of the adjective; present indicative active and present infinitive active of the a-stem verb; direct object . 12
VI. Irregular a- and o-stem adjectives; indirect object . 13
VII. Review of Group A.; present indicative passive of the a-stem verb; vocative 14
VIII. The consonant-declension; agreement of the appositive 15
IX. Adjectives of the consonant-declension; future indicative active of sum 16
X. The i-declension; extent of time and space . 17
XI. Adjectives of the i-declension . . 18
XII. The u-declension 19
XIII. Review of the declensions; irregular nouns . 21
XIV. Numeral adjectives 22
XV. Comparison of adjectives . 23
XVI. Irregular comparison 24
XVII. Personal and possessive pronouns . . . 25
XVIII. Demonstrative pronouns; is, ille, iste, ipse . 26
XIX. Demonstrative pronouns; hic, idem . . 27
XX. Relative, interrogative and indefinite pronoun . . 28
XXI. Inflection of the verb 28
XXII. Incomplete tenses of a-stem verbs; moods in independent sentences 29
XXIII. Incomplete tenses of e-stem verbs 30
XXIV. Incomplete tenses of consonant-stem and u-stem verbs . 31

XXV.	Incomplete tenses of short i-stem verbs	32
XXVI.	Incomplete tenses of long i-stem verbs	33
XXVII.	Complete tenses, active voice	34
XXVIII.	Verb-forms from the simple stem	35
XXIX.	The periphrastic conjugations	37
XXX.	Review of verbs; irregular verbs; **sum** and its compounds	38
XXXI.	Irregular verbs; **edo, fero**	39
XXXII.	Irregular verbs; **volo, nolo, malo**	40
XXXIII.	Irregular verbs; **do, eo, fio**	41
XXXIV.	Impersonal and defective verbs	42

EXERCISES ON SYNTAX.

XXXV.	Nominative, vocative and accusative cases	43
XXXVI.	Dative case	44
XXXVII.	Locative case	45
XXXVIII.	Genitive case; source and cause	46
XXXIX.	Genitive case; possessive and special uses	47
XL.	Ablative case proper	48
XLI.	Instrumental ablative	49
XLII.	Locative ablative	50
XLIII.	Comitative ablative	51
XLIV.	Ablative absolute; ablative with prepositions	52
XLV.	Use of the tenses	53
XLVI.	Subjunctive in dependent clauses	54
XLVII.	Subjunctive in dependent clauses (*continued*)	55
XLVIII.	Infinitive	56
XLIX.	Participles	57
L.	Gerund and gerundive	58
LI.	Supine	59
LII.	Forms of conditional sentences	60
LIII.	Indirect discourse	61
LIV.	Indirect discourse (*continued*)	62
LV.	Indirect discourse (*continued*)	63
LVI.	Relations of place	64
LVII.	Relations of place (*continued*)	65
LVIII.	Relations of time	66
LIX.	Relations of time (*continued*)	67
LX.	Caesar, B. G. I., cap. I.–IV. For miscellaneous review	68

LATIN EXERCISES.

EXERCISES.

EXERCISES ON FORMS.

I.

Preliminary.

Learn thoroughly Gr. 1–51, and practise to secure a good pronunciation and the habit of placing the accent rightly.

II.

The a-declension; Gr. 52–56.
Present indicative of the verb **sum** (to *be*).
Subject nominative.
Agreement of the finite verb.
Agreement of the predicate noun.

VOCABULARY.

Gallĭă, -ae, *Gaul* (now France).
lĭnguă, -ae, *tongue, speech, language.*
Belgae, -ārŭm (pl.), *Belgians.*
causă, -ae, *cause, reason.*
Gărumnă, -ae, *Garonne* (river).
Ăquītānĭă, -ae, *Aquitania* (now S. W. France).
ĭn (prep. with abl.), *in, on, among.*
ĭn (prep. with acc.), *into, to, towards, for.*

ē or ex (prep. w. abl.),[1] *out of, from.*
ăd (prep. w. acc.), *to, towards, for.*
ĕt (conj.), *and, also.*
nōn (adv.),[2] *not.*
sŭm, *[I] am.*
ĕs, *(thou) art.*
est, *(he, she, it) is.*
sŭmŭs, *(we) are.*
estĭs, *(you) are.*
sunt, *(they) are.*

* The personal pronoun-subject is expressed in Latin only when emphatic; in ordinary speech the verb-form shows the person and number of the subject.

EXERCISES.

1. in Galliā sum. 2. linguā³ Belgārum. 3. in Garumnam. 4. ad Garumnam. 5. causā es.⁴ 6. ex Aquitaniā. 7. sŭmus in Galliā. 8. ad Belgas. 9. Belgae causā sunt. 10. linguā Galliae linguā Belgārum nōn est. 11. in Belgīs. 12. in Galliā et in Aquitaniā. 13. ex Aquitaniā in Galliam.

1. We are the cause. 2. To the Belgians. 3. Out of Gaul. 4. In the language of the Belgians. 5. The Garonne is in Gaul and Aquitania. 6. The Garonne is not in [the land of]⁵ the Belgians. 7. He is not the cause. 8. There is no cause.⁶ 9. Out of Gaul into [the land of] the Belgians. 10. Toward the Garonne.

III.

The e-declension; Gr. 57–60.
Imperfect indicative of the verb sum (to *be*).

VOCABULARY.

rēs, rĕī, *thing, matter, circumstance.*
diēs, diēī (c.),* *day.*
fĭdēs, -ĕī, *faith, belief, promise.*
spēs, -ĕī, *hope.*
cŭm (prep. w. abl.), *with, along with.*
glōriă, -ae, *glory.*
cōpiă, -ae, *plenty, supply.*
cōpiae (pl.), *forces, troops.*

prōvincia, -ae, *province.*
nātūră, -ae, *nature, character.*
ĕrăm, (*I*) *was.*
ĕrăs, (*thou*) *wast.*
ĕrăt, (*he, she, it*) *was.*
ĕrāmŭs, (*we*) *were.*
ĕrātĭs, (*you*) *were.*
ĕrant, (*they*) *were.*

EXERCISES.

1. cum fĭdē. 2. erat spes gloriae. 3. fĭdĕi causā.¹ 4. cum provinciae copiīs. 5. in provinciā nōn est Garumnă. 6. causārum erat copiă. 7. rērum natūră. 8. cum Belgīs

---

* Gender is denoted by (M.), (F.), (N.) or (C.), but only when the noun is an exception to the rules given in the Grammar.

ērātis. 9. in copiīs provinciae Belgae ĕrant. 10. Belgae non sŭmus. 11. gloriă dīcī. 12. copiae Belgārum in provinciā sunt. 13. rērum causā.

1. The glory of the days. 2. You² are the glory of the province. 3. The troops of the province are among the Belgians. 4. There are troops in Gaul. 5. By the nature of glory. 6. With faith and hope.³ 7. He was in Aquitania with the Belgians. 8. For the sake of the province. 9. You were in Gaul for the sake of glory. 10. Out of the province into Gaul.

IV.

The o-declension; Gr. 61–69.
Questions.

VOCABULARY.

ănĭmŭs, -ī, *spirit, courage, mind.*
bellŭm, -ī, *war.*
Rhēnŭs, -ī, *Rhine* (river).
proelĭŭm, -ī, *battle.*
Gallī, -ōrŭm (pl.), *Gauls* (a people).
Germānī, -ōrŭm (pl.), *Germans.*
ĭnĭtĭŭm, -ī, *beginning.*
ā or ăb (prep. w. abl.),¹ *away from, from.*

regnŭm, -ī, *kingdom, kingly power.*
ăgĕr, ăgrī, *land, farm-land, field.*
frūmentŭm, -ī, *corn, grain* (often pl.).
fīlĭŭs, -ī, *son.*
pŏpŭlŭs, -ī, *a people, a nation.*
fīlĭă, -ae, *daughter*; (Gr. [54]).
impĕrĭŭm, -ī, *power, sway.*
trans (prep. w. acc.), *across, beyond.*

EXERCISES.

1. belli causā Gallī ĕrant. 2. ab initiō belli. 3. in agrō frumentum est. 4. in agrīs Gallōrum frumenti est copiă. 5. ab Rheno ad Garumnam. 6. cum filiīs et filiābus. 7. nōnnĕ in Galliā initiō belli ĕras? 8. nōn ĕram. 9. cum fĭdē et animō. 10. trans Rhenum in Germānis ĕrāmus. 11. estne copiă frumenti?

1. Was there plenty of corn? 2. There was. 3. In the beginning[2] of the war the Germans were in Gaul. 4. By the sway of Gaul. 5. By the nature of the land. 6. The glory of the war. 7. The spirit of the Belgians. 8. The peoples of Gaul. 9. From the Garonne to the Rhine. 10. Are you Gauls? 11. We are not. 12. Was the nature of the land the cause of the battle? [No.]

V.

Adjectives of the a- and o-declensions; Gr. 70.
Agreement of the adjective.
Present indicative active and present infinitive active of the a-stem verb.
Direct object.

VOCABULARY.

altŭs, -ă, -ŭm, *high, deep.*
ămīcŭs, -ă, -ŭm,[1] *friendly.*
angustŭs, -ă, -ŭm, *narrow.*
cŭpĭdŭs, -ă, -ŭm, *desirous.*
lātŭs, -ă, -ŭm, *broad.*
meŭs, -ă, -ŭm (Gr. 126), *my, mine.*
pugnārĕ, *to fight.*
occŭpārĕ, *to occupy, seize.*
importārĕ, *to import.*
Rhŏdănŭs, -i, *Rhone* (river).
tuŭs, -ă, -ŭm, *thy, thine, your.*

pugnŏ, (*I*) *fight.*
pugnās, (*thou*) *fightest.*
pugnăt, (*he, she, it*) *fights.*
pugnāmŭs, (*we*) *fight.*
pugnātĭs, (*you*) *fight.*
pugnant, (*they*) *fight.*
occŭpŏ, (*I*) *seize.*
occŭpās, (*thou*) *seizest.*
etc.   etc.
importŏ, (*I*) *import.*
etc.   etc.

EXERCISES.

1. trans Rhēnum pugnat. 2. pugnārĕ in Gallīs. 3. regni cupĭdus est. 4. popŭli[2] amīci sunt. 5. trans Rhenum popŭli amīci nōn sunt. 6. Galli amīci[3] Germānis nōn sunt. 7. Gallōrum amīci Germāni nōn sunt. 8. angustīne sunt Rhodănus et Rhenus? 9. Rhodănus angustus est; Rhenus, latus. 10. agrum amicōrum nōn occŭpo. 11. importāmus frumentum in Galliam.

EXERCISES ON FORMS. 13

1. You are importing things into the province. 2. Were the nations desirous of war? 3. Is the Rhine deep? 4. The Rhine is deep and broad. 5. My son was friendly to your daughter. 6. Were you friendly to my daughter? 7. To fight with the Gauls across the Rhone. 8. My friends were desirous of war. 9. We are seizing the lands of the Belgians. 10. Are you seizing the lands of my friends? 11. My friends are importing corn into Gaul. 12. We are desirous of glory.

VI.

Irregular a- and o-stem adjectives; Gr. 71, 72.
Indirect object.

VOCABULARY.

ălĭus, -ă, -ŭd,[1] *another*.
altĕr, -ă, -ŭm,[1] *the other* (of two).
tōtŭs, -ă, -ŭm, *whole, all*.
ūnŭs, -ă, -ŭm, *one*.
multŭs, -ă, -ŭm, *much*, pl. *many*.
magnŭs, -ă, -ŭm, *great, large*.

dŏ,[2] (*I*) *give*.
dărĕ, *to give*.
nuntĭŏ, (*I*) *announce, tell*.
nuntĭārĕ, *to announce, to tell*.
rīpă, -ae, *bank* (of a river).
vĭă, -ae, *way, road, path*.

EXERCISES.

1. totam provinciam occŭpat. 2. aliae viae sunt. 3. totīus belli causā ĕras. 4. Gallīs fĭdem dat. 5. aliud regnum occupāre. 6. multae viae in Galliā sunt. 7. Gallīs causam nuntiat. 8. altĕra viā augustā est. 9. ad ripam Rhodăni. 10. Gallis nuntiāmus belli magni initium. 11. alii pugnant, alii provinciam occŭpant. 12. crantne viae in provinciā?

1. The Rhine is broad and large. 2. We give the province to the Belgians. 3. Are the Germans seizing the province? [No.] 4. Are you not fighting in Gaul? 5. The troops are on the road. 6. Some are desirous of glory; others, of war. 7. The people give my son[3] the king-

dom. 8. In the whole province we are desirous of a battle. 9. There is one road in the province. 10. We give all Gaul to the Germans. 11. There is great hope of glory. 12. Courage gives the sway of Gaul to the Germans. 13. Was there a great war in Aquitania?

VII.

Review of Group A.
Present indicative passive of a-stem verbs.
Vocative.

VOCABULARY.

silvă, -ae, *forest.*
postĕrŭs, -ă, -ŭm, *following, next.*
Celtae, -ārŭm (pl.), *Celts.*
appellŏ, -ārĕ,[1] *call.*
mātūrŭs, -ă, -ŭm, *ripe.*
deŭs, -ī (Gr. 68), *god.*
grātiă, -ae, *popularity, favor.*
ā or ăb (prep. w. abl.), *by* (to express the doer).
nostĕr, -tră, -trŭm, *our, ours.*

ŏb (prep. w. acc.), *on account of, because of, for.*
victōriă, -ae, *victory.*
vīnŭm, -ī, *wine.*
appellŏr, (*I*) *am called.*
appellārĭs, (*thou*) *art called.*
appellātŭr, (*he, she, it*) *is called.*
appellāmŭr, (*we*) *are called.*
appellāmĭnī, (*you*) *are called.*
appellantŭr, (*they*) *are called.*

EXERCISES.

1. linguā nostrā Galli appellantur.[2] 2. alter Rhenus appellātur; alter, Rhodănus. 3. amīci appellamīni. 4. filiusne tuus imperii cupĭdus est? 5. nostrae filiae cupĭdae sunt gratiae. 6. Galli a Belgis Celtae appellantur. 7. Celtas Gallos appellāmus. 8. frumenta in agris nōn ĕrant matūra. 9. postĕro diē[3] proelium ĕrat in silvā Belgārum. 10. imperium ā dīs dătur. 11. multae res in Belgas nōn importantur. 12. proelium Gallīs a filio tuo nuntiātur.

1. Your son is telling [the news of] the battle to the Gauls. 2. The one[4] people is called Belgians; the other, Gauls. 3. You call the Belgians Gauls. 4. The nations

of Gaul are called Celts in the language⁵ of the Belgians.
5. Land is given to the Germans by the Celts. 6. You are desirous of war, Belgians.⁶ 7. They are fighting for⁷ many reasons, my son. 8. The gods are giving victory to our friends. 9. On the following day⁸ there was a battle in the forest. 10. Wine is not imported into [the country of] the Belgians. 11. We do not import our wine. 12. The grain⁹ is not ripe.

VIII.

The consonant-declension; Gr. 73–90.
Agreement of the appositive.

VOCABULARY.

adsŭm,¹ (*I*) *am present, am by.*
ădĕs, (*thou*) *art present, art by.*
 etc. etc.
absŭm,¹ (*I*) *am absent, am away.*
ăbĕs, (*thou*) *art absent, art away.*
 etc. etc.
lex, lēgĭs, *law.*
flūmĕn, -ĭnĭs, *river.*
virtūs, -ūtĭs, *manhood, courage, merit.*

hŏnŏr, -ōrĭs, *honor.*
cŭpĭdĭtās, -ātĭs, *desire, greediness.*
consŭl, -ŭlĭs, *consul.*
tempŭs, -ŏrĭs, *time.*
Caesăr, -ărĭs, *Caesar.*
mercātŏr, -ōrĭs, *trader, merchant.*
hūmānĭtās, -ātĭs, *culture, refinement.*
cīvĭtās, -ātĭs, *state.*
sōl, sōlĭs, *sun.*

EXERCISES.

1. tempŏre belli non adĕram. 2. nōnne consul ăbest? 3. regni cupidĭtas causā ĕrat belli. 4. Caesar ŏb cupiditātem gloriae pugnat. 5. mercatōres in Germānos multas res important. 6. cum fĭdē et virtūte. 7. Caesar consul lēgēs civitāti dat. 8. lēges natūrae ā deis dantur. 9. leges totīus Galliae multae ĕrant. 10. tempŏre proelii trans flumen in Germānīs ĕram. 11. honōris causā consŭles pugnant.

1. With Cæsar and the consuls. 2. With hope and courage. 3. Cæsar fights on one² bank of the river; the Germans on the other. 4. Corn is imported across the river by the traders. 5. Is Cæsar, the consul, seizing the land of the Belgians? 6. In the state of the Belgians are many rivers. 7. The courage of the traders is not great. 8. They were away from the province at the beginning of the war. 9. They are called great on account of courage and glory. 10. The courage of the Belgians is great. 11. We were absent from Gaul in the time³ of the war. 12. The gods give victory to the consul on account of [his] courage.

IX.

Adjectives of the consonant-declension; Gr. 91–93.
Future indicative active of the verb sum (to be).

VOCABULARY.

vĕtŭs, -ĕrĭs, *old, ancient.*
ultĕrĭŏr, -ĭŭs, *farther.*
cĭtĕrĭŏr, -ĭŭs, *nearer.*
mĭnŏr, -ŭs, *less, smaller.*
mājŏr, -ŭs, *larger, greater.*
quăm (conj.), *than.*

ĕr ō, (*I*) *shall be.*
ĕr ĭs, (*thou*) *wilt be.*
ĕr ĭt, (*he, she, it*) *will be.*
ĕr ĭmŭs, (*we*) *shall be.*
ĕr ĭtĭs, (*you*) *will be.*
ĕr unt, (*they*) *will be.*

EXERCISES.

1. in Galliā ulteriōre pugnant Belgae. 2. in silva cum Celtīs erimus. 3. Caesăris copiae in via ĕrant. 4. bellum erit in Gallia. 5. non erat causā belli in provinciā. 6. nōnne amīci Caesăris critis? 7. Belgae minus frumenti quam Galli important. 8. num Caesar consul erit? 9. provinciam occŭpant et belli cupĭdi sunt. 10. Gallia citerior Caesăris provincia erat. 11. vetĕris belli proelia multa et magna² erant.

1. The Rhine is larger than the Rhone. 2. Across the Rhine are larger forests than in Gaul. 3. The forests will be smaller. 4. The Germans' courage is greater than the Gauls'. 5. Will there not be a battle in the forest? 6. My friends will be present. 7. The whole people was present. 8. Farther Gaul is larger than Hither[3] Gaul. 9. The war will be greater than the old [war].[4] 10. My desire of war is less [than it was]. 11. A great battle is announced. 12. The gods give victory and glory in war. 13. On the banks of the Rhine were many large[2] forests. 14. Some are friendly, others are desirous of war.

X.

The i-declension; Gr. 94–105.
Extent of time and space.

VOCABULARY.

pars, -rtis, *part.*
fīnis, -nis (c.), *end;* pl. *bounds, lands.*
mons, -ntis (M.), *mountain.*
mors, -rtis, *death.*
urbs, -bis, *city.*
mensis, -is, *month.*
ignis, -is, *fire.*
dē (prep. w. abl.), *down from, from.*

cremō, -āre, *I burn.*
post (prep. with acc.), *after.*
multitūdō, -inis, *multitude.*
pătĕr, -tris, *father.*
annŭs, -i, *year.*
pax, pācis, *peace.*
ēnuntiō, -āre, *I announce.*
ămō, -āre, *I love.*
Germănĭă, -ae, *Germany.*

EXERCISES.

1. rem ēnuntiat. 2. res cnuntiātur. 3. filio meo res ēnuntiantur. 4. fines Belgārum magni ĕrant. 5. pars magnă igni cremātur. 6. Caesar urbem crĕmat. 7. consŭlis causā pacem ămo. 8. filius consŭlis amīcus Caesări erat. 9. multos annos in finĭbus Belgārum ĕram. 10. dē montĕ in flumen. 11. a filio meo pax enuntiātur. 12. num

montes Galliae majōres sunt quam nostri? 13. pater tuus urbis Galliae igni crĕmat. 14. post annos multos pax ēnuntiātur. 15. mors consŭlis enuntiātur.

1. The death of Caesar is announced. 2. A multitude of traders. 3. The cities of Gaul are large. 4. He is burning a part of the cities with fire. 5. I am friendly to the consul's son for Caesar's sake. 6. The greediness of the traders was the cause of the war. 7. I was in the land[1] of the Belgians many months. 8. There was a fire in the mountains [for] many days. 9. In the mountains there are many rivers. 10. Some of the traders were among the Belgians, others were across the river. 11. The honors of Caesar are many. 12. I was among the mountains one month. 13. We announce peace.

XI.

Adjectives of the i-declension; Gr. 106–108.

VOCABULARY.

omnis, -ĕ, *all; every.*
trēs, trĭă (pl.), *three.*
ŏrĭens, -ntĭs, *rising.*
ŏrĭens sōl, *east.*
făcĭlĭs, -ĕ, *easy.*
ăpŭd (prep. w. acc.), *among, with.*

impĕrō, -ārĕ, *I order, I levy (troops).*
lĕgĭō, -ōnĭs, *legion.*
altĭtūdō, -ĭnĭs, *height or depth.*
pĕr (prep. w. acc.), *through.*
mīlĕs, -ĭtĭs, *soldier.*

EXERCISES.

1. tres viae sunt per Galliam. 2. via facĭlis est per Belgas. 3. altĭtūdo flumĭnis mĭnor est. 4. trēs partes sunt omnis Galliae. 5. tota via angusta ĕrit. 6. In Galliā legio erat una. 7. tres legiōnes provinciae[1] impĕrat. 8. Caesăris gratiă apud milĭtes magna erat. 9. militĭbus fidem dămus. 10. postĕro die tres legiōnes

aběrant. 11. altitūdo montium magna erat. 12. omnes viae angustae sunt et flumīnum altitūdo magnā. 13. honor consŭlis major erat quam virtus. 14. virtūte et anĭmo honor et victoria militĭbus dantur.

1. We shall be desirous of peace. 2. The old forest is burning.[2] 3. I was in the city three days. 4. All the roads are narrow. 5. At the beginning of the war there were three legions in Gaul. 6. The popularity of Caesar was less among the Gauls than among the Germans. 7. The courage of the soldiers gives peace to the province. 8. One part of the road was narrow; the other part was easy. 9. The hope of glory gives courage to the soldiers. 10. I levy three legions on the province (lit. order to the province). 11. I was in the province three months. 12. There is an easy road through Gaul. 13. All the legions were present.

XII.

The u-declension; Gr. 109–113.

VOCABULARY.

cultŭs, -ūs, *civilization; refinement.*
lăcŭs, -ūs (Gr. [110]), *lake.*
mănŭs, -ūs (F.), *hand.*
occāsŭs, -ūs, *fall, setting* (of the sun).
occāsŭs sōlĭs, *sunset, west.*
sěnātŭs, -ūs, *senate.*
princĭpātŭs, -ūs, *leadership.*

Dumnŏrix, -ĭgĭs, *Dumnorix.*
Divĭtĭăcŭs, -ī, *Divitiacus.*
Orgetŏrix, -ĭgĭs, *Orgetorix.*
Pīsō, -ōnĭs, *Piso.*
Messālă, -ae, *Messala.*
mātrĭmōnĭŭm, -ī, *marriage.*
hăbĭtō, -āre, *I dwell.*

EXERCISES.

1. Dumnŏrix et Divitiăcus cum Caesăre pugnant. 2. a senātu amīcus appellor. 3. tres menses in Gallia ěram; annum unum in urbe. 4. post mortem Caesăris in Germania tres annos erāmus. 5. fidem inter se[1] dant.

6. Dumnŏrix igni² cremātur.   7. in urbe Belgārum habitāmus.   8. habitasne trans Rhodănum?   9. principātūs cupĭdus erat Messālā.   10. cultus provinciae major quam Gallōrum est.   11. Piso et Messāla tres mensīs aběrant in Gallia.   12. num in Gallia citĕriōre multos mensīs erĭtis?   13. pacem amat multitūdo.   14. popŭli causā pugnāmus.

1. The Belgians are distant from the culture and refinement of the province.   2. The Belgians dwell in one part of Gaul; the Gauls, in another.   3. Divitiacus is called friend by the senate.   4. After the death of Dumnorix, Piso was in the city [for] many months.   5. From the lake to the mountain.   6. Piso and Messala were consuls.   7. The depth of the river is less than [that] of the lake.   8. He gives his daughter in marriage³ to Dumnorix.   9. The consul, Messala, was on the mountain at⁴ sunset.   10. The lands of the Gauls are broad, ours are narrow.   11. He tells [the news of] the battle to the senate.   12. The leadership of Gaul is given to Cæsar by the people.

XIII.

Review of the declensions.
Irregular nouns; Gr. 114–117.

VOCABULARY.

lŏcŭs, -ī (Gr. [116]), *place.*
circŭm (prep. w. acc.), *around.*
dŏmŭs, -ūs (f.), (Gr. [115]), *house, home.*
sanguĭs, -ĭnĭs (m.), (Gr. [115]), *blood.*

ĭtĕr, -ĭtĭnĕrĭs (Gr. [115]), *journey, march, route.*
Helvētĭī, -ōrŭm, *Helvetians.*
vŏluntās, -ātĭs, *wish, consent.*
hĭĕmō, -ārĕ, *I am wintering.*

EXERCISES.

1. iter Helvetiōrum Caesări nuntiātur. 2. tres legiōnes circum urbem hiĕmant. 3. domus angusta ĕrat. 4. locus magnus est. 5. iter nōn facĭle erit. 6. itinĕra facilia sunt. 7. voluntāte Caesăris in Belgis habĭto. 8. regni cupiditāte[1] provinciam occupātis. 9. apud milĭtes hiĕmo. 10. iter vetus facĭle erat. 11. altĕro in loco proelium erat magnum. 12. agri milĭtĭbus a popŭlīs Galliae dantur. 13. initio belli spēs erat victoriae magna. 14. trans flumen via angusta est. 15. păter meus in urbe nōn habĭtat.

1. We are wintering among the Belgians. 2. The places are large and broad. 3. The Helvetians are on the march. 4. I dwell in Cæsar's house. 5. Around the places was much blood.[2] 6. The Rhine and the Garonne are large rivers. 7. We were in the place three years. 8. The houses are small. 9. We were at home.[3] 10. There is a road through the mountains. 11. Orgetorix was desirous of kingly power.. 12. The soldier was at home on the next day. 13. The legions winter among the Helvetians. 14. There was an easy route through Gaul. 15. Dumnorix and Divitiacus dwell among[4] the mountains.

XIV.

Numeral adjectives; Gr. 118.

VOCABULARY.

passŭs, -ūs, *step, pace.*
millĕ passuŭm, *mile* (1000 paces).
pēs, pĕdĭs (m.), *foot.*
prŏfectĭŏ, -ōnĭs, *departure, start.*
vīcŭs, -ī, *village.*
Alpēs, -ĭŭm, *Alps.*

confirm ārĕ, *to fix, appoint, set.*
confirm ō, *I appoint.*
etc.   etc.
hŏmŏ, -ĭnĭs, *man, person.*
rĕdĭtĭŏ, -ōnĭs, *coming back, return.*
Ităliă, -ae, *Italy.*

EXERCISES.

1. domum[1] reditiōnis spes.   2. vici omnēs crĕmantur.   3. profectiōnem in tertium annum lege confirmant.   4. dĕcem annos in Gallia ĕram.   5. millia passuum viginti tria silva abest.   6. flumen pĕdēs undeviginti altum erat.   7. in itinĕre copia frumenti legionĭbus dătur.   8. fratri tuo imperium Galli dant.   9. duae Galliae sunt; citerior in Italia est, ulterior trans Alpīs.   10. Gallia citerior minor est quam Gallia ulterior.   11. per Alpīs in Galliam mercatōres multas res important.   12. ob profectiōnem milĭtum pater tuus omnīs vicos crĕmat.   13. in vicis amīcis copiā erat frumenti.   14. vici amicōrum tuōrum cremantur.

1. The road is[2] three miles from the river.   2. There is one legion in Farther Gaul.   3. Our departure is fixed by law for[3] the third year.   4. The Alps are high mountains.   5. The Germans were in Gaul five months.   6. After the death of Orgetorix, the war was announced to my father by Piso.   7. Three months after the beginning of the war I was at home.[1]   8. Two legions are wintering in Gaul; the one among the Belgians, the other across the Garonne.   9. The city is[2] thirteen miles from the mountain.   10. On the seventh day[4] I shall be on the bank of the Rhine.

XV.

Comparison of adjectives; Gr. 119–123.

VOCABULARY.

nōbĭlĭs, -ĕ, *noble, of high birth.*
măgĭs (adv.), *more.*
diffĭcĭlĭs, -ĕ, *difficult, hard.*
maxĭmē (adv.), *most, very, especially.*
spērŏ, -ārĕ, *I hope, I expect.*
fortĭs, -ĕ, *brave.*
longē (adv.), *far, by far.*
mĭnŭs (adv.), *less.*
Rōmānŭs, -ă, -ŭm, *Roman.*
făcĭlĭs, -ĕ, *easy.*

EXERCISES.

1. unā ex parte[1] mons altissĭmus[2] est; altĕrā ex parte, flumen Rhenus; tertiā, Rhodănus. 2. flumĭna latissĭma multa sunt. 3. Piso in Helvetiis hiĕmat. 4. tempŏre belli magnus est honor milĭtum. 5. a senātu popŭli Romāni amīcus appellātur. 6. apud Romānos in ripa flumĭnis aderāmus. 7. difficillĭmum est[3] res in Belgas importāre. 8. itinĕra per Alpīs in Galliam erant. 9. altitūdo montium magna est. 10. via non est alia.

1. Among the Helvetians Orgetorix was far the noblest. 2. The Belgians are the bravest of all the Gauls. 3. To seize all Gaul is difficult. 4. The journey is very difficult. 5. There are many very high mountains in Gaul. 6. There are rivers in Gaul deeper than the Rhone. 7. The Rhine is broader than the Rhone. 8. The route through the Alps is harder. 9. We fight with the Romans. 10. The Germans are braver than the Gauls. 11. It is more difficult[3] to fight with the Romans than with the Belgians.

XVI.

Irregular comparison; Gr. [123].

VOCABULARY.

bŏnŭs, -ă, -ŭm, *good*.
mălŭs, -ă, -ŭm, *bad*.
parvŭs, -ă, -ŭm, *small*.
sĕnex (Gr. [115]), *old*.
jŭvĕnĭs (Gr. [96]), *young*.
extĕrŭs, -ă, -ŭm,[1] *outside, outer*.
dŭŏ, -ae, -ŏ (Gr. [72]), *two*.
infĕrŭs, -ă, -ŭm,[1] *lower, inferior*.
supĕrŭs, -a, -um,[1] *upper*.

intĕrĭŏr; intĭmŭs, *inner; inmost*.
prĭŏr; prīmŭs, *former; first*.
prŏprĭŏr; proxĭmŭs, *nearer; nearest, next*.
ultĕrĭŏr; ultĭmŭs, *further, furthest*.
Sēquăuī, -ōrŭm, *Sequanians (a tribe)*.
confirmō, -ārĕ, *make (peace)*.

EXERCISES.

1. ad inferiōrem partem flumĭnis Rheni. 2. cum proxĭmis civitatĭbus pacem confirmātis. 3. erant itinĕra duo; unum per Sequănos, angustum et difficĭle, altĕrum ' per provinciam nostram. 4. quam[2] maxĭmis itinerĭbus. 5. quam plurĭmas urbīs occŭpant. 6. tres partes[3] Helvetiōrum trans Rhodănum sunt. 7. per Alpīs erat proxĭmum[4] iter in Galliam ulteriōrem. 8. Helvetii primus popŭlus trans Rhodanum sunt. 9. in summo monte[5] multi milĭtes sunt. 10. nostri milĭtes fortiōres sunt. 11. flumĭna Galliae majōra quam Italiae sunt. 12. veterrĭma est urbs Helvetiōrum.

1. Nearer Gaul is smaller than Farther Gaul. 2. On the following day, Caesar was among the Sequanians. 3. I am making peace with as many states as possible.[2] 4. Caesar's desire of kingly power was less than Piso's. 5. The former soldiers were younger and braver. 6. There are older men in the neighboring[6] cities. 7. In the country of the Belgians are many large[7] cities. 8. The larger part of the multitude is on the road. 9. Victory is given to the braver men. 10. The Romans are called brave by our consuls. 11. The old route is better than the narrow road.

XVII.

Personal and possessive pronouns; Gr. 124-126.

VOCABULARY.

inter (prep. w. acc.), *between, among*.
ĕgŏ, etc., *I, me*, etc.
tū, etc., *thou, thee*, etc.
suŭs, -ă, -ŭm, *his, his own, her*, etc.

cāsŭs, -ūs, *chance, accident*.
suī, etc., *himself, herself*, etc.
nullŭs, -ă, -ŭm (Gr. 71), *no, no one*.
vestĕr, -tră, -trŭm, *your, yours*.

EXERCISES.

1. tu, mī fili, junior es quam ĕgŏ. 2. nostri anĭmi belli cupidi sunt. 3. principātum provinciae Caesar mihi dat. 4. et[1] ego[2] et tu, mi amīce, erāmus in silvā. 5. tibi nuntiat victoriam. 6. vobiscum[3] tres menses milĭtes ĕrant. 7. hostes inter se[6] pugnant. 8. victoria nostrārum legiōnum nuntiātur. 9. iter nobīs difficilius erit quam tibi. 10. Helvetii nos amīcos appellant. 11. vestri fīnes, amici, a Gallis occupantur. 12. omnes legiōnes nostrae cum amīcis tuis in Belgis pugnant. 13. senātus te amīcum populi appellat. 14. castra Caesăris meliōre in loco quam mea est.

1. You are too[4] desirous of war, my friends. 2. My legion is[5] four miles distant[5] from the Rhone. 3. At the time of your departure I was with Cæsar. 4. The lands of the Sequanians are broader than our [lands]. 5. Five years after the war, Orgetorix was with us in Farther Gaul. 6. It will be easy to seize your cities. 7. The Sequanians are fighting with one another.[6] 8. A part of the enemy is present in the city. 9. There are very many nations in the country[7] of the Germans. 10. The legions were present by chance.

XVIII.

Demonstrative pronouns; is, illĕ, istĕ, ipsĕ;
Gr. 127–132.

VOCABULARY.

incŏlă, -ae (m.), *inhabitant.*
sătĭs (adv.), *enough.*
nŏvŭs, -ă, -ŭm, *new.*
illĕ, illă, illŭd, *that.*

saepĕ (adv.), *often.*
ĭs, eă, ĭd, *this, that; he, she, it.*
istĕ, istă, istŭd, *that.*
ipsĕ, ipsă, ipsŭm, *self.*

EXERCISES.

1. Galliae incŏlae ipsōrum linguā Celtae, nostrā Galli appellantur. 2. cōrum omnium fortissĭmi sunt Belgae. 3. ad eos mercatōres saepe res important. 4. illi popŭli proxĭmi sunt Germānis. 5. eā de causā Helvetii fortissĭmi sunt omnium Gallōrum. 6. is locus angustus erat natūrā. 7. consul ipse abĕrat ā proelio. 8. mortem patris mei ipsam nuntiātis. 9. ad eas res satis[1] est annus. 10. mercatōres ipsi res istas in Belgas non important. 11. vinum a nobīs non importātur. 12. illīus urbis incŏlae res nullas important. 13. Belgae sunt Galliae popŭlus ultĭmus. 14. omnium milĭtum longe erat ille fortissĭmus.

1. These soldiers are braver than you. 2. He levies on the whole province a large number of soldiers. 3. For these reasons I shall be present with you. 4. At that time the journey through the Alps was very difficult. 5. The road itself is easier than yours. 6. This grain is not ripe. 7. His desire of honor is very great. 8. The height of that mountain is less than [that] of the Alps. 9. Dumnorix himself is desirous of a revolution.[2] 10. You are at home; I am desirous of a return home. 11. I am levying as many soldiers as possible[3] on the province. 12. They are fighting with him on the top of the mountain. 13. I was in that city three months.

XIX.

Demonstrative pronouns; hĭc, īdem; Gr. 133-137.

VOCABULARY.

consĭlĭum, -ī, *plan.*
castră, -ōrŭm (pl.), *camp.*
nāvĭs, -ĭs, *ship.*
lux, lūcĭs, *light.*

rĕgĭŏ, -ōnĭs, *region, country.*
hĭc, haec, hŏc, *this.*
ĭdĕm, eădĕm, ĭdĕm, *same.*

EXERCISES.

1. eōdem tempŏre apud vos adĕram. 2. haec via vetus est; illa est nova. 3. eădem nuntiantur ab aliis. 4. in ejusdem flumĭnis ripā urbs erat major. 5. ab iisdem nostra consilia hostĭbus enuntiantur. 6. primā luce ĕgo in summo monte eram. 7. hi milĭtes in Gallia hiĕmant; illi in vicĭs Alpium. 8. pacem cum civitatĭbus iisdem confirmāmus. 9. eo die tria millia passuum ab cōrum castris abĕram. 10. habĭto in ripa flumĭnis ejusdem. 11. naves ipsae eōdem in loco erunt. 12. eo tempŏre et ego et ille casu aderāmus. 13. via illa magis angusta quam difficĭlis est. 14. in castris majorĭbus multi milĭtes eo tempŏre erant.

1. The rivers of this region are broad. 2. The other mountain is higher than this. 3. I was present with you in that battle. 4. The depth of these rivers is great. 5. These things are told to me by the enemy. 6. My enemies are very many and their country[1] large. 7. The place was narrow and the road new and difficult. 8. The cities and villages are burned with fire. 9. Three ships of Caesar himself are burned by the same enemy. 10. There was no hope of peace. 11. I give you my promise. 12. This region is the best part of the land of the Belgians. 13. This mountain is[2] three miles distant[2] from the river. 14. The same men dwell across this river.

XX.

Relative, interrog. and indef. pronoun; Gr. 138–141.

VOCABULARY.

antĕ (prep. w. acc.), *before.*
ăcĭēs, -ēī, *edge, line of battle.*
effēmĭnō, *I weaken; effeminate.*
etc. etc.
quī, quae, quŏd, *who, which, that.*
nunc (adv.), *now.*

factĭŏ, -ōnĭs, *party, faction.*
părātŭs, -ă, -ŭm, *ready, prepared.*
quĭs, quae, quĭd, *who? which? what?*
quĭs, quae, quĭd, *any, any one.*

EXERCISES.

1. duo legiōnes, quae in castris ĕrant, in silva nunc pugnant. 2. iīdem, qui nobiscum in acie erant, in vicīs Helvetiōrum hiĕmant. 3. quis has res importat? 4. cui victoriā hostium nuntiātur? 5. mihi erit hoc ĭter difficilius quam tibi, qui es junior. 6. Galliae totīus factiōnes sunt duae. 7. omnis Galliae tres sunt partes, quarum una Aquitania appellātur. 8. mercatores ea important quae animos effemĭnant. 9. ad eam rem parāti sŭmus. 10. domum reditiōnis spes non est. 11. popŭli qui trans Rhenum habĭtant fortiōres sunt quam Galliae popŭli.

1. We, who are in camp, are ready for war. 2. There will be a battle in this village. 3. Those things which weaken the courage[1] of the Belgians are not imported. 4. You are seizing more land[2] than the enemy. 5. There is a large number of the enemy on that mountain. 6. Across the same river there is a multitude of our soldiers. 7. Before his return from the war, there will be a battle. 8. Cæsar calls his soldiers friends. 9. They give a promise to each other. 10. On the next day they burn the village which was on the bank of this river. 11. Who is not ready to fight with the enemy? 12. What troops are in the villages? 13. Is any one fighting in the forest? [No.]

XXI.

Inflection of the verb; Gr. 142–190.

XXII.

Incomplete tenses of a-stem verbs; Gr. 191–195.
Moods in independent sentences.

VOCABULARY.

commĕŏ, -ārĕ, *go and come; with ad, visit.*
spectŏ, -ārĕ, *look, look at, see.*
bellŏ, -ārĕ, *make war, war.*
compărŏ, -ārĕ, *prepare, make ready.*
concĭlĭŏ, -ārĕ, *gain, gain over, get.*
praestŏ, -ārĕ, *stand before, excel.*
văgŏr, -ārī (dep.),[1] *wander.*
arbĭtrŏr, -ārī (dep.),[1] *think, judge.*
cōnŏr, -ārī (dep.),[1] *try, attempt.*
incĭtŏ, -ārĕ, *rouse up, excite.*

EXERCISES.

1. mercatōres saepe ad Gallos commeant. 2. Belgae proxĭmi sunt Germānis qui trans Rhenum habĭtant. 3. ea comparāre conābar, quae importantur. 4. conēmur, mei amīci, urbem occupāre. 5. nuntiāte victoriam, mi pater, tuīs militĭbus. 6. spectant in orientem solem. 7. fīdes dăbĭtur[2] nobīs. 8. conabantur Orgetŏrix et Helvetii omnīs popŭlos Galliae incitāre. 9. hostes bellandi[3] cupĭdi erant. 10. civitas ob eam rem incitabĭtur. 11. Helvetii mīnus vagabantur quam alii popŭli Galliae. 12. Belgae extrēmis in finĭbus Galliae habitābant. 13. regnum in civitāte suā occupābit Orgetŏrix, cujus pater nobis amīcus multos annos erat.

1. Rouse up the men of this city. 2. My sons were trying to rouse up the states of Gaul. 3. The enemy were wandering through the country and cities of the Sequanians. 4. After the death of Orgetorix the Helvetians tried to seize the lands of all Gaul. 5. Orgetorix will be burned with fire by his own state. 6. Call him, my son, the friend of the Roman people. 7. Let us prepare all things for our return home. 8. May you be called brave! 9. May they be burned with fire! 10. May the gods give you glory! 11. In their own language they are called Celts; in ours, Gauls. 12. Traders visit[4] them least often and import wine and other things.

XXIII.

Incomplete tenses of e-stem verbs; Gr. 196–197.

VOCABULARY.

pertĭneō, -ērĕ, *pertain, belong, stretch.*
prohĭbeō, -ērĕ, *keep out, prohibit, stop.*
hăbeō, -ērĕ, *have.*
undīquĕ (adv.), *on all sides.*
mŏveō, -ērĕ, *move.*

vĭdeō, -ērĕ, *see.*
obtĭneō, -ērĕ, *hold, possess.*
contĭneō, -ērĕ, *hold in, bound.*
pătēō, -ērĕ, *extend.*
Jūră, -ae, *Jura* (a mountain).
quŏd (conj.), *because.*

EXERCISES.

1. Belgae pertĭnent ad inferiōrem partem flumĭnis Rheni. 2. undīque loci natūrā Helvetii continentur; unā ex parte¹ monte Jurā altissĭmo, qui est inter Sequănos et Helvetios; altera ex parte flumĭne Rheno, altissĭmo et latissĭmo. 3. profectio nostra in annum tertium lege confirmabātur. 4. postĕro die castra ex eo loco movent. 5. Caesar ei legiōni quam secum habēbat copiam frumenti comparābat. 6. haec in Belgas per provinciam importāmus quod aliŭd iter nullum habēmus. 7. urbs extrēma haec est et proxĭma Helvetiōrum finĭbus.

1. There are two routes by which² traders will visit³ us. 2. The Belgians kept traders out of their territories. 3. I will gain the royal power⁴ for you with my troops.² 4. The territories⁵ of the Helvetians were narrow. 5. The Helvetians had narrow territories, which extended two hundred and forty miles in length,⁶ one hundred and eighty in breadth.⁶ 6. You will attempt the same thing as⁷ I. 7. Did he move camp on that day? [No.] 8. Let us keep the enemy⁸ out of our territories. 9. Move camp often and report⁹ to me the battles you see.¹⁰ 10. The Gauls hold one part of the country; the Belgians, another. 11. Aquitania extended from the Garonne river to the mountains.

XXIV.

Incomplete tenses of consonant-stem and u-stem verbs;
Gr. 198, 199.

VOCABULARY.

incŏlŏ, -ĕrĕ, *dwell.*
divĭdŏ, -ĕrĕ, *divide, separate.*
gĕrŏ, -ĕrĕ, *manage, carry on, wage.*
praecēdŏ, -ĕrĕ, *precede, surpass.*
ōcĕănŭs, -ī, *ocean.*
aut (conj.), *or.*
aut... aut, *either... or.*
perdūcŏ, -ĕrĕ, *lead through, build, construct.*
nēmŏ, -ĭnĭs, *no one.*
fluŏ, fluĕrĕ, *flow.*

contendŏ, -ĕrĕ, *contend, fight, hasten, strive.*
influŏ, -ĕrĕ, *flow into.*
trĭbuŏ, -ĕrĕ, *assign, attribute.*
dēbeŏ, -ērē, *owe, ought.*
fĕrē (adv.), *almost.*
quŏtĭdiānŭs, -ă, -ŭm, *daily.*
fossă, -ae, *ditch.*
mūrŭs, -ī, *wall.*
cŭm (conj.), *when.*

EXERCISES.

1. flumen est quod per fines Sequanorum fluit. 2. Belgae proximi sunt Germanis, qui trans Rhenum incolunt, quā de causā[1] alios virtute praecedunt. 3. hujus regionis una pars, quam Galli obtinent, continetur Garumnā flumine, Oceano, finibus Belgarum. 4. Helvetii reliquos Gallos virtute praecedunt, quod fere quotidianis proeliis cum Germanis contendunt, cum aut suis finibus eos prohibent aut ipsi in eorum finibus bellum gerunt. 5. a lacu, qui in Rhodanum influit, ad montem Juram, qui fines Sequanorum ab Helvetiis dividit, murum et fossam perducit.

1. I keep all men out from the province; I allow[2] no one a passage.[2] 2. Cæsar hastened into the province by forced[3] marches. 3. He hastens through the Alps with these five legions by the shortest[4] route. 4. We attribute the victory to your courage. 5. He has a large number of soldiers about him.[5] 6. A wall and a ditch were constructed from

the lake to the river by that legion which Cæsar had with him.⁵ 7. There was a hard road⁶ between mount Jura and the river Rhone. 8. May you dwell at home in peace. 9. For this reason I was waging war in the land of the Germans. 10. The banks of the river which flows through our city are high.

XXV.

Incomplete tenses of short ĭ-stem verbs; Gr. 200–202.

VOCABULARY.

căpĭŏ, -ĕrĕ, *take, receive.*
suscĭpĭŏ, -ĕrĕ, *undertake.*
ērĭpĭŏ, -ĕrĕ, *rescue.*
dŏlŏr, -ōrĭs, *grief, sorrow.*
nōmĕn, -ĭnĭs, *name.*
frāter, -trĭs, *brother.*
făcĭŏ, -ĕrĕ, *do, make.*

conficĭŏ, -ĕrĕ, *do, accomplish, finish.*
perfĭcĭŏ, -ĕrĕ, *do, perform.*
afficĭŏ, -ĕrĕ, *move, affect.*
septentrĭŏ, -ōnĭs, *north* (usually pl.).

EXERCISES.

1. per eos omnēs Orgetŏrix se eripiēbat. 2. post ejus mortem, Helvetii iter facĕre conabuntur. 3. una pars initium capit¹ a flumĭne Rhodăno. 4. homĭnes bellandi cupĭdi magno dolōre afficiebantur. 5. capiāmus urbem. 6. hic locus ē reditiōne exercĭtūs nomen capiet. 7. quas in partes hostes iter faciunt? 8. ab iisdem nostra consilia et quae in castris geruntur hostĭbus ēnuntiantur. 9. initium pugnae Dumnŏrix faciēbat et milĭtes ejus. 10. eripĭte meum patrem, amīci mei! 11. Belgae spectant in septentriōnem et orientem solem. 12. Aquitania spectat inter occāsum solis et septentriōnes. 13. tune bellum cum Gallis gĕrēs?

· 1. I am making a journey through the province. 2. These things will be accomplished by us. 3. On the following day he undertook the matter. 4. The place takes its name from²

EXERCISES ON FORMS. 33

the victory of the Roman legions. 5. Does the river take its name from² the battle? [No.] 6. In the time of Cæsar many legions were rescued from² the hands of the enemy. 7. Let us try to take the city which the enemy rescued from² our hands. 8. It is hard to take a city that has a wall and ditch around it.³ 9. This matter was told to the Helvetians by us. 10. After his death the Helvetians tried to make the journey. 11. Orgetorix will give his daughter in marriage to Dumnorix, the brother of Divitiacus.

XXVI.

Incomplete tenses of long ī-stem verbs; Gr. 203, 204.

VOCABULARY.

věnĭŏ, -ĭrĕ, *come.*
commūnĭŏ, -ĭrĕ, *wall, fortify.*
interfĭcĭŏ, -ĕrĕ, *kill, slay.*
convěnĭŏ, -ĭre, *come together, assemble.*

sĭ (conj.), *if.*
pervěnĭŏ, -ĭre, *come through, arrive.*
vīs, vīs (Gr. [115]), *violence, force;* pl. *strength.*
ŭbĭ (conj.), *when, where.*

EXERCISES.

1. ad eam partem, quae in ripa fluminis habitābat perveniēbat. 2. eodem die milites ad ripam conveniēbant. 3. venīte ad me, filiae meae! 4. eōdem proelio, quo Helvetii filium interficiēbant, patrem interficiēbant. 5. Caesar uno die id faciet quod nos viginti diēbus facĭmus. 6. pacem cum Caesăre faciāmus! 7. in dolōrem veniātis, hostes! 8. urbs ab hostĭbus magnā vi communiebātur. 9. ea faciēmus quae nobis tribuuntur. 10. pacem cum proxĭmis civitātĭbus confirmāre Helvetii conabantur. 11. postěro die conveniunt ad ripam Rhodăni et castra in eo loco communiunt. 12. murum et fossam a flumĭne ad lacum perducāmus!

1. Cæsar is fortifying a camp on the top of the mountain. 2. Many soldiers come out of the city which you are fortify-

ing. 3. I shall arrive at the city within[1] the next ten days. 4. The enemy are slaying the traders themselves. 5. The enemy will burn with fire those who shall be taken in battle. 6. This[2] [news] is told us by the soldiers whom you rescued. 7. If you do[3] violence, I shall stop [you]. 8. When that day comes,[3] I shall allow you a passage through the city. 9. There is one legion [only] in farther Gaul; if the enemy assemble,[3] they will seize the whole region. 10. The Gauls are coming across the river and we shall all be slain.

XXVII.

Complete tenses, active voice; Gr. 205-207.

VOCABULARY.

pervĕnĭŏ, -īrĕ, -vēnī, *come, arrive.*
constĭtŭŏ, -tŭĕrĕ, -tŭī, *determine, decide on.*
spērŏ, spērārĕ, spērāvī, *hope, expect, hope for.*
pōnŏ, pōnĕrĕ, pŏsŭī, *place, pitch.*
făcĭŏ, făcĕrĕ, fēcī, *do,* etc.
paucŭs, -ă, -ŭm (comm. pl.), *few.*
interfĭcĭŏ, -ĕrĕ, -fēcī, *kill.*
mĭnĭmē (adv.), *least.*

perfĭcĭŏ, -ĕrĕ, -fēcī, *do, accomplish.*
convĕnĭŏ, -vĕnīrĕ, -vēnī, *assemble.*
căpĭŏ, căpĕrĕ, cēpī, *take,* etc.
hăbĕŏ, hăbērĕ, hăbŭī, *have,* etc.
dō, dărĕ, dĕdī, *give,* etc.
mittŏ, mittĕrĕ, mīsī, *send.*
gĕrŏ, gĕrĕrĕ, gessī, *wage,* etc.
hăbĭtŏ, -ārĕ, -āvī, *dwell.*
jŭbĕŏ, -ērĕ, jussī, *bid, order.*

EXERCISES.

1. post ejus mortem Helvetii id quod constituĕrat facĕre conabantur. 2. multa mihi dĕdĕras. 3. ad magnam partem legiōnis pervēnĕram, quae tria millia passuum a flumĭne castra ponēbat. 4. hi hostes consŭlem interfēcĕrant, et milĭtes ejus cēpĕrant. 5. si vos vim fēcerĭtis, ĕgo prohibēbo. 6. Caesar bellum trans Rhenum gessit. 7. ubi id quod constituisti perfēcĕris, vĕni domum ad nos. 8. quae in castris nostris geruntur, ea hostĭbus ille nuntiābit. 9. hi sunt trans Rhodănum primi.

EXERCISES ON FORMS. 35

1. I had ordered him to seize the city of the enemy.
2. The top of the mountain was occupied¹ by the soldiers.
3. Cæsar had arrived at the same time. 4. He has dwelt among the Sequanians many months. 5. Had you pitched your camp when I arrived? 6. If you assemble² at³ the bank of the river, I will give you a passage⁴ through the province. 7. There are few rivers in the Alps, which are very high mountains. 8. Of all these the Belgians are the bravest because traders visit them least often. 9. Aquitania extends from the Garonne river to the mountains and the ocean. 10. This circumstance was told¹ to the Helvetians.

XXVIII.

Verb-forms from the simple stem; Gr. 208, 209.

VOCABULARY.

pugnō, -nārĕ, -nāvī, -nātum.
occŭpō, -pārĕ, -pāvī, -pātum.
importō, -tārĕ, -tāvī, -tātum.
pertĭneō, -nērĕ, -nuī.
prohĭbeō, -bērĕ, -buī, -bĭtum.
mŏveō, -vērĕ, mōvī, mōtum.
cōnŏr, -ārī, -ātŭs.
vehĕmentĕr (adv.), *greatly, strongly.*

divĭdō, -dĕrĕ, -vīsī, -vīsum.
gĕrō, gĕrĕrĕ, gessī, gestum.
căpĭō, căpĕrĕ, cēpī, captum.
făciō, făcĕrĕ, fēcī, factum.
vĕnĭō, vĕnīrĕ, vēnī, ventum.
fluō, fluĕrĕ, fluxī.
trĭbuō, -uĕrĕ, -uī, -ūtum.
rŏgō, -ārĕ, -āvī, -ātum, *ask, ask for.*

EXERCISES.

1. facile factu¹ est iter perficĕre. 2. ad consŭles patrem mittit rogātum² pacem. 3. bellum gessĕrat in finĭbus hostium. 4. quae est causă belli quod gerĭmus? 5. nobilissĭmi cum Germānis pugnant. 6. milĭtes, ab hostĭbus capti, interficientur. 7. multae res, in Belgas importātae, animos eōrum effeminābant. 8. consul, magis cupiditāte imperii motus quam spe reditiōnis, urbem occŭpat. 9. multae res,

in fines nostros importātae, a militĭbus capiebantur. 10. quis haec a finĭbus Gallōrum prohĭbet? 11. nemo, dolōre motus, vim facĕre conabĭtur. 12. multi milĭtes, in proelio interfecti, domum mittebantur ad amīcos suos.

1. The city, having been seized by the legions, was burned. 2. I had come to ask[3] peace. 3. In many places the river flows through large forests. 4. The Belgians, effeminated by[4] imported things, are trying to wage war. 5. May the gods give you those things which you hope for! 6. This journey will be easy to make.[5] 7. I am greatly moved by Cæsar's death. 8. All kingdoms and cities are the gods'. 9. Let us wage war with the legions that have burned our homes. 10. With[4] that legion which he had with him and with[4] the soldiers who had assembled from[6] the province, Cæsar builds a wall from[7] the lake to Mt. Jura, which divides the territories[8] of the Sequanians from the Helvetians.

XXIX.

The periphrastic conjugations; Gr. 210-214.

VOCABULARY.

sŭm, essĕ, fŭi, fŭtūrŭs.
dō, dăre, dĕdī, dătŭm.
nuntĭŏ, -āre, -āvī, -ātŭm.
appellŏ, -āre, -āvī, -ātŭm.
crĕmŏ, -āre, -āvī, -ātŭm.
ēnuntĭŏ, -āre, -āvī, -ātŭm.
impĕrŏ, -āre, -āvī, -ātŭm.
hăbĭtŏ, -āre, -āvī, -ātŭm.
hĭĕmŏ, -āre, -āvī, -ātŭm.
confirmŏ, -āre, -āvī, -ātŭm.
praecēdŏ, -dĕre, -dī, -essŭm.
ērĭpĭŏ, -rĭpĕre, -rĭpuī, -reptŭm.

spērŏ, -āre, -āvī, -ātŭm.
effēmĭnŏ, -āre, -āvī, -ātŭm.
hăbeŏ, hăbēre, hăbuī, hăbĭtŭm.
obtĭneŏ, -ēre, -uī, obtentŭm.
pătcŏ, pătēre, pătuī.
commeŏ, -āre, -āvī, -ātŭm.
spectŏ, -āre, -āvī, -ātŭm.
concĭlĭŏ, -āre, -āvī, -ātŭm.
văgŏr, -āri, -ātŭs.
incŏlŏ, -ĕre, -uī.
contendŏ, -dĕre, -dī, -ntŭm.
commūnĭŏ, -nīre, -nīvī, -nītŭm.

EXERCISES.

1. iter mihi dătum est; ĭdem tibi dabĭtur. 2. conātus erat iter per Alpes facĕre. 3. captūrus sum illam urbem. 4. ea legiōne, quam mecum habeo, fines Gallōrum occupāre conar. 5. pars hostium Orgetorĭgis victoriā ad bellum mota erat. 6. per Alpes iter faciendum est. 7. Alpes minōres altae sunt. 8. tres legiōnes in Gallia ulteriōre hiemābant. 9. domi futūrus sum. 10. num dătūrus es iter per provinciam hostĭbus? 11. fuerasne in vetĕre urbe?

1. All Gaul is divided[1] into three parts. 2. This matter was announced to the Helvetians. 3. Orgetorix rescued himself through his friends. 4. The soldiers whom he had with him had come together out of the province. 5. Three legions which had wintered in Hither Gaul, hastened through the Alps into the province. 6. The Helvetians had killed Piso in the same battle. 7. If you make[2] peace with us, we will winter in Gaul. 8. I intend to winter in Gaul. 9. The soldiers have been rescued from[3] the hands of the Belgians. 10. The city must be seized by you. 11. A large part of the city had to be burned with fire.

XXX.

Review of verbs.
Irregular verbs; sŭm and compounds; Gr. 215–222.

VOCABULARY.

adsŭm, ădcssĕ, adfuī, adfūtūrŭs.
absŭm, ăbcssĕ, āfuī, āfŭtūrŭs.
prōsŭm, prōdessĕ, prōfuī, prōfŭtūrŭs, *be advantageous, useful.*
possŭm, possĕ, pŏtuī, *be able, can, have power or influence.*
praesŭm, praecessĕ, praefuī, praefŭtūrŭs, *be present,*[1] *be first, at the head.*
sŭpersŭm, sŭpĕressĕ, sŭperfuī, sŭperfŭtūrŭs, *be left over, survive.*
dūcŏ, dūcĕrĕ, duxī, ductŭm, *lead,* (also, *to marry*).
dēbeŏ, dēbērĕ, dēbuī, dēbĭtŭm, *owe, ought.*

EXERCISES.

1. bellum gerĕre non possŭmus, quod a provincia longe absŭmus. 2. omnia quae facĕre potestis, fecistis. 3. quis illud dīcĕre possit²? 4. mihi non prodest³ saepe cum iis qui in ripis flumĭnis habĭtant contendĕre. 5. adesse non facile est. 6. Sequānos praesentīs et absentīs incitāre conābar. 7. per provinciam iter vobis dăre non potĕro. 8. num potuĕrunt iter difficile facĕre? 9. si potĕro, apud vos adĕro.

1. Dumnorix had very much influence among the Helvetians, because he had married the daughter of Orgetorix from that state. 2. It had been advantageous to him to be able to move camp. 3. Be good and brave, my friends; our position⁴ is advantageous to us. 4. The whole multitude was present. 5. The whole state is divided⁵ into four parts. 6. Those who ought to be useful to us have moved camp and are not present. 7. He did in⁶ one day what the enemy did in⁶ twenty days. 8. The daughter of Orgetorix and one of his sons were taken.⁷ 9. One hundred and twenty thousand men⁷ survived.

EXERCISES ON FORMS. 39

XXXI.

Irregular verbs; ĕdo, fĕro; Gr. 223, 224.

VOCABULARY.

ĕdŏ, ĕdĕrĕ, ēdī, ēsŭm, *eat, consume.*
fĕrŏ, fĕrrĕ, tŭlī, lātŭm, *carry, bring, bear.*
infĕrŏ, infĕrrĕ, intŭlī, illātŭm, *carry on, make* (war).
diffĕrŏ, diffĕrrĕ, distŭlī, dilātŭm, *differ.*
confĕro, confĕrrĕ, contŭlī, collātŭm, *collect, bring together, compare;*
  se conferre, *to betake one's self, go.*
rĕfĕrŏ, rĕfĕrrĕ, rĕtŭlī, rĕlātŭm, *carry back;* pedem referre, *retreat.*
jŭbeŏ, jŭbērĕ, jussī, jussŭm.
impĕdīmentŭm, -ī, *hindrance;* pl. *baggage.*
hostĭs, -ĭs (c.), *enemy.*

EXERCISES.

1. bellum inferre non possunt. 2. Dumnŏrix, cujus frater Divitiăcus eo tempŏre principātum in civitāte obtinēbat, idem conāri potĕrat. 3. erat una per Sequănos via, quā īre non potĕrant. 4. frumentum non contulĕrant, quod dăre debēbant.[1] 5. ager Germanōrum conferri non potest cum agro Gallōrum. 6. contendēbant pedem referre. 7. jubēbat partem mīlitum impedimenta in unum locum conferre; partem pedem referre. 8. hi omnes inter se[2] linguā diffĕrunt. 9. trans flumen in agros hostium se contulĕrant.

1. The Helvetians brought their baggage together to one place. 2. He ordered the ships to be brought together into one place. 3. For this reason they could not make war on[3] their enemies. 4. I shall bring together many men, and make war on the nations beyond the Rhine.[4] 5. The seventh and tenth legions did not retreat. 6. Let us retreat, soldiers, if the enemy are[5] many. 7. The baggage will be brought together. 8. . You ought to go to the camp of the Germans. 9. Who can make war on us? 10. A few can stop the soldiers from [their] march in those places. 11. The soldiers that we had levied came together in a few days.

XXXII.

Irregular verbs; vŏlo, nōlo, mālo; Gr. 225.

VOCABULARY.

auxĭlĭum, -ĭ, *help, aid.*
undĕ (adv.), *whence, from which.*
văcŏ, -ārĕ, -āvī, -ātŭm, *be empty, be vacant.*
discēdŏ, -dĕrĕ, -cessī, -cessŭm, *depart, go out or away.*

vŏlŏ, vellĕ, vŏluī, *to wish, be willing.*
nōlŏ, nollĕ, nōluī, *to be unwilling.*
mālŏ, mallĕ, māluī, *to prefer, choose rather, wish more.*
fŭgă, -ae, *flight.*

EXERCISES.

1. nolēbam pedem referre. 2. noli bellum Romānis, amīcis nostris, inferre. 3. in eam partem Helvetii se conferent, ubi eos esse voluĕris. 4. voluĕrat totam Galliam occupāre. 5. malo trans Rhenum bellum Germānis inferre quam in Galliā. 6. num vis illud suscipĕre? 7. pars militum pedem referre vult. 8. faciāmus omnia quae facĕre volŭmus. 9. quid vultis, amici? 10. maluit ab hostĭbus interfĭci quam pedem referre. 11. ii qui ad ripas venĕrant, pedem referre quam bellum gerĕre malēbant.

1. Dumnorix wished to have great influence[1] with[2] the Sequani. 2. We, who were across the river, were not able to bring help to our [friends]. 3. I did not wish to say this to many men. 4. He did not wish that place from which the Helvetians had departed to be empty. 5. Many prisoners[3] were brought into the city. 6. I had rather[4] be taken than save myself by flight. 7. Do you prefer to be slain [rather] than be taken [prisoner]? 8. Many were taken and slain, who were unwilling to rescue themselves by flight. 9. The flight of the enemy had given us the victory. 10. The city which we wished to take was given to us by the consent of the inhabitants. 11. The journey will have to be performed. 12. I am unwilling to retreat; I prefer to fight.

XXXIII.

Irregular verbs; do, eo, fio; Gr. 226-229.

VOCABULARY.

eō, īrĕ, īvī (iī), ĭtŭm, *go.*
fīō, fĭĕrī, (factŭs), *be made, become, happen.*
transĕō, transīrĕ, transiī, transĭtŭm,[1] *go over, cross.*
lintĕr, -trĭs (c.), *boat, skiff.*

rătĭs, -ĭs, *raft.*
aufĕrō, aufĕrrĕ, abstŭlī, ablātŭm, *take away.*
ădeō, ădīrĕ, ădiī, ădĭtŭm, *go to, go near, approach, visit.*
pāgŭs, -ī, *district, canton.*

EXERCISES.

1. multa fīunt quae non volŭmus. 2. id si fīet magno cum pericŭlo provinciae erit. 3. ii qui flumen transiĕrant suis[2] auxilium ferre non potĕrant. 4. spes gloriae major facta erat. 5. via per Alpes angusta est; alio itinĕre transeāmus. 6. in finĭbus Sequanōrum, qui trans Rhodănum incŏlunt, bellum gerēbam. 7. num hostes possunt amīci fĭĕri? 8. Caesar popŭlos adīre volēbat, qui trans Rhenum incŏlunt. 9. nolī hostes cum militĭbus adīre.

1. The Helvetians were crossing this river by[3] [means of] boats and rafts. 2. The beginning of that flight was made by Dumnorix and his horsemen. 3. Let us cross this river. 4. The hope of a return home has been taken away. 5. At the beginning of the war, there were large forces in the province. 6. It is very difficult to cross a river by [means of] boats and rafts. 7. A large river, which we were crossing, flows into the lake. 8. Do not cross the Rhine, legions; the enemy are numerous and brave. 9. The whole state is divided into four cantons. 10. There is a river which flows through the territories of the Sequani into the Rhone. 11. If they try[4] to cross, he will be able to prevent [them].

XXXIV.

Impersonal and defective verbs; Gr. 230–235.

VOCABULARY.

lǐcĕt, lǐcēre, lǐcuǐt, *is permitted, one may.*
ŏportĕt, -tēre, -tuǐt, *is proper, right; one ought, it behooves.*
nĕqvĕ (or nĕc), *and not, nor.*

nĕqvĕ ... nĕqvĕ, *neither ... nor.*
ăbĕō, -ire, -ĭi, -ĭtŭm, *go away, depart.*
Haeduī, -ōrŭm, *Hæduans,* (a Gallic nation).

EXERCISES.

1. id facĕre per me[1] lĭcĕt tibi. 2. oportet cum hostibus contendĕre. 3. tres legiōnes in Galliam mittam. 4. Rhodānus in lacum fluit. 5. castra proxĭmo die mōvit. 6. plures hostium capientur. 7. bellum in Haeduis gessĕrat. 8. multa bella gesta erant. 9. iter per provinciam non dăbo. 10. si id fecerĭtis, multa millia homĭnum interficientur. 11. malo id facĕre quam bellum inferre. 12. apud nos fortes sunt milĭtes multi. 13. tres annos in provincia fuĕrat.

1. The land of the Belgians extends many miles to the east. 2. Do[2] not attribute the victory to me, soldiers; the gods have given us victory. 3. Rescue yourselves from[3] the hands of the enemy, if you can, my sons. 4. The consul had taken many cities. 5. Peace will come when the enemy are[4] slain. 6. Let us rescue ourselves, Piso. 7. By daily battles one ought to bring peace. 8. It is neither permitted nor proper to make war on[5] friends. 9. You may[6] cross the river, my friends; the enemy have departed. 10. The soldiers whom you had levied did not assemble. 11. The Helvetians are trying to make a march through our province.

EXERCISES ON SYNTAX.

XXXV.

Nominative, vocative and accusative cases; Gr. 253-268.

VOCABULARY.

tergŭm, -ĭ, *back.*
audĕō, -ērĕ, ausŭs,[1] *dare.*
ĭtă (adv.), *thus, in this way.*
pollĭceŏr, -ērī, -ĭtŭs, *promise.*
vertō, -ĕrĕ, vertī, versŭm, *turn.*
dīcō, -ĕrĕ, -xī, -ctŭm, *say.*

hĭbernŭs, -ă, -ŭm, *of winter, wintry.*
hĭbernă, -ōrum, *winter quarters.*
auxĭlĭă, -ōrum, *auxiliaries.*
flăgĭtō, -ārĕ, -āvī, -ātŭm, *demand.*
hostĭs, -ĭs, *enemy.*
castră, -ōrŭm, *camp.*

EXERCISES.

1. cōrum qui domum rediĕrunt census habĭtus est. 2. ita dies circĭter quindĕcim iter fecĕrunt. 3. tres copiārum partes[2] Helvetii id flumen[3] transduxĕrant. 4. omnes hostes terga vertērunt. 5. relĭquos omnes nostri interfecērunt. 6. Caesar in hiberna in Sequănos[4] exercĭtum deduxit. 7. paucos dies morātur. 8. primam et secundam aciem in armis esse, tertiam castra munīre jussit. 9. hic locus ab hoste circĭter passus sescentos, uti dictum est, abĕrat. 10. salūtem suam Gallōrum equitatui committĕre non audēbat. 11. hunc montem murus arcem efficit.

1. He made haste to go to Bibracte. 2. Caesar demanded of the Haeduans[5] the corn[5] which they had promised. 3. Thus they made [their] march [for] fifteen days. 4. He left two legions and a part of the auxiliaries there. 5. On the same day[6] he moved camp. 6. For[7] five successive days Caesar led forth his troops in front of his camp. 7. He thought himself able[8] to do this without danger. 8. While he was waiting[9] a few days, a panic seized the whole army. 9. He hastened toward Ariovistus by forced marches.

XXXVI.

Dative case; Gr. 269–272.

VOCABULARY.

contĭnentĕr (adv.), *constantly.*
cūră, -ae, *care.*
summŭs, -ă, -ŭm, *highest, greatest.*
collŏquĭŭm, -ī, *conference, talk.*

ūsŭs, -ūs, *use, advantage.*
mūnītĭō, -ōnĭs, *fortification.*
făcultās, -ātĭs, *supply.*
ĭtĕrŭm (adv.), *again, a second time.*

EXERCISES.

1. proxĭmi sunt Germānis, qui trans Rhenum incŏlunt, quibuscum¹ continenter bellum gerunt. 2. Helvetiis est in animo² per agrum Sequanōrum iter facĕre. 3. ob eas causas ei munitiōni³ quam fecĕrat T. Labiēnum legātum praefēcit. 4. his omnibus rebus unum repugnābat. 5. omnium rerum quae ad bellum usui⁴ erant summa erat in eo oppĭdo facultas. 6. decĭma legio per tribūnos milĭtum ei gratias egit. 7. dies colloquio dictus est, ex eo die quintus. 8. is sibi legatiōnem ad civitātes suscēpit. 9. itĕrum colloquio diem constituit. 10. haec mihi sunt curae.

1. This matter will be cared for by Caesar (lit., will be for a care to C.). 2. We have nothing left⁵ except the soil of our land. 3. Dumnorix was in command of the cavalry which the Haeduans had sent to Caesar's aid.⁶ 4. The Helvetians are neighbors of⁷ the province and of the Allobroges. 5. What business⁸ has Caesar or the Roman people in my Gaul? 6. The Roman people pardoned the Arverni and did not reduce [them] to a province.⁹ 7. Caesar had favored¹⁰ this legion, and trusted¹⁰ [it] on account¹¹ of [its] courage. 8. They arrived in the country of the Lingones on the fourth day. 9. Caesar ordered two lines to repulse the enemy, the third [one] to finish the work.

XXXVII.

Locative case; Gr. 273, 274.

VOCABULARY.

collĭs, -ĭs (M.), *hill.*
conscrībŏ, -ĕrĕ, -psī, -ptŭm, *levy (troops).*
collŏcŏ, -ārĕ, -āvī, -ātŭm, *post, place.*
cĕlĕrĭtĕr (adv.), *quickly.*

subdūcŏ, -ĕrĕ, -xī, -ctŭm, *withdraw.*
postquăm (conj.), *after.*
prō (prep. w. abl.), *before, for, in proportion to, etc.*
sōlŭs, -ă, -ŭm (Gr. 71.), *alone.*

EXERCISES.

1. et domi et in reliqua Gallia plurĭmum potĕrat.[1] 2. postquam id[2] animum advertit, copias suas Caesar in proxĭmum collem subdūcit. 3. in summo jugo duas legiōnes, quas in Gallia citeriōre conscripsĕrat, et omnia auxilia collocāvit. 4. provincia mea haec est Gallia, sicut illa vestra. 5. celerĭter concilium dimittit, Liscum retĭnet; quaerit ex solo ea[3] quae in conventu dixerat. dicit liberius atque audacius. 6. ob eam causam, quamdiu potui, tacui. 7. pro multitudĭne homĭnum et pro gloria belli atque fortitudĭnis, angustos fines habēmus.

1. On the next day, because two days remained, he hastened to go to Bibracte. 2. There was nothing at home. 3. The number of those who returned home was found out [to be] one hundred and ten thousand.[4] 4. The Sequanians had admitted Ariovistus within their country. 5. The river Dubis as [if] drawn by a pair of compasses surrounds almost the whole town. 6. I came into Gaul earlier than the Roman people [did]. 7. The Suevi who had come to the banks of the Rhine began to return home. 8. The kind of fight in which the Germans had trained themselves was this. 9. At sunset Ariovistus led his troops back to camp.

XXXVIII.

Genitive case; source and cause; Gr. 275-284.

VOCABULARY.

ūmittŏ, -ĕrĕ, -īsī, -issŭm, *lose.*
accĭpĭŏ, -ĕrĕ, -cēpī, -ceptŭm, *receive.*
nŭmĕrŭs, -ī, *number.*
pĕdĕs, -ĭtĭs, *foot-soldier.*

cădŏ, -ĕrĕ, cĕcĭdī, cāsŭm, *fall.*
ĕquĕs, -ĭtĭs, *horseman.*
oblīviscŏr, -iscī, -lĭtŭs, *forget.*
pellŏ, -ĕrĕ, pĕpŭlī, pulsŭm, *drive, defeat.*

EXERCISES.

1. horum omnium fortissimi sunt Belgae. 2. triduī[1] viam processērunt hostes. 3. reminiscĕre et vetĕris incommŏdi popŭli Romāni et pristīnae virtūtis Helvetiōrum. 4. vetĕris contumeliae oblivisci volebat. 5. tridui viam processit. 6. pauci de nostris[2] cadunt. 7. equĭtum millia erant sex; totīdem numĕro[3] pedītes velocissimi ac fortissimi. 8. Haedui eorumque clientes semel atque itĕrum[4] cum his contendĕrunt armis; magnam calamitātem pulsi accepērunt; omnem nobilitātem, omnem senātum, omnem equitātum amisērunt.

1. All Gaul is divided into three parts, one of which the Belgians inhabit. 2. No one receives more sorrow[5] from[6] that [fact] than I. 3. We are not aware of any wrong. 4. Do not forget the injuries which they have inflicted on the Haeduans and their allies. 5. At first about fifteen thousand of these crossed the Rhine; they are now in Gaul to the number of one hundred and twenty thousand. 6. He attacked them and slew a large part of them. 7. Our [men] waited three days on account of the wounds of the soldiers. 8. Those through whose country the enemy had gone brought them back. 9. By the panic of these [men] even the soldiers and centurions were disturbed.

EXERCISES ON SYNTAX. 47

XXXIX.

Genitive case; possessive and special uses; Gr. 285-291.

VOCABULARY.

āvertŏ, -ĕrĕ, -tī, -sŭm, *turn away, turn aside.*
cognoscŏ, -ĕrĕ, -ōvī, -ĭtŭm, *learn ; perf. know.*
postrīdĭē (adv.), *the next day, on the morrow.*
praemittŏ, -ĕrĕ, -īsī, -īssŭm, *send ahead.*
ămīcĭtĭă, -ae, *friendship.*
ĭbī (adv.), *there.*
posteā (adv.), *afterwards.*
sĕquŏr; -ī, -cūtŭs, *follow.*

EXERCISES.

1. postridie ejus diēi¹ iter ab Helvetiis avertit. 2. ibi filia Orgetorigis atque unus e filiis captūs est.² 3. ii, qui ex urbe amicitiae causā Caesārem secūti erant, non magnum in re militāri³ usum habebant. 4. Divitiăci summum in popŭlum Romānum studium cognoverat. 5. P. Considius qui rei militāris peritissimus habebatur et in exercĭtu L. Sullae et postea in M. Crassi fuerat, cum exploratoribus praemittĭtur. 6. ea res per fugitīvos L. Aemilii, decuriōnis equĭtum Gallorum, nuntiatur. 7. ipse Dumnŏrix rerum novarum cupĭdus est.

1. The place takes its name from the slaughter of the Roman army. 2. The feelings⁴ of Divitiacus were hurt by his brother's punishment. 3. Neither his coming nor [that] of Labienus was known. 4. On account of the excellence of the land, the Germans who dwell across the Rhine, will cross over from their own country into the country of the Helvetians. 5. On the next day he hastened to go to Bibracte, the largest town of the Haeduans. 6. I shall not overlook the wrongs of the Haeduans. 7. Caesar cheered the spirits of the Gauls by his words. 8. Led by the desire of kingly power, Orgetorix made a conspiracy of the nobility. 9. The Helvetians, moved by his sudden arrival, send envoys to him.

XL.

Ablative case proper; Gr. 292–296.

VOCABULARY.

abstĭneŏ, -ērĕ, -uī, -tentŭm, *hold off, refrain.*
corpŭs, -ŏrĭs, *body.*
dēsistŏ, -ĕrĕ, dēstĭtī, -stĭtŭm, *cease from, leave off.*
ingens, -ntĭs, *great, huge.*

affĕrŏ, -ferrĕ, attŭlī, allātŭm, *bring.*
cōgŏ, cōgĕrĕ, coēgī, coactŭm, *compel.*
ēdūcŏ, -ĕrĕ, -xī, -ctŭm, *lead out.*
mōs, -ōrĭs, *custom, habit.*

EXERCISES.

1. Labiēnus nostros expectabat proelioque abstinebat. 2. a Bibracte, oppido Haeduorum longē maximo, non amplius milibus passuum octodĕcim aberat. 3. moribus suis Orgetorĭgem ex vincŭlis causam dicĕre coëgērunt. 4. Dumnŏrix gratiā et largitione apud Sequănos plurĭmum potĕrat. 5. negotio desistĕre non potĕram. 6. ob eam rem ex civitāte profūgi et Romam ad senātum vēni. 7. ea res Caesari non minōrem quam ipsa victoria voluptātem attŭlit. 8. duae fuērunt Ariovisti uxōres, una quam domo secum eduxerat, altera quam in Gallia duxerat.

1. They had gone from home. 2. The enemy are trying to keep our army from the march. 3. By their flight the rest of the cavalry was frightened. 4. He was trying to shut Cæsar off from the corn which was supplied from the Sequanians and Hæduans. 5. Ariovistus, king of the Germans, has seized a third part of their land, which is the best of all Gaul. 6. He now orders the Sequanians to leave the second third part. 7. Mettius was found and brought back to him. 8. Ariovistus sent sixteen thousand men with all the cavalry. 9. On the next day, Cæsar, according to his custom, led his forces out of both camps. 10. All the enemy turned their backs and did not cease to flee. 11. On the next day they arrived at the Rhine.

XLI.

Instrumental ablative; Gr. 297, 298.

VOCABULARY.

aequŭs, -ă, -ŭm, *equal, level.*
nĭhĭl (indeclinable), *nothing.*
ŏpŭs, -ĕris, *work.*
tĭmŏr, -ōrĭs, *fear, panic.*
vescŏr, -ī, *feed on, eat.*
ĕtĭăm (adv.), *also, even.*
ōrūtĭō, -ōnĭs, *speech, talk.*
tēlŭm, -ī, *missile, weapon.*
ūtor, -ī, ūsŭs, *use.*
vox, -ōcĭs, *voice, talk, words.*

EXERCISES.

1. hac oratiōne adducti, inter se fidem et jus jurandum dant. 2. ea legiōne quam secum habebat, militibusque, qui ex provincia convenĕrant, murum fossamque perdūcit. 3. opĕris munitione et militum concursu et telis hostes repulsi sunt. 4. eo frumento¹ quod flumine Arăre² navibus subvexerat, uti non potĕrat. 5. domi nihil erat quo¹ vesci potĕrant. 6. horum vocibus ac timōre etiam ii qui magnum in castris usum habebant, milĭtes centurionesque quique³ equitatui⁴ praeĕrant perturbabantur. 7. hic locus aequo spatio ab castris Ariovisti et Caesăris abĕrat.

1. Elated by this battle, the Helvetians began to resist more boldly. 2. Induced by the lack of all things, we sent ambassadors to you about a surrender. 3. He filled the whole mountain with men. 4. We do not contend by means of trickery, or depend upon artifice. 5. Our [men] got possession of the baggage and camp. 6. This town was fortified by the nature of [its] situation. 7. The Hæduans did not make use of the help of the Roman people in the wars that they had with me. 8. Much⁵ was said by Cæsar. 9. Broken by these defeats, the Hæduans have been compelled to give hostages to the Sequanians. 10. They fought⁶ with their swords. 11. We wish Gaul, though conquered in war,⁷ to use its own laws.

XLII.

Locative ablative; Gr. 299-303.

VOCABULARY.

cōnātŭs, -ūs, *attempt.*
ĭnĭmīcŭs, -ă, -ŭm, *unfriendly, hostile.*
nonnullŭs, -ă, -ŭm, *some, a few.*
tempĕrō,-ārĕ,-āvī,-ātŭm,*refrain.*

dējĭcĭō, -ĕrĕ, -jēcī, -jectŭm, *cast down.*
injūrĭă, -ae, *wrong, injury.*
prīdĭē (adv.), *on the day before.*
vădŭm, -ī, *shoal, ford.*

EXERCISES.

1. hic pagus unus, patrum nostrorum memoriā, L. Cassium, consŭlem interfecerat, et ejus exercĭtum sub jugum miserat. 2. pridie proelium non commiserant. 3. ex eo proelio circiter millia centum et triginta superfuĕrunt eāque totā nocte continenter iĕrunt. 4. totis castris[1] testamenta obsignabantur. 5. inter fines Helvetiorum et Allobrŏgum Rhodănus fluit isque nonnullis locis[1] vado transĭtur. 6. homĭnes inimīci nobīs non temperabunt ab injuria. 7. Helvetii ea spe dejecti, hoc conātu destitĕrunt. 8. nunc sunt in Gallia multa millia.

1. These all differ from one another[2] in language, customs [and] laws. 2. At daybreak he was not far away from the camp of the enemy. 3. They join battle with the cavalry of the Helvetians in an unfavorable place. 4. On all these days Ariovistus kept his army in camp.[3] 5. Records were found in the camp of the Helvetians and brought to Caesar. 6. He ordered them to await his arrival in that place. 7. They attacked our [men] on the right flank.[4] 8. On the next day he turned his course from the Helvetians. 9. Early in the night[5] about six thousand men of that canton which is called Verbigenus left the camp of the Helvetians, and hastened toward the Rhine and the country of the Germans.

XLIII.

Comitative ablative; Gr. 304, 306.

VOCABULARY.

anceps, -ipitis (Gr. [115.]), *doubtful.*
consuesco, -ĕrĕ, -ēvī, -ētŭm,[1] *get used, be wont.*
pĕtō, pĕtĕrĕ, pĕtīvī, -ītum, *ask, beg.*

diū (adv.), *long.*
collŏquŏr, -i, -cūtŭs, *talk with, converse.*
dux, dŭcĭs, *guide, leader.*
lēnĭtās, -ātĭs, *gentleness, slowness.*
vĭgĭlĭă, -ae, *watch.*

EXERCISES.

1. flumen est Arar, quod per finīs Haeduorum in Rhodănum influit incredibĭli lenitāte. 2. omnes qui adĕrant magno fletu auxilium a Caesăre petere coepērunt. 3. ancipĭti proelio diu pugnatum est.[2] 4. ea omnia injussu[3] Caesăris et civitātis fecerat. 5. per C. Valerium, cui[4] summam omnium rerum fidem[5] habebat, cum eo colloquĭtur. 6. de[6] tertia vigilia T. Labiēnum, cum duābus legionibus et iis ducibus qui iter cognoverant, montem adscendĕre jubet. 7. eo die quo consuerat intervallo[7] hostes sequĭtur et millia passuum tria ab eorum castris castra ponit.

1. Caesar hastened to this city by forced marches. 2. Dumnorix, the brother of Divitiacus, was meant by this speech of Liscus. 3. Dumnorix, [a man] of the greatest boldness, is desirous of a revolution. 4. He himself hastened to the enemy in the fourth watch by the same route by which they had gone. 5. At daybreak neither his arrival nor [that] of Labienus, as he afterward learned from prisoners, was known. 6. Meanwhile he drew up a line of battle of the four legions half way up[8] the hill. 7. He was not more than a mile and a half[9] from the enemy's camp. 8. The Sequanians have received Ariovistus into[10] their country, and all their towns are in his power. 9. The Germans are of huge size of body and of incredible courage.

XLIV.

Ablative absolute; ablative with prepositions; Gr. 307, 308.

VOCABULARY.

cornū, -ūs, *horn, wing.*
indūcō, -ĕrĕ, -xī, -ctŭm, *lead on, induce.*
confīdō, -ĕrĕ, -fīsŭs, (Gr. [210] (g)), *trust in, confide.*

nox, noctĭs, *night.*
invĕnĭō, -īrĕ, -vēnī, -ventŭm, *come upon, find.*
prŏfĭcīscŏr, -ī, -fectŭs, *start, set out.*

EXERCISES.

1. Orgetŏrix, M. Messālā et M. Pisōne consulibus, regni cupiditate inductus conjurationem nobilitatis fecit. 2. his rebus cognĭtis, Caesar Gallorum animos confirmavit. 3. bello Helvetiorum confecto, totīus fere Galliae legāti ad Caesărem gratulatum[1] convenērunt. 4. nullam partem noctis itinĕre intermisso in fines Lingŏnum die quarto pervenērunt. 5. eorum satisfactione accepta et itinĕre exquisīto per Divitiācum, de quarta vigiliā profectus est. 6. ipse a dextro cornu[2] proelium commīsit. 7. perpauci aut viribus[3] conlisi tranare contendērunt aut lintribus inventis sibi salūtem repererunt.

1. They could not go by this way, because the Sequanians were unwilling. 2. After this council was dismissed the same chief men of the states returned to Caesar. 3. After driving[4] back our cavalry, they formed a phalanx and came up to our first line. 4. After giving this answer, he left. 5. Calling together their chiefs, a large number of whom he had in camp, he blames them severely. 6. When Caesar's arrival was known, Ariovistus sent envoys to him. 7. When the camp had been fortified, he left two legions there; the remaining four he led back to the larger camp. 8. By the delivery of this speech[5] the minds of all were changed. 9. He allowed all the rest to surrender after they had delivered the hostages, arms and deserters.

XLV.

Use of the tenses; Gr. 309-312.

VOCABULARY.

castellŭm, -ī, *fort, redoubt.*
noudŭm (adv.), *not yet.*
dispōnō, -nĕrĕ, -pŏsuī, -pŏsĭtŭm, *place, post.*

prīnceps, -cĭpĭs, *leading, chief.*
praesĭdĭŭm, -ī, *garrison, defence.*
rĕvertō, -ĕrĕ, -vertī, -versŭm, *return* (also deponent).

EXERCISES.

1. ea res enuntiata est. 2. post ejus mortem nihilo[1] minus Helvetii id quod constituerant facere conantur. 3. Allobroges nondum bono animo[2] in populum Romanum videbantur. 4. milites, quos imperaverat, conveniebant. 5. eo opere perfecto praesidia dispōnit, castella commūnit. 6. ubi ea dies quam constituerat cum legātis venit, legati ad eum reverterunt. 7. legatos ad eum mittunt, cujus legatiōnis Divico princeps fuit, qui dux Helvetiorum fuerat. 8. hac oratione habita, conversae sunt omnium mentes. 9. Helvetii castra movebunt.

1. This district was called Tigurinus; for all the Helvetian state is divided[3] into four districts. 2. The Helvetians were crossing this river. 3. Setting[4] out from camp with three legions, he came to that part which had not yet crossed the river. 4. While this was[5] going on, the horsemen of Ariovistus threw missiles at our men. 5. He began battle on the right wing, because he had noticed these facts. 6. Then at last the Germans from necessity led out their forces from the camp and posted them at equal intervals, tribe by tribe. 7. I dare not go into that part of Gaul without an army. 8. The Sequani must endure all tortures. 9. The enemy charged suddenly and swiftly.

XLVI.

Subjunctive in dependent clauses; Gr. 322-333.

VOCABULARY.

ălĭquĭs, -quă, -quĭd, *some one, any one.*
exĕō, -īrĕ, -ĭī, -ĭtŭm, *go out, depart.*
impĕtŭs, -ūs, *attack.*
ŏcŭlŭs, -ī, *eye.*
plăcĕō, -ērĕ, -uī, -ĭtŭm, *please.*
scĭō, -scīrĕ, -scīvī, -scītum, *know.*

custōs, -ōdĭs, *guard, sentinel.*
hortŏr, -ārī, -ātŭs, *urge.*
lŏquŏr, -ī, -cūtŭs, *speak, talk.*
persuādĕō, -ērĕ, -sī, -sŭm, *persuade.*
vĕl, *or.*
vĕl . . . vĕl, *either . . . or.*

EXERCISES.

1. civitati persuāsit ut de finibus suis cum omnibus copiis exīrent. 2. Arar in Rhodănum influit incredibĭli lenitate, ita ut ocŭlis, in utram partem fluat,[1] judicari non possit. 3. placuit ei ut ad Ariovistum legatos mittĕret qui ab eo postulārent uti aliquem locum colloquio dicĕret. 4. equitātum qui sustinēret hostium impĕtum, misit. 5. per eos, ne causam dicĕret, se eripuit. 6. petit atque hortatur ut vel ipse de eo statuat vel civitatem statuere jubeat. 7. Dumnorĭgi custōdes ponit ut, quae agat,[1] quibuscum loquatur,[1] scire possit.

1. There was no doubt that[2] the Helvetians were the most powerful of all Gaul. 2. He sent [men] to find out[3] what[4] the character of the mountain was. 3. There were two ways by which they could[4] go out from home. 4. Divitiacus with many tears began to beg Cæsar not to decide on anything too severe toward his brother. 5. He warns Dumnorix to avoid all suspicions for the future. 6. He ordered the Allobroges to furnish them a supply of corn. 7. I am the only [one] who could[5] not be brought to take an oath or give my children [as] hostages. 8. Our men attacked the enemy so vigorously when the signal was given, that no room was given for throwing the javelins at the enemy.[6]

XLVII.

Subjunctive in dependent clauses (*continued*).

VOCABULARY.

hōrǎ, -ae, *hour*.
intellěgō, -ěrě, -xī, -ctǔm, *know, understand*.
prĭusquăm (conj.), *before*.
vŏcō, -ārě, -āvī, -ātǔm, *call*.

EXERCISES.

1. Helvetii, cum id intellegěrent, legātos ad eum mittunt. 2. id ubi Caesar resciit, quorum per fīnīs ierant, his, uti reducěrent, imperavit. 3. hoc toto proelio, cum[1] ab hora septǐma ad vespěrum pugnatum sit, aversum[2] hostem viděre nemo potuit. 4. priusquam quicqvam conarētur, Divitiacum ad se vocavit. 5. diutius cum nostrorum impětus sustinēre non possent, alteri, ut coeperant, in montem se recepērunt; alteri ad impedimenta et carros suos se contulērunt. 6. vehementer eas incusavit quod quaerěrent[3] quam in partem[4] aut quo consilio ducerentur.

1. At daybreak, when the top of the mountain was held by Labienus, Considius runs up to Cæsar. 2. When this had been reported to Cæsar, he hastened to start from the city. 3. When the day which he had set came, he gave no one a passage through the province. 4. When they could not persuade them, they sent ambassadors to Dumnorix the Hæduan, in order to gain their request from the Sequanians through his intercession.[5] 5. He could not use that corn which he had brought up the Arar,[6] because the Helvetians had turned their course from the river. 6. He accuses them strongly, because he is not aided by them. 7. Before he made[7] any attempt he ordered Divitiacus to be summoned to him.

XLVIII.

Infinitive; Gr. 334–342.

VOCABULARY.

ăgŏ, ăgĕrĕ, ēgī, actŭm, *do, deal, talk.*
ŏportĕt, -ērĕ, -uĭt, *it is proper, one ought.*
pŏtiŏr, pŏtīrī, potītŭs, (Gr. [297]), *get, get control of.*
intĕrĭm (adv.), *meanwhile.*

vălĕŏ, -ērĕ, -uī, -ĭtŭm, *be strong, be able.*
auctōrĭtās, -ātĭs, *authority, influence.*
sī (conj.), *if.*
plebs, plēbĭs, (Gr. [98]), *people, common people.*

EXERCISES.

1. perfacĭle est, cum virtūte omnibus[1] praestēmus, totīus Galliae imperio[2] potiri.   2. intĕrim quotidie Caesar Haeduos frumentum flagitare.   3. Liscus dicit esse nonnullos quorum auctorĭtas apud plebem plurimum valeat.   4. Caesări cum id nuntiatum esset, eos per provinciam nostram iter facere conari, matūrat ab urbe proficisci.   5. Ariovistus respondit, si quid Caesar velit, illum ad se venire oportēre.   6. Ariovistus ad Caesărem legatos mittit velle[3] se de his rebus agere cum eo.   7. pauci, viribus confīsi, tranare contendērunt.   8. per exploratores Caesar cognovit montem a suis tenēri.

1. He did not wish these things to be discussed while more [persons] were present.[4]   2. It is dangerous for the Germans[5] to get used to cross the Rhine.   3. He saw that the Haeduans were held under[6] the sway of the Germans.   4. When Caesar learned that they kept[7] in camp, he chose a place suitable for a camp six hundred paces beyond them.   5. The Suevi, who had come to the banks of the Rhine, began to return home.   6. Word was brought to Caesar that the horsemen of Ariovistus were coming nearer to the hill and throwing stones and javelins at our men.   7. Caesar promised to care[8] for the matter, [saying] that he had great hope that Ariovistus would put an end[9] to his injuries.

XLIX.

Participles; Gr. 343–347.

VOCABULARY.

convertō, -ĕrĕ, -vertī, -versŭm, *turn, change.*
flĕō, flērĕ, flēvī, flētŭm, *weep.*
prōjĭcĭō,-ĕrĕ,-jēcī,-jectŭm,*throw.*
tandĕm (adv.), *at last, at length.*
ĕō (adv.), *thither.*

ōrŏ, -ārĕ, -āvī, -ātŭm, *beg, pray, ask.*
mens, -ntĭs, *mind, reason.*
sŏcĭŭs, -ī, *friend, ally.*
vulnŭs, -ĕrĭs, *wound.*
verbŭm, -ī, *word.*

EXERCISES.

1. Bojos, receptos[1] ad se, socios sibi adsciscunt. 2. persuādent finitĭmis, uti eodem usi consilio cum iis proficiscantur. 3. haec cum pluribus verbis flens a Caesăre petĕret, Caesar consolatus rogat finem orandi faciat.[2] 4. tandem vulneribus defessi et pedem referre et quod mons subĕrat circiter mille passuum eo se recipere coepērunt. 5. hoc toto proelio aversum[3] hostem vidēre nemo potuit. 6. Bojos petentibus[4] Haeduis ut in finibus suis collocarent concessit. 7. ea re impetrata, sese omnes flentes Caesări ad pedes projecērunt.

1. Caesar learned that Considius, in his fright,[5] had reported to him what he had not seen.[6] 2. After encouraging his men, Caesar joined battle. 3. The Helvetians who had betaken themselves to the mountain, began again to make a stand, when they saw this.[7] 4. Our [men] having waited three days on account of the wounds of the soldiers and the burial of the slain, could not pursue them. 5. After the lapse[8] of three days he began to follow them himself with all his forces. 6. When he had noticed this, he called[9] a council and severely upbraided them. 7. He treated those who were brought back as enemies.[10] 8. The Ubii, who dwell nearest the Rhine,[11] pursued[12] them [while they were] frightened, and slew a large number of[13] them.

L.

Gerund and gerundive; Gr. 348, 349.

VOCABULARY.

cūrŏ, -ārĕ, -āvī, -ātŭm, *care for, attend to.*
instrŭŏ, -ŭĕrĕ, -uxī, -uctŭm, *draw up, arrange.*
pandŏ, -dĕrĕ, -dī, pansŭm and passŭm, *extend, stretch out.*
servĭtūs, -ūtĭs, *slavery.*

trādŏ, -dĕrĕ, -dĭdī, -dĭtŭm, *give over, surrender.*
ĭnĭtĭŭm, -ī, *beginning.*
mŭlĭĕr, -ĕrĭs, *woman.*
pons, -ntĭs, *bridge.*
pŏtestās, -ātĭs, *power, opportunity.*

EXERCISES.

1. mercatores ea important quae ad effeminandos animos pertinent. 2. pontem in Arāre faciendum curat. 3. colloquendi Caesări causa visa non est. 4. reperiebat in quaerendo[1] Caesar initium ejus fugae factum esse a Dumnorĭge, atque ejus equitibus. 5. ad eas res conficiendas, Orgetŏrix delegĭtur. 6. mulĭeres in proelium proficiscentis milites passis manibus flentes implorabant ne se in servitūtem Romanis tradĕrent. 7. P. Crassus tertiam aciem nostris subsidio misit. 8. aciem instruxit hostibusque pugnandi potestātem fecit.[2] 9. dixit id se sui muniendi non Galliae impugnandae causa facere.

1. As the hope of returning home had been lost,[3] we were the more prepared to undergo[4] all dangers. 2. The highest zeal and eagerness for waging war sprang up. 3. The tenth legion affirmed that it was perfectly ready to wage war. 4. Caesar stops[5] speaking and returns to his [men]. 5. Caesar went to Nearer Gaul to hold the assizes.[6] 6. The enemy charged so suddenly and quickly that no room was given for throwing[7] their javelins at the enemy. 7. The town was so fortified by the nature of its position that it gave a great opportunity for prolonging a war. 8. He said that he ought to suspect that Caesar, because he had an army in Gaul, had [it] to crush him.[8]

LI.

Supine; Gr. 350–352.

VOCABULARY.

conspĭcĭŏ, -ĕrĕ, -exi, -cctŭm, *see, perceive.*
exīstĭmŏ, -ārĕ, -āvī, -ātŭm, *think, believe.*
fortūnă, -ae, *fortune.*

sŭpĕrŏ, -ārĕ, -āvī, -ātŭm, *conquer, overcome.*
indĕ (adv.), *thence, from there.*
tentŏ, -ārĕ, -āvi, -ātŭm, *try, test.*

EXERCISES.

1. Haedui, cum se suaque ab iis defendere non possent, legatos ad Caesarem mittunt rogatum auxilium. 2. perfacile factu esse illis probat conata perficere. 3. eos cum apud se in castris Ariovistus conspexisset, conclamavit, quid ad se venirent.[1] 4. Ariovistus respondit Haeduos sibi quoniam belli fortunam tentassent et armis superati essent stipendiarios esse factos. 5. legati veniebant questum sese ne obsidibus quidem[2] datis pacem redimere potuisse. 6. neque sibi homines feros ac barbaros temperaturos[3] existimabat, quin,[3] cum omnem Galliam occupassent, ut ante Cimbri Teutonique fecissent, in provinciam exirent atque inde in Italiam contenderent.

1. The Hæduans came to complain because the Harudes, who had lately been brought over into Gaul, were laying[4] waste their country. 2. I fled from the state and came to Rome to ask help. 3. He blamed them severely, [saying that] Ariovistus had most eagerly sought the friendship of the Roman people, when he was consul.[5] 4. He resolved to send[6] envoys to Ariovistus to ask him to name some place for a conference, [saying] that he wished to treat with him about the most important interests of each. 5. Cæsar promised to care[7] for this matter, [saying] that he had great hope that Ariovistus, led by his kindness and influence, would put[7] a stop to his wrongs.

LII.

Forms of conditional sentences; Gr. 446–456.

EXERCISES.

1. si quid vultis, ad Idus Aprilis revertimini. 2. si vim facere conentur, prohibeat Caesar. 3. id si fiet, magno cum periculo provinciae erit. 4. id si fiat, magno cum periculo provinciae sit. 5. id si factum esset, magno cum periculo provinciae fuisset. 6. si Romani superent, nobis libertatem eripiant. 7. si Romani superabunt, nobis libertatem eripient. 8. si quid accidat Romanis, summam in spem regni obtinendi Dumnorix venit.[1] 9. si quid mihi[2] a Caesare opus esset, ego ad eum venissem; si quid ille me vult, illum ad me venire oportet. 10. si nemo sequatur, tamen ego cum sola decima legione eam.

1. If they try to cross against my will, I shall stop them. 2. If they should try to cross, I should stop them. 3. If they were trying to cross, I should stop them. 4. If they had tried to cross, I should have stopped them. 5. I will make peace with you, if hostages are given me by you. 6. If hostages had been given me, I should have made peace with the enemy. 7. If anything happens to him, no one will think that it has not been done by my consent. 8. If anything were happening, all would think that it was done by my consent. 9. If you wish to be free from blame, bring back the fugitives. 10. If this be told, we shall come into the severest torture. 11. If this should be told to Ariovistus, I do not doubt[3] that[4] he would inflict[5] punishment on the hostages. 12. If this had been told me, I should have inflicted punishment on you. 13. A wall, put around this mountain, makes [it] a fort. 14. Considius says that the mountain which Caesar wished to be seized by Labienus is held by the enemy.

LIII.

Indirect discourse; Gr. 457–478.

EXERCISES.

1. tres jam copiarum partes Helvetii id flumen[1] transduxerunt.

Caesar certior factus est tres jam copiarum partes Helvetios id flumen transduxisse.

2. sunt nonnulli quorum auctoritas apud plebem plurimum valet.

Liscus dicit esse nonnullos quorum auctoritas apud plebem plurimum valeat.

3. scio illa esse vera nec quisquam ex eo plus quam ego doloris capit.

Divitiacus dixit scire se illa esse vera nec quenquam ex eo plus quam se doloris capere.

4. mons quem a Labieno occupari voluisti ab hostibus tenetur; id a Gallicis armis atque insignibus cognovi.

Considius dicit montem quem a Labieno occupari voluerit ab hostibus teneri; id se a Gallicis armis atque insignibus cognovisse.

---

1. They are trying to march through our province.

Word was brought to Caesar that they were trying to march through our province.

2. We intend to march through the province without any[2] harm, because we have no other road.

They sent ambassadors to him to say that they intended to march through the province without any harm because they had no other road.

3. Men of hostile spirit, if the privilege of marching through the province be given, will not refrain from wrong and harm.

He did not think that men of hostile spirit, if the privilege of marching through the province were given, would refrain[3] from wrong and harm.

LIV.

Indirect discourse (*continued*).

EXERCISES.

1. si pacem populus Romanus cum Helvetiis faciet in eam partem ibunt atque ibi erunt ubi tu eos constitueris[1] atque esse volueris;[1] sin bello persequi perseverabis, reminiscere et veteris incommodi populi Romani et pristinae virtutis Helvetiorum.

is ita cum Caesare agit; si pacem populus Romanus cum Helvetiis faceret in eam partem ituros atque ibi futuros Helvetios ubi eos Caesar constituisset atque esse voluisset; sin bello persequi perseveraret, reminisceretur et veteris incommodi populi Romani et pristinae virtutis Helvetiorum.

2. eo mihi minus dubitationis datur quod eas res quas vos commemoravistis memoria teneo.

his Caesar ita respondit; eo sibi minus dubitationis dari quod eas res quas legati Helvetii commemorassent memoria teneret.

---

1. Do not cause this place where we stand[2] to take [its] name from the defeat of the Roman people and the slaughter of [their] army.

[He told him] not to cause that place where they stood to take its name from the defeat of the Roman people and the slaughter of their army.

2. The Helvetians have been taught by their forefathers to be[3] in the habit of receiving[4] hostages, not of giving; of that fact the Roman nation is a witness.

Divico answered that the Helvetians had been taught by their forefathers to be in the habit of receiving hostages, not of giving; that the Roman nation was a witness of that fact.

LV.

Indirect discourse (*continued*).

EXERCISES.

1. Caesari renunciatur Helvetiis esse in animo per agrum Sequanorum et Haeduorum iter in Santonum fines facere qui non longe a Tolosatium finibus absunt[1] quae civitas est[1] in provincia.

2. Liscus dicit hos seditiosa atque improba oratione multitūdinem deterrere ne frumentum conferant quod praestare debeant.

3. Caesar reperit Dumnorigem odisse Romanos quod eorum adventu potentia ejus deminuta et Divitiacus frater in antiquum locum gratiae atque honoris sit restitutus.

4. eodem die ab exploratoribus certior factus hostes sub monte consedisse milia passuum ab ipsius castris octo, qualis esset natura montis et qualis in circuitu ascensus qui cognoscerent misit. renunciatum est facilem esse.

1. Divitiacus the Haeduan spoke for[2] them, [saying] that all Gaul was divided into two parties[3]; that the Haeduans held the leadership of one of these, the Arverni of the other; that after these had fought[4] with each other for[5] the power many years, it came to pass that the Germans were hired[6] by the Arverni; that at first about fifteen thousand of these crossed the Rhine; that now there were in Gaul one hundred and twenty thousand.

2. He said that he was the only one out of the whole state of the Haeduans who could not be brought to take the oath, or give his children as hostages; that for this reason[7] he had fled from the state, and had come to Rome to the senate to ask aid, because he alone was not held either[8] by an oath or by hostages.

LVI.

Relations of place.

Place where; locative, Gr. 273; ablative, Gr. 299; with prepositions, Gr. 308.

Place to which; accusative, Gr. 265; with prepositions, Gr. 268.

Place from which; ablative, Gr. 293; with prepositions, Gr. 308.

EXERCISE.

1. Belgae a cultu atque humanitate longissime absunt, minimeque ad eos mercatores saepe commeant. 2. aut suis finibus eos prohibent, aut ipsi in eorum finibus bellum gerunt. 3. civitati persuasit ut de finibus suis cum omnibus copiis exirent. 4. trium mensium molita cibaria sibi quemque domo efferre jubent. 5. Rhodanus nonnullis locis vado transitur. 6. ex eo oppido pons ad Helvetios pertinet. 7. Caesari cum id nuntiatum esset, eos per provinciam nostram iter facere conari,[1] maturat ab urbe proficisci et quam maximis potest itineribus in Galliam ulteriorem contendit et ad[2] Genuam pervenit. provinciae toti quam maximum potest militum numerum imperat — erat omnino in Gallia ulteriore legio una — pontem, qui erat ad Genuam, jubet rescindi. 8. interea ea legione quam secum habebat, militibusque, qui ex provincia convenerant, a lacu Lemanno, qui in flumen Rhodanum influit, ad montem Juram, qui fines Sequanorum ab Helvetiis dividit, millia passuum decem novem murum in altitudinem pedum sedecim fossamque perducit. 9. eo autem frumento quod flumine[3] Arare navibus subvexerat propterea minus[4] uti poterat, quod iter ab Arare Helvetii averterant a quibus discedere nolebat. 10. non solum domi sed etiam apud finitimas civitates largiter potest. 11. Diviacus dixit ob eam rem se ex civitate profugisse et Romam ad senatum venisse auxilium postulatum.

LVII.

Relations of place (*continued*).

EXERCISE.

1. hic locus aequo fere spatio ab castris Ariovisti et Caesaris aberat. eo, ut erat dictum, ad colloquium venerunt. legionem Caesar, quam equis devexerat, passibus ducentis ab eo loco constituit. 2. ultra eum locum, quo in loco Germani consederant, circiter passus sescentos ab iis, castris idoneum locum delegit acieque triplici instructa ad eum locum venit. 3. ipse a dextro cornu, quod eam partem minime firmam hostium esse animadverterat, proelium commisit. 4. hoc proelio trans Rhenum nuntiato Suevi, qui ad ripas Rheni venerant, domum reverti coeperant; quos Ubii, qui proximi Rhenum incolunt, perterritos insecuti magnum ex his numerum occiderunt. Caesar una aestate duobus maximis bellis confectis maturius paulo quam tempus anni postulabat, in hiberna in Sequanos exercitum deduxit; hibernis Labienum praeposuit; ipse in citeriorem Galliam ad conventus agendos profectus est. 5. Belgae ab extremis Galliae finibus oriuntur, pertinent ad inferiorem partem fluminis Rheni, spectant in septentrionem et orientem solem. Aquitania a Garumna flumine ad Pyrenaeos montes et eam partem oceani, quae est ad[1] Hispaniam, pertinet; spectat inter occasum solis et septentriones. 6. biduo post Ariovistus ad Caesarem legatos mittit; velle se de his rebus quae inter eos agi coeptae neque perfectae essent agere cum eo; uti aut iterum colloquio diem constitueret, aut, si id minus vellet, e suis legatis aliquem ad se mitteret. colloquendi Caesari causa visa non est, et eo magis, quod pridie ejus diei Germani retineri non poterant quin in nostros tela conjicerent. legatum e suis sese magno cum periculo ad eum missurum et hominibus feris objecturum existimabat. commodissimum visum est C. Valerium Procillum ad eum mittere.

LVIII.

Relations of time.
Time when or within which; Gr. 301.
Time during which; Gr. 266, 302.
Dates; Gr. 487–497.
Ablative absolute; Gr. 307.
Temporal clauses; Gr. 330.

EXERCISE.

1. die constituta causae dictionis, Orgetorix omnem suam familiam undique coegit. 2. cum civitas jus suum exsequi conaretur, Orgetorix mortuus[1] est. 3. ubi jam se ad eam rem paratos esse arbitrati sunt, vicos incendunt. 4. diem dicunt, qua die ad ripam omnes conveniant. is dies erat a. d.[2] V. Kal. Apr. L. Pisone, A. Gabinio consulibus. 5. ut spatium intercedere posset, dum milites quos imperaverat convenirent,[3] legatis respondit diem[4] se ad deliberandum sumpturum; si quid vellent ad[5] Id. Apr. reverterentur. 6. in fines Vocontiorum die septimo pervenit. 7. legationis Divico princeps fuit, qui bello Cassiano[6] dux Helvetiorum fuerat. 8. ita dies circiter quindecim iter fecerunt. 9. pluribus praesentibus eas res jactari nolebat. 10. itaque prius quam quicquam conaretur,[7] Divitiacum ad se vocari jubet. 11. de tertia vigilia T. Labienum summum jugum montis adscendere jubet. 12. post quam id animum advertit copias suas Caesar in proximum collem subducit. 13. hoc toto proelio, cum ab hora septima ad vesperum pugnatum sit, aversum hostem videre nemo potuit. 14. ea tota nocte continenter ierunt; nullam partem noctis itinere intermisso in fines Lingonum die quarto pervenerunt, cum et propter vulnera militum et propter sepulturam occisorum nostri triduum morati eos sequi non potuissent.

LIX.

Relations of time (*continued*).

EXERCISE.

1. prima[1] nocte e castris Helvetiorum egressi ad Rhenum finesque Germanorum contenderunt. 2. paucis mensibus ante Harudum millia hominum xxiii ad eum venerant. 3. futurum est[2] paucis annis ut omnes ex Galliae finibus pellantur. 4. dum paucos dies ad Vesontionem rei frumentariae commeatusque causa moratur, timor omnem exercitum occupavit. 5. haec cum animadvertisset, vehementer eos incusavit. 6. dixit Ariovistum se consule cupidissime populi Romani amicitiam appetisse. 7. factum ejus hostis periculum patrum nostrorum memoria; factum etiam nuper in Italia servili tumultu. 8. septimo die, cum iter non intermitteret, ab exploratoribus certior factus est Ariovisti copias a nostris millibus passuum quattuor et viginti, abesse. 9. biduo post Ariovistus ad Caesarem legatos mittit. 10. ex eo die dies continuos quinque Caesar pro castris suas copias produxit, ut, si vellet Ariovistus proelio contendere, ei potestas non deesset. Ariovistus his omnibus diebus exercitum castris continuit. 11. ubi ne tum quidem eos prodire intellexit, circiter meridiem exercitum in castra reduxit. tum demum Ariovistus partem suarum copiarum, quae castra minora oppugnaret,[3] misit. acriter utrimque usque ad vesperum pugnatum est. solis occasu suas copias Ariovistus multis et inlatis et acceptis vulneribus in castra reduxit. 12. ubi cum castris se tenere Caesar intellexit, ne diutius commeatu prohiberetur, ultra eum locum quo in loco Germani consederant, circiter passus sescentos ab iis, castris idoneum locum delegit acieque triplici instructa ad eum locum venit. primam et secundam aciem in armis esse, tertiam castra munire jussit.

LX.

For miscellaneous questions in review.

EXERCISE.

CAESAR, BELL. GALL. I., CAP. I.–IV.

I. Gallia est omnis divisa in partes tres; quarum unam incolunt Belgae, aliam Aquitania, tertium qui[1] ipsorum[2] lingua Celtae, nostra Galli appellantur. hi omnes lingua, institutis, legibus inter se differunt. Gallos ab Aquitanis Garumna flumen, a Belgis Matrona et Sequana dividit.[3] horum omnium fortissimi sunt Belgae, propterea quod a cultu atque humanitate provinciae longissime absunt, minimeque ad eos mercatores saepe commeant atque ea quae ad effeminandos animos pertinent, important, proximique sunt Germanis, qui trans Rhenum incolunt, quibuscum continenter bellum gerunt. qua de causa[4] Helvetii quoque reliquos Gallos virtute praecedunt, quod fere cotidianis proeliis cum Germanis contendunt, cum aut suis finibus eos prohibent, aut ipsi in eorum finibus bellum gerunt. eorum una pars quam Gallos obtinere dictum est,[5] initium capit a flumine Rhodano; continetur[6] Garumna flumine, Oceano, finibus Belgarum; attingit etiam ab[7] Sequanis et Helvetiis flumen Rhenum; vergit[8] ad septentriones. Belgae ab extremis Galliae finibus oriuntur, pertinent ad inferiorem partem fluminis Rheni, spectant[9] in septentrionem et orientem solem. Aquitania a Garumna flumine ad Pyrenaeos montes et eam partem Oceani, quae est ad Hispaniam, pertinet; spectat inter occasum solis et septentriones.[10]

II. Apud[11] Helvetios longe nobilissimus fuit et ditissimus Orgetorix. Is M. Messala et M. Pisone consulibus regni cupiditate inductus conjurationem nobilitatis fecit et civitati persuasit, ut de finibus suis cum omnibus copiis exirent; perfacile esse,[12] cum virtute omnibus praestarent, totius Galliae imperio[13] potiri. id hoc[14] facilius eis persuasit quod undique loci natura Helvetii continentur; una ex[15] parte flumine Rheno latissimo et altissimo, qui agrum Helvetium a Germanis dividit; altera ex parte monte Jura altissimo qui est inter Sequanos et Helvetios; tertia lacu Lemanno et flumine Rhodano, qui provinciam nostram ab Helvetiis dividit. his rebus[16] fiebat, ut et minus late vagarentur, et minus facile finitimis bellum inferre possent; qua de causa homines bellandi cupidi magno dolore adficiebantur. pro[17] multitudine autem hominum et pro gloria belli atque fortitudinis angustos se fines habere arbitrabantur, qui in longitudinem millia passuum CCXL in latitudinem CLXXX patebant.

III. His rebus adducti et auctoritate Orgetorigis permoti constituerunt ea quae ad proficiscendum pertinerent comparare, jumentorum et carrorum quam maximum numerum coëmere, sementes quam maximas facere, ut in itinere copia frumenti suppeteret, cum proximis civitatibus pacem et amicitiam confirmare. ad eas res conficiendas biennium sibi satis esse duxerunt, in tertium annum profectionem lege confirmant. ad eas res conficiendas Orgetorix deligitur. is sibi[18] legationem ad civitates suscepit. in eo itinere persuadet Castico, Catamantaloedis filio, Sequano, cujus pater regnum in Sequanis multos annos obtinuerat et a senatu populi Romani amicus appellatus erat, ut regnum in civitate sua occuparet, quod pater ante habuerat; itemque Dumnorigi Haeduo, fratri Divitiaci, qui eo tempore principatum in civitate obtinebat ac maxime plebi acceptus[19] erat, ut idem conaretur persuadet, eique filiam suam in matrimonium dat. perfacile factu esse illis probat conata perficere, propterea quod ipse suae civitatis imperium obtenturus esset; non esse dubium, quin totius Galliae plurimum Helvetii possent; se suis copiis suoque exercitu illis regna conciliaturum confirmat. hac oratione adducti inter se fidem et jus jurandum dant et regno occupato[20] per tres potentissimos ac firmissimos populos totius Galliae[21] sese potiri posse sperant.

IV. Ea res Helvetiis per indicium enuntiata. moribus suis Orgetorigem ex vinclis causam dicere[22] coëgerunt. damnatum[23] poenam sequi oportebat, ut igni cremaretur. die constituta causae dictionis[24] Orgetorix ad judicium omnem suam familiam,[25] ad hominum milia decem, undique coëgit et omnes clientes obaeratosque suos quorum magnum numerum habebat, eodem conduxit; per eos ne[26] causam diceret, se eripuit. cum civitas ob eam rem incitata armis jus suum exsequi conaretur multitudinemque hominum ex agris magistratus cogerent, Orgetorix mortuus est;[27] neque abest suspicio, ut Helvetii arbitrantur, quin ipse sibi mortem consciverit.[28]

NOTES.

[The exercises are numbered for convenience of reference, but it is not intended that each shall be a separate lesson, though most of them will be found of the proper length for a single recitation. Some, however, contain matter which should be slowly learned and digested. Such are the topics included under the head of "Preliminary" and of "Inflection of the Verb." In all cases, however, the teacher should divide the work according to the needs and capabilities of his class.

The references to the Grammar at the head of each exercise include only the head matter in larger print, which should be thoroughly and completely memorized. In connection with each lesson the notes should be carefully read over, and, when necessary, explained and illustrated by the teacher. In particular, the teacher should assure himself that all the technical terms of grammar employed are made perfectly clear to the pupils by repeated definition and explanation. Such terms often suggest only the vaguest ideas to a beginner, and time spent in giving an exact knowledge of them is spent to the best advantage possible. In some cases, especially in the lessons on syntax, portions of the notes should be memorized. Such cases are left to the judgment of the teacher, as no directions can be given that will suit all classes.

Besides the references to the Grammar, the pupil should be required to commit to memory the vocabularies, giving the Latin word when the teacher gives the English, or *vice versa*. The English sentences should be written out in Latin, copied on the blackboard, corrected, and given orally as a review along with the following lesson. Such a method is a very exacting one for both teacher and pupil, but is after all the shortest, since it brings in the end far better results with far less work. All the words used in the exercises on forms are given in the vocabularies, that the pupil may have as much time as possible to gain a perfect mastery of the inflections; words used in the exercises on syntax must often be looked for in the index at the end of the book. The omission is intentional, its object being to give the pupil practice in finding words in an alphabetical vocabulary. Few teachers are aware how large a part of the two or three hours spent in translating a page of a Latin author is spent by the beginner in the mechanical task of searching out words in his lexicon. A little more expertness in finding a word will certainly be no loss to the pupil when he takes up his Cæsar or Cicero.

The teacher should not confine himself to the exercises given here, but should give various oral exercises, taking a short sentence and varying it; changing the number or person of the subject, the tense, mood or voice of the verb, etc. That there should be constant practice in repeating and writing inflectional forms is so self-evident that it is unnecessary to dwell upon it here. Moreover, from the very first the pupil should be trained to notice the ending of the inflected words. Such a habit, formed at the beginning, will do much to prevent the blundering in translation that always results from a disregard of the meaning and force of flectional syllables. Too great stress cannot be given at the beginning to the difference between English and Latin in their methods of expressing the relation of words to one another, the former chiefly by prefixing something to the significant word; the latter, by adding something. The pupil should be made to see at the very beginning that in *virtutis*, for example, it is the final syllable that expresses the relation which is expressed in English by the preposition "of"; and the rest of the word which gives the meaning "courage."]

I.

The preliminary definitions and principles should be taken slowly and carefully, and special pains should be taken with pronunciation and accent. As soon as the pupil has memorized the rules of quantity and accent, he should be given practice in pronouncing words, pointing out long and short syllables, etc. Any page of the exercises will furnish material for such training. The teacher may, if he chooses, assign certain portions to be read over in advance as a part of the lesson, and require the pupil to point out all syllables, the quantity of which can be determined by inspection.

The rules of euphony of vowels and consonants may properly be omitted in the reading of the notes, until flectional forms, that serve to illustrate them, are reached. Such will be found chiefly in the consonant-declension and the verb.

II.

Rules of Syntax. (To be carefully memorized.)
The nominative is used as the subject of a finite verb.
The finite verb agrees with its subject in person and number.
The predicate-noun agrees with the subject in case.

(The teacher should assure himself that every pupil has a clear and definite idea of the meaning of "subject," "finite verb," "agrees," "predicate-noun," etc.)

1. ē stands only before consonants; ex before both consonants and vowels.—2. nōn precedes the word it limits.—3. The Latin has no articles. causa, for example, may be translated *cause, a cause,* or *the cause,* as the sense of the passage requires.—4. The verb of a Latin sentence is more commonly at the end.—5. Words in brackets are to be omitted in translating into Latin.—6. The Latin has no words corresponding to the English introductory *there* and *it*. These words should therefore be omitted in translating into Latin. "There is no cause" becomes in Latin "cause is not" (i.e. does not exist).

III.

1. causā (abl.) means "*for the sake*," and stands after the genitive that limits it; e.g. gloriae causā, *for glory's sake, for the sake of glory.* —2. *You* may be translated into Latin by either the singular or the plural. In the earlier exercises the pupil should write both forms.— 3. use cum.

IV.

Questions answered by *yes* or *no* are indicated in Latin, not as in English, by putting the verb before the subject, but by the use of the interrogative particles -nĕ and nŭm.

A question is asked by appending -nĕ to the prominent or emphatic word, which is regularly put first in the sentence; e.g. estne causa? "*Is* there a cause?" causane est? "Is there a *cause?*"

The insertion of a negative word, as in English, shows that the answer *yes* is expected. -nĕ is appended to the negative as the prominent word. nōnne causa est? "Is there not a cause?"

Num is used when the answer *no* is expected. It stands regularly at the beginning of the sentence. num causa est? "Is there a cause?" (= There is no cause, is there?).

Answers are usually given by repeating some words of the question.

1. ā stands only before consonants; ăb before both vowels and consonants.—2. Abl. without a prep. Compare No. 7 of the Latin exercise.

V.

Rules of Syntax.

The adjective agrees with the noun it limits in gender, number and case.
The accusative is used as the direct object of an action.

The inflection of an a-stem verb in the pres. ind. act. is given in the vocabulary. The pupil should carefully learn the endings. Take notice that **occupo** and **importo** are inflected in the same way as **pugno**. The pres. infin. act. (ending -ārĕ) is also given.

The Latin has no progressive or emphatic forms of conjugation. **pugnat** may be translated "*he fights,*" "*he is fighting,*" or "*he does fight,*" according to the connection.

1. Adjectives are often used substantively as in English; e.g. **amicus** = a friendly man; i.e. a friend. — 2. **populi** may be either gen. sg. or nom. pl. here. Translate the sentence in both ways. — 3. Translate **amici** in this sentence as an adjective, but in the following one as a noun.

VI.

Rule of Syntax.

The dative is used as the indirect object.

(The teacher should make the meaning of "indirect object" perfectly clear by repeated illustration.)

1. **alius . . . alius** = one . . . another; **alii . . . alii** = some . . . others; **alter . . . alter** = the one . . . the other. — 2. **do** is peculiar in having ă in the endings -ămŭs, -ătĭs, while other a-stem verbs have -āmŭs, -ātĭs. So in the infin. **dărĕ**. — 3. i.e. *to my son;* indirect object.

VII.

Rule of Syntax

The vocative is used to denote the person or thing spoken to.

1. Verbs meaning "call," "name," etc., take two direct objects as in English, one of which becomes subject when the verb is passive; the other a predicate-noun. — 2. "They are called," etc. **Galli** is the predicate-noun, not the subject. — 3. "On the next day." — 4. See VI., note 1. — 5. Compare No. 1 of the Latin exercise. — 6. The nominative is regularly used for the vocative in the plural, and in the singular when there is no separate vocative form. — 7. Use **ob**. — 8. Compare No. 9 of the Latin exercise. — 9. Use the plural.

VIII.

Rule of Syntax.

The appositive agrees with the noun it limits in case.

Before going on with the exercises, the pupil should thoroughly master this lesson, and be able to inflect any consonant stem, on knowing the nom. and gen. sg. and the gender. 1. adsŭm and absŭm are inflected like sŭm; ăd or ăb being prefixed to each form. — 2. Compare VI., note 1, and notice that alter, not alius, is used when only two things are spoken of. — 3. Compare No. 1 of the Latin sentences.

IX.

1. Less of corn; i.e. less corn. — 2. "Many and great" = the English "many great," etc. — 3. Hither Gaul; i.e. nearer Gaul, — the valley of the Po. — 4. "Old" must agree with the understood noun, "war."

X.

Rule of Syntax.

The accusative is used to denote extent of time or space.

This lesson also needs special care. The teacher should require the pupil to tell the class of each i-stem; to repeat the endings until they are entirely familiar, and to consult the lists in [99] whenever a new i-stem is met with, to determine its form in doubtful cases.
1. Use pl. of fĭnĭs.

XI.

1. "Orders to the province," i.e. levies on, etc.; orders the province to furnish. — 2. "Is burning," i.e. is being burned. Use passive.

XII.

1. inter se, "mutually." Translate *each other* or *one another*, preceded by *to, for, from*, or any preposition that the English idiom requires. — 2. See Gr. [99]. — 3. Translate "*for marriage*"; *in* with acc. — 4. Use abl. without a prep.

XIII.

Time will be saved by stopping on the review of the declensions until the pupils have thoroughly mastered them.

The irregularities of the words given in the vocabulary should be learned from [115] and [110]; other irregular nouns should be learned in the same way as they are met with hereafter.

1. Translate "from" or "because of."—2. Translate "much of blood." Compare IX., note 1.—3. At home; **domi**, locative.—4. Use **in**.

XIV.

The first ten numerals should be learned, also *centum* and *mille*, and the method of formation of the others noticed.
1. The acc. **domum** means "home," "homeward"; the locative **domi**, "at home."—2. Use **abest**.—3. Use **in** w. acc.—4. Abl. without a prep.

XV.

1. "On one side."—2. "Very high." The superlative often means "very."—3. "It is very hard, etc." Literally, "to import, etc., is very hard." The infinitive is used, as in English, as subject, but there is no introductory word. Compare II., note 6. An infinitive thus used, being an indeclinable noun, is neuter, and the predicate-adjective must agree with it in the neuter singular.

XVI.

1. **exterus, inferus** and **superus** are rarely found in the positive.—2. **quam** before a superlative emphasizes it; e.g. **quam maximus**, "the very greatest," "the greatest possible."—3. "Three fourths."—4. "The nearest route," i.e. shortest.—5. **summus mons** = "top of the mountain." So **imus mons** = foot of the mountain.—6. Translate "nearest cities."—7. Translate "many and large."

XVII.

1. **et ... et** = both ... and.—2. **ego et tu** is the usual order of the personal pronouns in Latin.—3. **cum** is appended to the ablative case of the personal pronouns; **vobiscum** = cum vobis.—4. Express *too* by using the comparative.—Use **abest**.—6. **inter se**; see XII., note 1.—7. Use **fines**.

XVIII.

When used adjectively **is, ille** and **iste** correspond nearly to the English *this* or *that*; **ipse** to *self* (*myself, himself*, etc., according to the word it limits). All of them are often used substantively, and are translated by *he, she* or *it*; **ipse**, being emphatic, may be translated by emphasizing the English pronoun, or by adding *self*.
1. **satis** is often used with the verb "*be*" as an indeclinable predicate-adjective.—2. **res novae**, "new things," a change in government, revolution.—3. See XVI., note 2.

XIX.

Hic, when used adjectively, means *this;* **idem,** *same.* Both are often used substantively, and, like **is** and **ille,** have the general force of personal pronouns; *he, she, it.*
1. Use **fines.** — 2. Use **absum.**

XX.

Rule of Syntax.

The relative pronoun agrees with its antecedent in gender, number and person.
1. Translate "minds." — 2. Translate "more of land,". **plus agri.**

XXI.

The preliminary lessons on verbal inflections may be taken in connection with Lessons XXII. to XXIX., instead of memorizing the whole at once. But the teacher should see that all of this preliminary matter is thoroughly mastered before leaving the verb and passing to the exercises in Syntax.

The lessons that follow on the verb-forms should not be taken too rapidly. The pupil should master the lists of verbal endings thoroughly, and the teacher should give him practice in repeating these rather than in repeating the model verb given in the foot-notes. There should be constant practice in analyzing the verb-forms into their elements of stem, sign, and suffix, until the pupil can tell any one of them at a glance. Constant practice in writing inflections on the board is of course indispensable.

XXII.

Rules of Syntax.

The indicative is used to make a statement directly.
The indicative is used to ask a question directly.
The imperative is used to give a command directly.
The subjunctive is used to make a statement doubtfully.
The subjunctive is used to ask a question doubtfully.
The subjunctive is used to give a command doubtfully (e.g. in *exhortations, wishes, requests,* or *mild commands*).

1. Deponent verbs are to be translated as active forms. — 2. **do, dăre,** has short **ă** as stem vowel. Gr. 226. — 3. The gerund corresponds to the English verbal noun in *-ing.* — 4. visit, **commeo ad;** lit. "travel to."

XXIII.

1. See XV., note 1.—2. Abl. without a prep.—3. See XXII., note 4.—4. royal power; regnum.—5. fines.—6. Use in w. acc.—7. "The same thing which I" [attempt]; idem quod, etc.—8. Use plur.—9. nuntio.—10. Use fut. In English the present tense is often used, as here, of actions really future in time, especially in subordinate clauses. The Latin is more exact in the use of the tenses. Notice also that the relative pronoun is omitted in this sentence in English, but must be inserted in the Latin; "battles which you shall see."

XXIV.

1. "for which reason," or simply "therefore."—2. "give a journey."—3. "great marches."—4. "nearest route."—5. "him" refers to the subject; use the proper case of sui. The prep. cum is appended to the abl. case of the personal pronouns. See XVII., note 3.—6. Use iter.

XXV.

1. "Takes its beginning from"; i.e. begins at...—2. Use e or ex.—3. Compare XXIV., note 5.

XXVI.

1. Use ablative without a prep.—2. "This news" = these things, haec.—3. Use future. Compare XXIII., note 10.

XXVII.

The forms of verbs given in the vocabulary are the first three of the "principal parts." See Gr. 168, 169.

1. Use imperf. tense.—2. Use future perf. The "assembling" is to be finished before the "giving."—3. "to the bank"; ad w. acc.—4. See XXIV., note 2.

XXVIII.

The force and construction of the forms from the simple stem cannot be clearly given until the pupil has gone further, as most of them have no corresponding forms in English. Meanwhile the supine may be translated by the English infinitive, and the fut. act. participle by "about to." The perf. pass. participle corresponds to the English pass. participle; e.g. dătus = "given," or "*having been given*"; dătūrus, "about to give," etc.

From this point the teacher should require the principal parts of all verbs, and the form of each stem, with the manner of formation of

NOTES. 79

the present and perfect stems as shown in the Gr. 158–162 and 164–167. Verbs in the vocabularies, without any meaning added, have been already defined in preceding vocabularies.
1. "easy to do." — 2. "to ask for." — 3. Compare the second Latin sentence. — 4. Abl. without a prep. — 5. **factu.** — 6. Use c. — 7. Use a. — 8. **fines.**

XXIX.

1. i.e. is now divided; has been divided. Use the perf. tense. The present would mean "is being divided," "is now undergoing division." — 2. Use future perf. Compare XXIII., note 10, and XXVII., note 2. — 3. Use c.

XXX.

1. The pres. part. **praesens** usually means "present," perhaps because **adsum** lacks the participle. — 2. "would be able"; see Gr. 317. — 3. "it is not advantageous, etc." — 4. **locus.** — 5. Perfect tense. — 6. Abl. without a prep. — 7. Use the singular. A finite verb sometimes agrees with the nearest subject, and is understood with the others. — 8. "One hundred and twenty thousands of men."

XXXI.

1. **debebant,** "were under obligation." As the English *ought* has no past tense, some other expression of the same force must be used here. — 2. "from one another." — 3. Use dative case to express *on* here. — 4. Translate "nations which are beyond the Rhine." — 5. Use fut. tense.

XXXII.

1. Translate "to be able very much" (**plurimum**). — 2. "with," **apud.** — 3. "many taken enemies." — 4. Pres. **malo,** I prefer. Translate "rather . . . than" by **quam.**

XXXIII.

1. Compounds of **eo** almost always drop the v of the perfect stem. See Gr. [12] (c). — 2. "to their friends." — 3. Abl. without a prep. — 4. Future tense.

XXXIV.

1. **per me,** "for all of me," "as far as I am concerned." — 2. Use **nolite** with the infin., "be unwilling to, etc." — 3. Use c. — 4. Use future perf. — 5. Compare XXXI., note 3. — 6. "you may" = "it is permitted to you."

Exercises on Syntax.

[The exercises on syntax given here are not enough to give the pupil a thorough training, but are intended to cover the more important and common constructions, and give him enough familiarity with them to begin the translation of a Latin author. The teacher should keep in mind the fact that constant repetition is the only way to make a principle familiar to the learner, and also that pupils find such repetition and training much less irksome at the beginning of their study than later.]

XXXV.

1. **audeo** is semi-deponent; see Gr. [210] (*g*). — 2. **tres partes** = three-fourths. — 3. See Gr. [208]. — 4. Translate **in Sequanos** "among the Sequani." — 5. See Gr. [262], end. — 6. Abl. without a prep. — 7. "For" is often used in English to express extent of time and space. — 8. Translate "thought himself to be able," etc. — 9. Use **dum** with present tense.

XXXVI.

1. **quibuscum**; see XVII, note 3. — 2. "The Helvetians have in mind," Gr. 270. — 3. Dat. with a compound of **prae**, Gr. [269], end. — 4. "advantageous," lit. "for an advantage." Gr. [272]. — 5. Translate "nothing of left," i.e. of remainder, **nihil reliqui**. — 6. "for an aid to Cæsar." — 7. "neighboring to." — 8. "what of business." — 9. "into a province," **in** with acc. — 10. See Gr. [269]. — 11. "on account of," **propter**.

XXXVII.

1. ("was able very much," i.e.) "had great influence." — 2. See Gr. [208]. — 3. ("asks from him alone those things," i.e.) questions him privately about, etc. — 4. Translate "one hundred and ten of thousands."

XXXVIII.

1. **tridui**, see Gr. [284]. — 2. See Gr. [284], near end. — 3. (foot-soldiers equally many in number, i.e.) "the same number of foot-soldiers." — 4. "once and again" i.e. repeatedly, several times. — 5. Translate "more of sorrow." — 6. Use **ex**.

XXXIX.

1. See Gr. [285], end. — 2. See Gr. [257]. — 3. **res militaris** = warfare. — 4. feelings; **animus**, lit. soul, mind.

XLI.

1. See Gr. [297]. — 2. See Gr. [297], end. — 3. "and those who." The antecedent is often implied in the relative. — 4. See Gr. [269], end.

NOTES. 81

—5. Translate "many things," multa.—6. Translate "it was fought." See Gr. [234].—7. "In war." bello; lit. "by war."

XLII.

1. See Gr. [299].—2. inter se.—3. Use abl. without a prep. The Latin uses an abl. of means; "kept in his army by means of the camp." —4. aperto latere; "on the open (i.e. undefended) side." The left side was covered by the shield.—5. prima nocte; in the first part of the night.

XLIII.

1. The perfect means "am wont"; plup. "was wont," etc. —2. See Gr. [234].—3. injussu (found only in the abl.) means "with the no-order," i.e. without the order of, etc. —4. Translate "in whom." —5. "faith of all things," i.e. confidence in all matters.—6. "in the third watch." —7. "at what interval he was wont," i.e. at the interval, at which, etc.—8. in colle medio; lit. on the middle of the hill. Medius, like summus, imus, primus, etc., sometimes refers to a part of the word it limits. Compare XVI., note 5.—9. "a thousand and five hundred paces." —10. intra fines.

XLIV.

The pupil should carefully read Gr. [307] and take note of the different ways of translating the ablative absolute. The absolute construction, though not common in English, is a favorite one in Latin. In some of the sentences given in the exercise more than one way of translation is possible, and the teacher should require the pupil to give them all, and tell the modification expressed,— time, cause, concession, etc.

1. gratulatum is supine.— 2. on the right wing. — 3. viribus may be dative (Gr. [269]) or ablative (Gr. [297]). Both cases are found with confido.—4. Active forms in English must often be changed to the passive in translating into Latin, since the Latin has no perfect active participle. So here, translate "our cavalry having been driven back." — 5. "This speech having been delivered."

XLV.

Illustrations of "sequence of tenses" will come in the next exercise and the following, when the subjunctive in subordinate clauses has been introduced.

1. nihil is usually found only in nom. and acc., but a regularly declined o-stem is found in the old Latin, and the abl. nihilo occurs with

minus to denote degree of difference.—2. Supply **esse.** Certain forms of **sum** are often omitted. For **bono animo,** see Gr. 305.—3. Use perf.—4. Translate "having set out." The Latin is more exact than the English in the use of tenses. The perfect must be used here, because the *setting out* takes place before the *coming.* A present participle would imply that it took place at the same time.—5. Use present. See Gr. [309].

XLVI.

[The exercises given in this and the next lesson are too few to give the necessary training on subjunctive uses, but the following lessons will contain illustrations, and the teacher should require a reason for every subjunctive met with from this time forth. Subjunctives in conditional sentences are purposely omitted, that the various forms of conditional sentences may be given together in a later lesson.

The pupil should take notice that the English usually expresses purpose by the infinitive, and should translate accordingly. Most of the explanation necessary is left to the teacher, who should give minute and patient training on the moods until the pupil has formed the habit of noticing the force of a subjunctive, and the modification of thought expressed by its use.]

1. See Gr. 323.—2. **quin.** See Gr. [326].—3. Use rel. pr. and compare No. 3 of the Latin exercise.—4. Use **qualis.**—5. Subj. A clause of characteristic. See Gr. [326].—6. "room of throwing... was not given."

XLVII.

1. "although."—2. an enemy turned away, i.e. an enemy fleeing. —3. What difference of meaning would the indicative give? See Gr. [328].—4. "In what direction."—5. Translate "he [being] intercessor"; abl. abs.—6. Abl. See Gr. [297], end.—7. Compare No. 4 of the Latin exercise.

XLVIII.

1. See Gr. [269], end.—2. See Gr. [297].—3. **velle** is the object of a verb of saying implied in **legatos mittit.** Insert "saying" in translation. —4. Use abl. abs.—5. i.e. "that the Germans should get used," etc. Notice the use of "for" in English before an infinitive phrase. The sentence can mean also that crossing is dangerous for the Germans, in which case "Germans" would be dative. Write it in both ways.—6. Translate "in the sway."—7. i.e. kept themselves there. Translate accordingly.—8. After verbs of *promising*, etc., the exactness of the Latin

requires the future. As there is no future infinitive, the pres. infin. of the act. periphrastic conjugation must be used, as it is nearly equivalent to a future. Translate "that the matter was going to be for a care to him." — 9. Translate "make an end for his injuries," and notice that a future form, as in the first part, is required.

XLIX.

1. Translate receptos as an independent clause. So usi, in the next sentence, as if in the same construction as proficiscantur. — 2. ut is omitted. See Gr. [325], mid. — 3. "a fleeing enemy." The participle is equivalent to a simple adjective. — 4. Translate petentibus by a relative clause. — 5. Translate "frightened." — 6. Subj. See Gr. 322. — 7. "having seen this," conspicati. — 8. "three days having intervened." — 9. "a council having been called together, he upbraided," etc. — 10. Translate "held the brought-back [ones] in the number of enemies." — 11. See Gr. [268], end. — 12. "having pursued ... slew," etc. — 13. of them; ex his.

L.

1. "in the course of his inquiry." The abl. without a prep. would mean "by inquiring." — 2. "made the enemy a chance," or in English idiom, "gave them a chance to fight." — 3. Use abl. abs. "The hope of a return home having been taken away." — 4. "for undergoing," ad with gerundive. — 5. "makes an end of speaking." — 6. ad with gerundive; a common way of expressing purpose. — 7. Translate "room of throwing." — 8. sui opprimendi causā. The genitive of the gerund or gerundive, with causā, is often used to express purpose. For sui, see Gr. [348].

LI.

1. In translating, insert "asking" before the last clause. It is implied in conclamavit. For the mood, see Gr. 323. — 2. quidem emphasizes the word before it. Translate "not even by giving hostages." — 3. Translate "refrain from going on, etc." — 4. Subj. See Gr. [328]. — 5. Use abl. abs. Translate "he" by se. Why ? — 6. placuit ei ut mitteret; lit. it pleased him to send. — 7. See XLVIII., note 8.

LII.

1. venit in spem, "entertains a hope." Notice that expressions of hoping, doubting, etc., are modified by the same form of condition as hypothetical statements. — 2. "if I had any need." Gr. 270. — 3. See note 1 above. — 4. Use quin; Gr. [326].

LIII.

The left-hand column in this exercise, and the following, contains sentences in the direct form; the other contains the same sentences made dependent on verbs of *saying*, etc. The teacher should call the attention of the pupil to the changes of tense required by the rule of sequence, as well as the changes of mood.—1. See Gr. [268].—2. Use ullus.—3. When a fut. indic. becomes infin. the act. periphrastic infin. must be used, as the future lacks the infin.

LIV.

1. These verbs are fut. perf.—2. Perf. " where we have taken our stand"; constitimus.—3. ut w. subj.—4. infinitive.

LV.

The pupil should be required to change all the sentences of these exercises to the direct form.

1. Notice that the relative clauses at the end are not a part of what is said to Cæsar, but are remarks added by the writer. They are in the indicative, therefore. See Gr. [322], end.—2. pro.—3. Translate "that there were two parties of all Gaul."—4. Use impf. " When they [had fought and] were [still] fighting many years.—5. de, concerning.—6. " summoned by means of pay."—7. " on account of this thing."—8. "bound neither by an oath, nor," etc.

[The remaining lessons, LVI. to LX., are intended to give additional drill on the various ways of expressing time and place in Latin, and at the same time to serve as a general review of the more common constructions of syntax. Many of the sentences in them are repeated from previous lessons. Not only the head matter, but also the notes of the Grammar, should be studied in connection with them.]

LVI.

1. See Gr. 339.—2. ad with the name of a town means *to* or *in* the vicinity of.—3. See Gr. [297], end.—4. minus often has the same force as non.

LVII.

1. See LVI., note 2.

LVIII.

1. The adj. mortuus, dead, with the verb sum, supplies the lacking tenses of morior.—2. a. d. = ante diem.—3. See Gr. [330].—

4. "a while." — 5. ad with dates means *about.* — 6. Cassian war, i.e. war with Cassius. — 7. See Gr. [330], mid.

LIX.

1. "early in the night." — 2. "it will come to pass." — 3. See Gr. 325.

LX.

1. **qui = ii qui,** as often. "those who." — **ipsorum** = an emphatic "their." — 3. See Gr. [267], end. — 4. "for this reason." The rel. clause is the favorite construction in Latin, and is often used where the English idiom requires a demonstrative. — 5. "which it has been said that the Gaul's occupy." — 6. "is bounded." — 7. "off the Sequani"; i.e. on that side of the country where the Sequani dwell. So a **dextra** means "on the right," etc. — 8. "slopes"; i.e. extends. — 9. "they look to the north"; i.e. their country stretches away in a northerly direction. — 10. The whole phrase means "north-west." — 11. **apud** before the name of a man means "at the house of"; before the name of a people, "in the country of," "among." — 12. Insert "saying" which is implied in **persuasit.** — 13. See Gr. [297]. — 14. **hoc . . . quod,** "for the reason that." — 15. "on" one side. — 16. See Gr. 295. — 17. "in proportion to," "considering." — 18. **sibi suscepit,** "took on himself." — 19. See Gr. 344. **plebi acceptus** = popular. — 20. "when they have seized," or "after seizing," abl. abs. expressing time. See Gr. [307]. — 21. See Gr. [290]. — 22. "compel him to plead in chains," i.e. arrest and bring to trial. — 23. **damnatum** limits the understood object of **sequi.** "it was right that the punishment should overtake the condemned [criminal], i.e. the law required this punishment to be inflicted on him if he were found guilty. — 24. "appointed day of the pleading," i.e. day set for the pleading, or for his trial. — 25. **familia,** slaves; not family in the English sense. — 26. escaped trial, lit. rescued himself in order not to plead his case. — 27. died. The adj. **mortuus** supplies the place of the lacking participle of **morior,** and with the verb **sum** has the same meaning as the complete tenses. — 28. The Latin expression for "committed suicide."

LATIN INDEX.

A.

A. = **Aulŭs.**

ā (prep. w. abl.), *from, away from; by* (to denote the agent); **a dextro cornu,** *on the right wing.*

ăb (prep. w. abl.), *from, away from, by.*

ăbeō, -īrĕ, -ĭī, -ĭtŭm, to *go away, depart.*

abstĭneō, -tĭnērĕ, -tĭnuī, -tentŭm, to *hold off, abstain, refrain.*

absŭm, ăbessĕ, āfuī, āfŭtŭrŭs, to *be away, be absent, be distant.*

ac (conj.), *and.*

acceptŭs, -ă, -ŭm, *acceptable;* **plēbī acceptŭs,** *popular.*

accĭdō, -cĭdĕrĕ, -cĭdī, to *happen.*

accĭpĭō, -cĭpĕrĕ, -cēpī, -ceptŭm, to *receive.*

ăciēs, -ēī, *edge; line* (of battle); *army* (in order of battle).

acrĭtĕr (adv.), *sharply, fiercely.*

ăd (prep. w. acc.), *to, toward; for; near, adjoining.*

addūcō, -dūcĕrĕ, -duxī, -ductŭm, to *lead, move, influence.*

ădeō, -īrĕ, -ĭī, -ĭtŭm, to *go to, go near, approach, visit.*

adfĕrō, -ferrĕ, -tŭlī, -lātŭm, to *bring, bring on.*

adfĭcĭō, -fĭcĕrĕ, -fēcī, -fectŭm, to *affect.*

adscendō, -scendĕrĕ, -scendī, -scensŭm, to *ascend.*

adsciscō, -sciscĕrĕ, -scīvī, -scītŭm, to *take to, join to* (*one's self*).

adsŭm, ădessĕ, adfuī, adfŭtūrŭs, to *be present, be by.*

adventŭs, -ūs, *coming, arrival.*

advertō, -vertĕrĕ, -vertī, -versŭm (Gr. [268]), to *turn to;* **ănĭmŭm advertĕrĕ,** to *turn the mind to, notice.*

Aemĭlĭŭs, -ī, *Æmilius.*

aequŭs, -ă, -ŭm, *equal, even, level.*

aestās, -ātĭs, *summer.*

affĕrō; see **adfĕrō.**

afflcĭō, -fĭcĕrĕ, -fēcī, -fectŭm, see **adfĭcĭō.**

ăgĕr, agrī (Gr. 66), *land, farmland, country.*

ăgō, ăgĕrĕ, ēgī, actŭm, to *do, deal,* to *hold, conduct,* to *talk.*

ălĭquĭs, -quă, -quĭd (Gr. 141), *some one.*

ălĭŭs, -ă, -ŭd (Gr. 71), *another;* **ălĭŭs ... ălĭŭs,** *one ... another,* **ălĭī ... ălĭī,** *some ... others.*

Allŏbrŏgēs, -ŭm, *Allobroges* (a Gallic tribe).

Alpēs, -ĭŭm (F.), *Alps.*

altĕr, -ă, -ŭm (Gr. 71), *the other;* **altĕr ... altĕr,** *the one ... the other;* pl. **altĕrī ... altĕrī,** *one party ... the other party.*

altĭtŭdō, -ĭnĭs, *height, depth.*

altŭs, -ă, -ŭm, *high, deep.*

ămĭcĭtĭă, -ae, *friendship.*

ămĭcŭs, -ă, -ŭm, *friendly,* often as a noun, **amicus,** *friend.*

āmittō, -mittĕrĕ, -mīsī, -missŭm, to *lose.*

ămō, -ārĕ, -ăvī, -ātŭm, to *love.*

LATIN INDEX.

amplius (adv.), *more.*
anceps, -cipitis (Gr. [115]), *double, doubtful.*
angustus, -ă, -ŭm, *narrow.*
animadvertō, -vertĕrĕ, -vertī, -versŭm, to *notice.*
animŭs, -ī, *spirit, mind, courage.*
annŭs, -ī, *year.*
antĕ (prep. w. acc.), *before.*
antĕ (adv.), *before, formerly.*
antĕ diĕm (Gr. [268]), *the day before.*
antīquŭs, -ă, -ŭm, *ancient, old.*
appellō, -ārĕ, -āvī, -ātŭm, to *call.*
appĕtō, -pĕtĕrĕ, -pĕtīvī, -pĕtītŭm, to *seek.*
Aprīlīs, -īs, *April;* īdūs aprīlēs, *Apr.* 13 (Gr. 496).
ăpŭd (prep. w. acc.), *among, with.*
Aquītānĭă, -ae, *Aquitania* (S. W. France).
Aquītānŭs, -ă, -ŭm, *Aquitanian.*
Arăr, -ărīs (Gr. [102]), the *Arar* (river, now *Saone*).
arbĭtrŏr, -ārī, -ātŭs, to *think, judge.*
Ariovistŭs, -ī, *Ariovistus* (a German king).
armă, -ōrŭm, *arms.*
arx, arcīs, *fort, citadel.*
ascendō, -scendĕrĕ, -scendī, ascensŭm; see adscendō.
ascensŭs, -ūs, *ascent.*
atquĕ (conj.), *and.*
attingō, -tingĕrĕ, -tĭgī, -tactŭm, to *reach to, touch.*
auctōrītās, -ātīs, *authority, influence.*
audācĭŭs (adv.), *more boldly.*
audeō, audērĕ, ausŭs (Gr. [216]), to *dare.*
aufĕrō, auferrĕ, abstŭlī, ablātŭm, to *take away.*
aut (conj.), *or;* aut ... aut, *either ... or.*

autĕm (conj.), *but, moreover.*
auxĭlĭŭm, -ī, *help, aid;* pl. auxĭlĭă, *auxiliary troops.*
āvertō, -vertĕrĕ, -vertī, -versŭm, to *turn away, turn aside;* āversŭs, *turned away, fleeing.*

B.

barbărŭs, -ă, -ŭm, *barbarous.*
Belgae, -ārŭm, *Belgians.*
bellō, -ārĕ, -āvī, -ātŭm, to *war, make war.*
bellŭm, -ī, *war.*
Bĭbractĕ, -īs (N.) (Gr. [100]), *Bibracte* (a town).
bĭduŭm, -ī, *two days.*
bienniŭm, -ī, *two years.*
Bojī, -ōrŭm, *Boii* (a tribe).
bŏnŭs, -ă, -ŭm (Gr. [123]), *good.*

C.

C. = Gaius.
cădō, cădĕrĕ, cĕcĭdī, cāsum, to *fall, happen.*
Caesăr, -ărīs, *Cæsar.*
călămĭtās, -ātīs, *defeat, misfortune.*
căpĭō, căpĕrĕ, cēpī, captŭm, to *take, receive.*
carrŭs, -ī, *cart.*
Cassĭānŭs, -ă, -ŭm, *Cassian, of Cassius.*
Cassĭŭs, -ī, *Cassius.*
castellŭm, -ī, *fort, redoubt.*
Castĭcŭs, -ī, *Casticus.*
castră, -ōrŭm, *camp.*
cāsŭs, -ūs, *fall, chance, accident.*
Catamantaloedīs, -īs, *Catamantaloedis.*
causă, -ae, *cause, reason;* abl. causā, *for the sake;* causam dīcere, to *plead one's cause, be tried.*
cĕlĕrĭtĕr (adv.), *quickly.*
Celtae, -ārŭm, *Celts.*
censŭs, -ūs, *census, count.*

LATIN INDEX. 89

centŭm, *hundred.*
centŭrĭŏ, -ōnĭs, *centurion.*
certĭŏr, -ĭŭs, *more certain;* certĭōrĕm făcĕrĕ, *to make (one) more certain,* to *inform;* certĭŏr fĭĕrī, *to be informed.*
cĭbārĭă, -ōrŭm, *food;* cĭbārĭă mōlĭtă, *ground food;* i.e. *meal.*
Cimbrī, -ōrŭm, *Cimbri.*
circĭtĕr (adv.), *about.*
circuĭtŭs, -ūs, *circuit.*
circŭm (prep. w. acc.), *around, about.*
cĭtĕrĭŏr, -ĭŭs (Gr. [123]), *nearer.*
cīvĭtās, -ātĭs, *state.*
clĭens, -ntĭs, *client.*
cŏĕmŏ, -ĕmĕrĕ, -ēmī, -ēmptum, to *buy up, buy.*
[cœpĭŏ, cœpĕrĕ], cœpī, cœptŭm, to *begin.* (The incomplete tenses are found only in old Latin.)
cognōscŏ, -noscĕrĕ, -nōvī, -nĭtŭm, to *learn;* perf. cognōvī, to *know.*
cōgŏ, cōgĕrĕ, coēgī, coactŭm, to *collect, compel.*
collĭs, -ĭs (m.), *hill.*
collŏcŏ, -ārĕ, -āvī, -ātŭm, to *place, post, settle* (a colony).
collŏquŏr, -lŏquī, -lŏcūtŭs, to *talk with, converse.*
collŏquĭŭm, -ī, *conversation, conference.*
commeātŭs, -ūs, *provisions, supplies.*
commĕmŏrŏ, -ārĕ, -āvī, -ātŭm, to *tell, relate.*
commĕŏ, -ārĕ, -āvī, -ātŭm, to *go and come;* commeo ad, to *visit.*
committŏ, -mittĕrĕ, -mīsī, -missŭm, to *entrust, commit,* to *join* (battle).
commŏdŭs, -ă, -ŭm, *fit, useful, proper.*
commūnĭŏ, -īrĕ, -īvī, -ītŭm, to *wall in, fortify.*

compărŏ, -ārĕ, -āvī, -ātŭm, to *prepare, make ready.*
cōnātŭm, -ī (a thing attempted), *attempt.*
cōnātŭs, -ūs, *attempt.*
concēdŏ, -cēdĕrĕ, -cessī, -cessŭm, to *grant, allow.*
concĭlĭŏ, -ārĕ, -āvī, -ātŭm, to *gain, gain over, get.*
concĭlĭŭm, -ī, *council.*
conclāmŏ, -ārĕ, -āvī, -ātŭm, to *cry out.*
concursŭs, -ūs, *assembling, coming together.*
condūcŏ, -dū cĕrĕ, -duxī -ductŭm, to *bring together, bring along.*
confĕrŏ, -ferrĕ, -tŭlī, -lātŭm, to *collect, bring together,* to *compare;* sē conferrĕ, to *betake one's self, go.*
conflcĭŏ, -fĭcĕrĕ, -fēcī, -fectŭm, to *do, accomplish, finish.*
confīdŏ, -fīdĕrĕ, -fīsŭs (Gr. [216]), to *trust, confide in.*
confirmŏ, -ārĕ, -āvī, -ātŭm, to *fix, appoint;* to *strengthen, encourage;* to *make* (peace); to *assure, promise.*
conjĭcĭŏ, -jĭcĕrĕ, -jēcī, -jectum, to *throw;* se conjicere, *betake one's self.*
conjūrātĭŏ, -ōnĭs, *conspiracy, league.*
cōnŏr, -ārī, -ātŭs, to *try, attempt.*
conscĭscŏ, -scīcĕrĕ, -scīvī, -scītŭm; sĭbī mortĕm conscĭscĕrĕ, to *kill one's self.*
conscrībŏ, -scrībĕrĕ, -scripsī, -scriptŭm, to *levy* (troops).
Consĭdĭŭs, -ī, *Considius.*
consīdŏ, -sīdĕrĕ, -sēdī, -sessŭm, to *settle, encamp.*
consĭlĭŭm, -ī, *plan.*
consōlŏr, -ārī, -ātŭs, to *console, cheer, encourage.*

conspĭcĭō,-spĭcĕrĕ,-spexī,-spectŭm, to *see, perceive.*
constĭtuō, -ŭĕrĕ, -uī, -ūtŭm, to *determine, decide on, appoint, place.*
consuescō, -suescĕrĕ, -suēvī, suētŭm, to *get used;* perf. consuevi, to *be wont.*
consŭl, -ŭlĭs, *consul.*
contendō, -tendĕrĕ, -tendī, -tentŭm, to *strive, hasten;* to *contend, fight.*
contĭnentĕr (adv), *continually, constantly.*
contĭneō, -tĭnērĕ, -tĭnuī, to *hold in, bound, keep in.*
contĭnuŭs, -ă, -ŭm, *successive.*
contŭmēlĭă, -ae, *insult.*
convĕnĭō, -vĕnīrĕ, -vēnī, -ventŭm, to *come together, meet, assemble.*
conventŭs, -ūs, *meeting, assembly;* pl. *assizes.*
convertō, -vertĕrĕ, -vertī, -versŭm, to *turn, change.*
cōpĭă, -ae, *plenty, supply.* In pl. copiae, *forces, troops.*
cornū,-ūs, *horn, wing*(of an army).
corpŭs, -ŏrĭs, *body.*
cōtĭdĭānŭs, -ă, -ŭm ; see quotid.
Crassŭs, -ī, *Crassus.*
cremō, -ārĕ, -āvī, -ātŭm, to *burn, set on fire.*
cultŭs, -ūs, *civilization, refinement.*
cŭm (prep. w. abl.), *with, along with.*
cŭm (conj.) (Gr. [328], [329], [330]), *when, since, because, although.*
cŭpĭdissĭmē (adv.), *most eagerly.*
cŭpĭdĭtās, -ātĭs, *desire, greed.*
cŭpĭdŭs, -ă, -ŭm, *desirous, fond.*
cūră, -ae, *care.*
cūrō, -ārĕ, -āvī, -ātŭm, to *care for, attend to.*
custōs, -ōdĭs, *guard, sentinel.*

D.

damnō, -ārĕ, -āvī, -ātŭm, to *condemn.*
dē (prep. w. abl.), *down from, from, concerning, about;* dē quartā vĭgĭlĭā, *in the fourth watch, in the course of . . .*
dēbeō, -ērĕ, -uī, -ĭtŭm, to *owe, ought.*
dĕcĕm, *ten.*
dĕcĭmŭs, -ă, -ŭm, *tenth.*
dĕcŭrĭō, -ōnĭs, *decurion* (a military officer).
dēdūcō, -dūcĕrĕ, -duxī, -ductŭm, to *lead, lead down.*
dēfendō, -fendĕrĕ, -fendī, -fensŭm, to *defend.*
dēfētiscŏr, -fētiscī, -fessŭs, to *grow weary;* part. dēfessŭs, *tired, worn out.*
dējĭcĭō, -jĭcĕrĕ, -jēcī, -jectŭm, to *cast down, throw away;* partic. dējectŭs, *disappointed.*
dēlĕgō, -lĕgĕrĕ, -lēgī, -lectŭm, to *choose.*
dēlībĕrō, -ārĕ, -āvī, -ātŭm, to *deliberate, consider.*
dēlĭgō ; see dēlĕgō.
dēmĭnuō, -ŭĕrĕ, -uī, -ūtŭm, to *lessen.*
dēmŭm (adv.), *at last, at length.*
dēsistō, -sistĕrĕ, -stĭtī, destĭtŭm,to *cease from,leave off, desist.*
dēsŭm, deessĕ, dēfuī, dēfūtūrŭs, to *be wanting, be lacking.*
dēterreō, -ērĕ, -uī, -ĭtŭm, to *frighten;* to *hinder.*
deŭs, -ī (Gr. 68), *god.*
dĕvĕhō, -vĕhĕrĕ, -vexī, -vectŭm, to *bring down, bring.*
dextĕr, -ă, -ŭm; also, -tra, -trum, *right, on the right hand; as* a noun, dextră, *the right hand, the right side* or *flank.*
dīcō, dīcĕrĕ, dixī, dictŭm, to *say, tell, appoint, plead* (one's cause).

LATIN INDEX. 91

dictĭŏ, -ōnĭs, *pleading.*
diēs, ēi (c.), *day ; a while.*
diffĕrō, -ferrĕ, -distŭlī, -dīlā-tŭm, to *differ.*
difficĭlĭs, -ĕ (Gr. 121), *hard, difficult.*
dīmittŏ, -mittĕrĕ, -mīsī, missŭm, to *dismiss.*
dīs, dītĭs, *rich.*
discēdŏ, -cēdĕrĕ, -cessī, -cessŭm, to *depart, go out or away.*
dispōnŏ, -pōnĕrĕ, -pŏsuī, -pŏsĭtŭm, to *arrange, place, post.*
diŭ (adv.), *long.*
diūtĭŭs (adv.), *longer.*
Dīvĭcō, -ōnĭs, *Divico.*
dīvĭdŏ, -vĭdĕrĕ, -vīsī, -vīsŭm, to *divide, separate.*
Dīvĭtĭăcŭs, -ī, *Divitiacus.*
dŏ, dărĕ, dĕdī, dătŭm (Gr. 226), to *give, grant.*
dŏlŏr, -ōrĭs, *grief, sorrow.*
dŏmŭs, -ūs (F.) (Gr. [115]), *house, home ;* dŏmī, *at home ;* dŏmŭm, *home, homewards.* (Gr.[273] and [265].)
dŭbĭtātĭŏ, -ōnĭs, *doubt.*
dŭbĭŭs, -ă, -ŭm, *doubtful ;* non est dubium, *there is no doubt.*
dŭcentī, -ae, -ă, *two hundred.*
dūcŏ, dūcĕrĕ, duxī, ductŭm, to *lead, bring ;* to *think, regard ;* dūcĕrĕ In mātrĭmōnĭŭm, or often dūcĕrĕ alone, to *marry* (said of the man).
dŭm (conj.) (Gr. [330]), *while.*
Dumnŏrīx, -ĭgĭs, *Dumnorix.*
duŏ, -ae, -ŏ (Gr. [72]), *two.*
dux, dŭcĭs, *guide, leader.*

E.

ē (prep. w. abl.), *out of, from.*
ĕdŏ, ĕdĕrĕ, ēdī, ēsŭm (Gr. 223), to *eat, consume.*

ēdūcŏ, -dūcĕrĕ, -duxī, -ductŭm, to *lead out, lead forth, bring.*
effēmĭnŏ, -ārĕ, -āvī, -ātŭm, to *weaken, effeminate.*
effĕro, -ferrĕ, extŭlī, ēlātŭm, to *bring forth, bring.*
effĭcĭŏ, -fĭcĕrĕ, -fēcī, -fectŭm; to *make, render.*
ĕgŏ (Gr. 125), *I, me.*
ēgrĕdĭŏr, -grĕdī, -gressŭs, to *go out, set forth.*
ēnuntĭŏ, -ārĕ, āvī, -ātŭm, to *announce, tell, bring news of.*
eŏ, īrĕ, īvī or iī, ĭtŭm (Gr. 227), to *go.*
eō (adv.), *thither.*
eōdĕm (adv.), to *the same place.*
ĕquĕs, -ĭtĭs, *horseman, horse-soldier.*
ĕquĭtātŭs, -ūs, *cavalry.*
ērĭpĭŏ, -rĭpĕrĕ, -rĭpuī, -reptŭm, to *take away ;* to *rescue.*
ĕt (conj.), *and ;* ĕt . . . ĕt, *both . . . and.*
ĕtĭăm (adv.), *also, even.*
ex (prep. w. abl.), *out of, from.*
exeŏ, -īrĕ, -iī, -ĭtŭm, to *go out, go forth, depart.*
exercĭtātĭŏ, -ōnĭs, *training, skill.*
exercĭtŭs, -ūs, *army.*
existĭmŏ, -ārĕ, -āvī, -ātŭm, to *think, believe.*
expectŏ, -ārĕ, -āvī, -ātŭm, to *wait for.*
explōrātŏr, -ōrĭs, *spy, scout.*
exquīrŏ, -quīrĕrĕ, -quīsīvī, -quīsītŭm, to *search out, inquire, inquire into.*
exsĕquŏr, -sĕquī, -sĕcūtŭs, to *carry out, execute.*
extĕrŭs, -ă, -ŭm (Gr. [123]), *outside, outer.*
extĭmŭs, -ă, -ŭm (Gr, [123]), *outermost, farthest.*
extrēmŭs, -ă, -ŭm (Gr. [123]), *outermost, farthest.*

LATIN INDEX.

F.

făcĭlĕ (adv.), *easily.*
făcĭlĭs, -ĕ (Gr. 121), *easy.*
făcĭlĭŭs (adv.), *more easily.*
făcĭŏ, făcĕrĕ, fēcĭ, factŭm, to *make, do.*
factĭŏ, -ōnĭs, *party, faction.*
făcultās, -ātĭs, *supply.*
fămĭlĭă, -ae (Gr. [54]), *household.*
fĕrē (adv.), *almost, nearly.*
fĕrŏ, ferrĕ, tŭlĭ, lātŭm (Gr. 224), *to bear, bring, carry.*
fĕrŭs, -ă, -ŭm, *wild, savage.*
fīdēs, ēī, *faith, belief, promise.*
fīlĭă, -ae (Gr. [54]), *daughter.*
fīlĭŭs, -ī (Gr. 67), *son.*
fīnĭs, -ĭs (c.) (Gr. [90]), *end;* pl. fīnēs, *bounds, land, territories, country.*
fĭnĭtĭmŭs, -ă, -ŭm, *neighboring;* as a noun, *neighbor.*
fīo, fĭĕrī [factŭs] (Gr. 229), *to be made, become, happen.*
firmŭs, -ă, -ŭm, *firm, strong.*
flāgĭtŏ, -ārĕ, -āvī, -ātŭm, to *demand, ask for.*
fleŏ, flērĕ, flēvī, flētŭm, to *weep.*
flētŭs, -ūs, *weeping.*
flŭmĕn, -ĭnĭs, *river.*
flŭŏ, flŭĕrĕ, fluxī, to *flow.*
fortĭs, -ĕ, *bold, brave.*
fortĭtūdŏ, -ĭnĭs, *courage, fortitude.*
fortūnă, -ae, *luck, fortune.*
fossă, -ae, *ditch, moat.*
frātĕr, -trĭs (Gr. 80), *brother.*
frūmentārĭŭs, -ă, -ŭm, *of corn;* rēs frūmentārĭă, *corn supply.*
frūmentŭm, -ī, *corn, grain.*
fŭgă, -ae, *flight.*
fŭgĭtīvŭs, -ă, -ŭm, *fleeing;* as a noun, fŭgĭtīvŭs, *deserter, runaway.*

G.

Găbīnĭŭs, -ī, *Gabinius.*
Gallŭs, -ī, *a Gaul;* pl. Gallī, *the Gauls.*
Gallĭă, -ae, *Gaul* (now *France*).
Gallĭcŭs, -ă, -ŭm, *Gallic.*
Gărumnă, -ae (m.), the *Garonne* (river).
Gĕnuă, -ae, *Genera.*
Germānĭă, -ae, *Germany.*
Germānŭs, -ă, -ŭm, *German;* usually pl. Germānī, the *Germans.*
gĕrŏ, gĕrĕrĕ, gessī, gestŭm, *to manage, carry on, wage* (war).
glōrĭă, -ae, *glory, honor.*
grātĭă, -ae, *favor, popularity;* pl. grātĭae, *thanks;* grātĭās ăgĕrĕ, to *give thanks, thank.*
grātŭlŏr, -ārī, -ātŭs (Gr. [269]), to *congratulate.*

H.

hăbeŏ, -ērĕ, -uī, -ĭtŭm, to *have, hold; deliver* (a speech).
hăbĭtŏ, -ārĕ, -āvī, -ātŭm, to *dwell.*
Haeduŭs, -ă, -ŭm, *Hæduan;* pl. Haeduī, the *Hæduans* (a Gallic tribe).
Harūdēs, -ŭm, *Harudes.*
Helvetĭŭs, -ă, -ŭm, *Helvetian;* pl. Helvetiī, the *Helvetians.*
hībernă, -ōrŭm (neut. pl. of hībernŭs), *winter quarters.*
hĭbernŭs, -ă, -ŭm, *of winter, wintry.*
hĭc, haec, hŏc (Gr. 134), *this; he, she,* &c.
hĭĕmŏ, -ārĕ, -āvī, -ātŭm, to *winter.*
Hispānĭă, -ae, *Spain.*
hŏmŏ, -ĭnĭs, *man, human being.*
hŏnŏr, -ōrĭs, *honor.*
hōră, -ae, *hour.*
hortŏr, -ārī, -ātŭs, to *urge.*

LATIN INDEX. 93

hostIs, -Is, *enemy.*
hūmānĭtās, -ātĭs, *culture, refinement.*

I.

Ĭbĭ (adv.), *there, in that place.*
īdĕm, eădĕm, Ĭdĕm (Gr. 137), *same.*
idōneŭs, -ă, -ŭm, *fit, suitable.*
Idūs, -uŭm (F.), *Ides* (Gr. 490).
ignĭs, -ĭs (Gr. [99]), *fire.*
illĕ, illă, illŭd (Gr. 131), *that, he, she, &c.*
impĕdīmentŭm, -ĭ, *hindrance;* pl. impedimenta, *baggage.*
impĕrĭŭm, -ĭ, *power, sway, military authority.*
impĕrŏ, -ārĕ, -āvī, -ātŭm, to *order, command, levy* (troops).
impĕtrŏ, -ārĕ, -āvī, -ātŭm, to *gain, gain a request.*
impĕtŭs, -ūs, *attack.*
implōrŏ, -ārĕ, -āvī, -ātŭm, to *beg, pray.*
importŏ, -ārĕ, -āvī, -ātŭm, to *import, bring in.*
imprŏbŭs, -ă, -ŭm, *bad, wicked.*
impugnŏ, -ārĕ, -āvī, -ātŭm, to *attack.*
In (prep.) w. abl., *in, on, among;* w. acc., *into, to, toward, for.*
incendŏ, -cendĕrĕ, -cendī, -censŭm, to *set fire to, burn.*
incĭtŏ, -ārĕ, -āvī, -ātŭm, to *rouse up, excite.*
incŏlă, -ae, *inhabitant.*
incŏlŏ, -cŏlĕrĕ, -cŏluī, to *dwell.*
incommŏdŭm, -ĭ, *misfortune, defeat.*
incrēdĭbĭlĭs, -ĕ, *incredible.*
incūsŏ, -ārĕ, -āvī, -ātŭm, to *blame.*
indĕ (adv.), *thence, from there.*
indĭcĭŭm, -ĭ, *information.*
indūcŏ, -dūcĕrĕ, -duxī, -ductŭm, to *lead on, induce; lead.*
infĕrĭŏr, -iŭs (Gr. [123]), *lower.*

infĕrŏ, -ferrĕ, -tŭlī, -lātŭm, to *carry on, wage* (war); to *inflict* (wounds).
infĕrŭs, -ă, -ŭm (Gr. [123]), *lower, inferior.*
influŏ, -fluĕrĕ, -fluxī, to *flow into, empty* (of a river).
ingens, -ntĭs, *huge, great.*
inĭmīcŭs, -ă, -ŭm, *unfriendly, hostile.*
inĭtĭŭm, -ĭ, *beginning.*
injūrĭă, -ae, *wrong, injury.*
injussū, *without orders.*
insĕquŏr, -sĕquī, -sĕcūtŭs, to *pursue, attack.*
insignĭă, -iŭm, *equipments, insignia.*
instĭtūtŭm, -ĭ, *custom.*
instruŏ, -struĕrĕ, -struxī, -structŭm, to *draw up, arrange.*
intellĕgŏ, -lĕgĕrĕ, -lexī, -lectŭm, to *know, understand.*
intĕr (prep. w. acc.), *between, among;* intĕr sē, *mutually, with each other, with one another, &c.* See XII. note 1.
intercēdŏ, -cēdĕrĕ, -cessī, -cessŭm, to *intervene.*
intĕreă (adv.), *meanwhile.*
interfĭcĭŏ, -fĭcĕrĕ, -fēcī, -fectŭm, to *slay, kill.*
intĕrĭm (adv.), *meanwhile.*
intĕrĭŏr, -iŭs (Gr. [123]), *inner, interior.*
intermittŏ, -mittĕrĕ, -mīsī, -missŭm, to *leave off.*
intervallŭm, -ĭ, *interval, distance.*
intĭmŭs, -ă, -ŭm (Gr. [123]), *inmost.*
invĕnĭŏ, -vĕnīrĕ, -vēnī, -ventŭm, to *come upon, find.*
ipsĕ, ipsă, ipsŭm (Gr. 132), *self, he himself, &c.*
īre, to *go;* see eo.
Ĭs, eă, ĭd (Gr. 129), *this* or *that, he, &c.*

istĕ, istă, istŭd (Gr. 130), *that, he.*
Ită (adv.), *thus, in this way, so;*
ita ut, *so that.*
Ităquĕ (conj.), *therefore.*
Ităliă, -ae, *Italy.*
Ităm (adv.), *also, likewise.*
Itĕr, Itinĕris (Gr. [115]), *journey, march, route.*
Itĕrŭm (adv.), *again, a second time.*

J.

jactŏ, -ārĕ, -āvī, -ātŭm, to *discuss.*
jăm (adv.), *already, at length.*
jŭbeŏ, jŭbĕrĕ, jussī, jussŭm, to *bid, order.*
jŭdĭcĭŭm, -ī, *trial.*
jŭdĭcŏ, -ārĕ, -āvī, -ātŭm, to *judge, decide.*
jŭgŭm, -ī, *yoke, ridge* (of a hill), *hill.*
jŭmentŭm, -ī, *yoke animal, beast of burden.*
jŭnĭŏr (Gr. [123]), *younger.*
Jūră, -ae, *Jura* (a mountain).
jūrŏ, -ārĕ, -āvī, -ātŭm, to *swear.*
jūs, jūrĭs, *right;* jus jurandum, *oath.*
jŭvĕnĭs, -ĭs (Gr. [96], [123]), *young;* as a noun, a *youth.*

K.

Kal. = Kalendae, *Calends* (first day of the month, Gr. 490).

L.

L. = Lūcĭŭs.
Lăbĭēnŭs, -ī, *Labienus.*
lăcŭs, -ūs (Gr. [110]), *lake.*
largĭtĕr (adv.), *largely;* largiter posse, to *have great power or influence.*
largĭtĭŏ, -ōnĭs, *free giving, liberality; bribery.*
lātē (adv.), *widely.*
lātĭtūdŏ, -ĭnĭs, *breadth, width.*

lātŭs, -ă, -ŭm, *broad, wide.*
lătŭs, -ĕrĭs, *side, flank.*
lēgātĭŏ, -ōnĭs, *embassy.*
lēgātŭs, -ī, *deputy; lieutenant, envoy, embassador.*
lĕgĭŏ, -ōnĭs, *legion.*
Lĕmannŭs, -ī (Lake) *Leman; Lake of Geneva.*
lēnĭtās, -ātĭs, *gentleness, slowness.*
lex, lēgĭs, *law.*
lībĕrĭŭs (adv.), *more freely.*
lībertās, -ātĭs, *freedom.*
lĭcet, lĭcērĕ, lĭcuĭt, lĭcĭtŭm, *it is permitted, one may.*
Lĭngŏnēs, -ŭm, *Lingones.*
linguă, -ae, *tongue, speech, language.*
lintĕr, -trĭs (c.) (Gr. 102), *boat, skiff.*
Liscŭs, -ī, *Liscus.*
lŏcŭs, -ī (Gr. [116]), *place, position, situation.*
longē (adv.), *far, by far.*
longissĭmē (adv.), *farthest, very far.*
longĭtūdŏ, -ĭnĭs, *length.*
lŏquŏr, lŏquī, lŏcūtŭs, to *speak, talk.*
lux, lūcĭs, *light;* primă lux, *daybreak.*

M.

M. = Marcus.
măgĭs (adv.), *more.*
măgĭstrātŭs, -ūs, *magistrate.*
magnĭtūdŏ, -ĭnĭs, *size.*
magnŭs, -ă, -ŭm (Gr. [123]), *great, large.*
mājŏr, -ŭs (Gr. [123]), *larger, greater.*
mālŏ, mallĕ, māluī (Gr. 225), to *prefer, choose, wish more.*
mălŭs, -ă, -ŭm (Gr. [123]), *bad.*
mănŭs, -ūs (F.), *Hand.*
mātrĭmōnĭŭm, -ī, *marriage;* in matrimonium ducere, *to marry.*

LATIN INDEX. 95

Matrōnă -ae (M.), *Marne* (river).
mātūrĭŭs (adv.), *earlier*.
mātūrō, -ārĕ, -āvī, -ātŭm, to *make haste, hasten*.
mātūrŭs, -ă, -ŭm (Gr. [121]), *ripe*.
maxĭmē (adv.), *most, very*.
maxĭmŭs, -ă, -ŭm (Gr. [123]), *greatest, very great*.
mĕlĭŏr, -ĭŭs (Gr. [123]), *better*.
mĕmŏrĭă, -ae, *memory*.
mens, -ntĭs, *mind, reason*.
mensĭs, -ĭs (Gr. [96]), *month*.
mercātŏr, -ōrĭs, *trader, merchant*.
mĕrīdĭēs, -ēī (M.), *noon, midday*.
Messālă, -ae, *Messala*.
meŭs, -ă, -ŭm (Gr. 126), *my, mine*.
mīlĕs, -ĭtĭs, *soldier*.
mīlĭtārĭs, -e, *military;* res mīlĭtarĭs, *military matters, warfare*.
millĕ (Gr. [118]), *thousand;* millĕ passuŭm (a thousand paces), *a mile*.
mĭnĭmē (adv.), *least*.
mĭnĭmŭs, -ă, -ŭm (Gr. [123]), *least, smallest*.
mĭnŏr, -ŭs (Gr. [123]), *less, smaller*.
mĭnŭs (adv.), *less*.
mittō, mittĕrĕ, mīsī, missŭm, to *send*.
mŏlō, -ĕrĕ, -uī, -ĭtum, to *grind*.
mons, -ntĭs (M.), *mountain, mount*.
mŏrŏr, -ārī, -ātŭs, to *wait*.
mors, -rtĭs, *death*.
mortuŭs, -ă, -ŭm, *dead*.
mōs, mōrĭs, *custom, usage*.
mŏveō, mŏvērĕ, mōvī, mōtŭm, to *move*.
mŭlĭĕr, -ĕrĭs, *woman*.
multĭtūdō, -ĭnĭs, *multitude, great number*.
multŭs, -ă, -ŭm (Gr. [123]), *much;* pl. *many*.
mūnĭō, -īrĕ, -īvī, -ītŭm, to *fortify, defend*.
mūnītĭō, -ōnĭs, *fortification*.
mūrŭs, -ī, *wall*.

N.

nātūră, -ae, *nature, character*.
nāvĭs, -ĭs (Gr. [99]), *ship*.
nē (adv. and conj.), *not;* ne...
quidem, *not even;* as conj. w. subj., *in order that* . . . *not, lest*. (See Gr. [325], 424).
nĕ (interrog. particle) (Gr. 427).
nĕc (conj.), *nor*. See neque.
nĕgōtĭŭm, -ī, *business, task*.
nēmō, -ĭnĭs, *no one*.
nĕquĕ (conj.), *and not, nor;* neque . . . neque, *neither* . . . *nor*.
nĭhĭl (indeclinable), *nothing*.
nĭhĭlŭm, -ī (rare), *nothing;* abl. nĭhĭlo mĭnŭs, *nevertheless*.
nōbĭlĭs, -ĕ, *noble, of good birth*.
nōbĭlĭtās, -ātĭs, *nobility*.
nōlō, nollĕ, nōluī (Gr. 225), to *be unwilling*.
nōmĕn, -ĭnĭs, *name*.
nōn (adv.), *not*.
nōndŭm (adv.), *not yet*.
nōnnullŭs, -ă, -ŭm, *some, a few*.
nostĕr, -tră, -trŭm, *our, ours*.
nŏvĕm, *nine*.
nŏvŭs, -ă, -ŭm, *new;* res novae, *a revolution, change of government*.
nox, noctĭs, *night*.
nullŭs, -ă, -ŭm (Gr. 71), *no, no one*.
nŭm (interrog. particle), (see Gr. 429).
nŭmĕrŭs, -ī, *number*.
nunc (adv.), *now*.
nuntĭō, -ārĕ, -āvī, -ātŭm, to *announce, tell, report*.
nūpĕr (adv.), *lately, recently*.

O.

ŏb (prep. w. acc.), *on account of, because of, for*.
ŏbaerātŭs, -ă, -ŭm, *indebted;* as subst., *a debtor*.

obliviscŏr, oblivisci, oblitŭs (Gr. 280), to *forget*.
obsēs, -ĭdĭs, *hostage*.
obsignŏ, -ārĕ, -āvī, -ātŭm, to *seal, make* (a will).
obtĭneŏ, -tĭnērĕ, -tĭnuī, -tentŭm, to *hold, possess ; to get, obtain*.
occāsŭs, -ūs, *fall, setting* (of the sun); occasus solĭs, *sunset, west*.
occĭdŏ, -cĭdĕrĕ, -cĭdī, -cīsŭm, to *slay, kill ;* occĭsī, *the slain, the dead*.
occŭpŏ, -ārĕ, -āvī, -ātŭm, to *seize, occupy*.
ōceănŭs, -ī,' *ocean*.
octŏ, *eight*.
octōdĕcim, *eighteen*.
ŏcŭlŭs, -ī, *eye*.
ōdī, ōdissĕ, ōsŭs (Gr. [235]), to *hate*.
omnīnō (adv.), *altogether, in all, only*.
omnĭs, -ĕ, *all, every*.
ŏportĕt, ŏportērĕ, ŏportuīt, *it is proper, it behooves, one ought*.
oppĭdŭm, -ī, *town, walled town*.
oppugnŏ, -ārĕ, -āvī, -ātŭm, to *attack*.
optĭmŭs, -ă, -ŭm (Gr.[123]), *best*.
ŏpŭs, -ĕrĭs, *work*.
ŏpŭs (indecl.) (Gr. [297]), *need*.
ōrātĭŏ, -ōnĭs, *speech, talk*.
Orgetŏrix, -ĭgĭs, *Orgetorix*.
ŏriens, -ntĭs, *rising ;* oriens sol, *east*.
ŏrĭŏr, -īrī, ortŭs (Gr. [216] (*h*)), to *rise ;* to *begin*.
ōrŏ, -ārĕ,-āvī,-ātŭm,to *beg, pray, ask*.

P.

P. = Publĭŭs.
pāgŭs, -ī, *district, canton*.
pandŏ, pandĕrĕ, pandī, passŭm and pansŭm, to *stretch out, extend*.

părātŭs,-ă, -ŭm, *prepared, ready*.
pars, -rtĭs, *part ;* In utrăm partĕm, *in which direction, which way*.
parvŭs, -ă, -ŭm, *small*.
passŭs, -ūs, *pace, step*.
păteŏ, pătērĕ, pătuī, to *lie open, extend, stretch*.
pătĕr, -trĭs (Gr. 80), *father*.
paucŭs, -ă, -ŭm (usually pl.), *few*.
paulō (adv.), *a little*.
pax, pācĭs, *peace*.
pĕdĕs, -ĭtĭs, *footman, foot-soldier*.
pējŏr, -ŭs (Gr. [123]), *worse*.
pellŏ, pellĕrĕ, pĕpŭlī, pulsŭm, to *drive, repulse, defeat; drive out*.
pĕr (prep. w. acc.), *through, by means of*.
perdūcŏ, -dūcĕrĕ, -duxī, -ductŭm, to *lead through, build, construct* (e.g., a wall).
perfăcĭlĭs, -ĕ, *very easy*.
perfĭcĭŏ, -fĭcĕrĕ, -fēcī, -fectŭm, to *do, perform, accomplish*.
pĕrīcŭlŭm, -ī, *trial, test ; danger*.
pĕrītŭs, -ă, -ŭm, *knowing* (of), *skilled* (in).
permŏveŏ, -mŏvērī, -mōvī, -mōtŭm, to *move strongly, move*.
perpaucŭs, -ă, -ŭm, *very few*.
persĕquŏr, -sĕquī, -sĕcūtŭs, to *follow, pursue*.
persĕvērŏ, -ārĕ, -āvī, -ātŭm, to *persevere, continue*.
persuādeŏ, -suādĕrĕ, -suāsī, -suāsŭm (Gr.[209]), to *persuade*.
perterreŏ, -ērĕ, -uī, -ĭtŭm, to *frighten*.
pertĭneŏ, -tĭnērĕ, -tĭnuī, to *stretch, extend ;* to *pertain, belong*.
perturbŏ, -ārĕ, -āvī, -ātŭm, to *disturb, frighten*.
pervĕnĭŏ, -vĕnīrĕ, -vēnī, -ventŭm, to *come through, arrive*.

LATIN INDEX. 97

pēs, pĕdĭs, *foot;* pedem referre, to *retreat.*

pessĭmŭs, -ă, -ŭm (Gr. [123]), *worst.*

pĕtō, pĕtĕrĕ, pĕtīvī, pĕtītŭm, to *ask, beg, seek.*

Pīsō, -ōnĭs, *Piso.*

plăceō, -ērĕ, -uī, -ĭtŭm (Gr. [269]), to *please;* placuit ei, *he resolved.*

plebs, plēbĭs, *common people, people.*

plūrĭmŭm (adv.), *very much, greatly.*

plūrĭmŭs, -ă, -ŭm (Gr. 123), *most.*

plūs (Gr. [92] and [123]), *more,* or often simply *many.*

poenă, -ae, *penalty, punishment.*

pollĭceōr, -ērī, -ĭtŭs, to *promise.*

pōnō, pōnĕrĕ, pŏsuī, pŏsĭtŭm, to *place, pitch* (a camp).

pons, -ntĭs (M.), *bridge.*

pŏpŭlŭs, -ī, a *people,* a *nation.*

possŭm, possē, pŏtuī (Gr. [222]), to *be powerful, have influence, be able, can.*

post (prep. w. acc.), *after.*

post (adv.), *afterwards.*

posteā (adv.), *afterwards.*

postĕrŭs, -ă, -ŭm (Gr. [123]), *following, next after.*

postquăm or post quam (conj.), *after.*

postrēmŭs,-ă,-ŭm(Gr.[123]),*last.*

postrīdiē (adv.), *on the next day, on the morrow.*

postŭlō, -ārĕ, -āvī, -ātŭm, to *demand, ask; require.*

postŭmŭs,-ă,-ŭm(Gr.[123]),*last.*

pŏtens, -ntĭs, *powerful.*

pŏtentĭă, -ae, *power, might.*

pŏtestās, -ātĭs, *power; opportunity.*

pŏtĭŏr, pŏtīrī, pŏtītŭs (Gr. [216] (h)), to *get control of, get, gain.*

praecēdō, -cēdĕrĕ, -cessī, -cessŭm, to *precede, surpass.*

praefĭcĭō, -fĭcĕrĕ, -fēcī, -fectŭm, to *put over, put in charge of.*

praemittō, -mĭttĕrĕ, -mīsī, -missŭm, to *send ahead.*

praepōnō,-pōnĕrĕ,-pŏsuī,-pŏsĭtŭm, to *put in charge, place in command.*

praesens, -ntĭs, *present.*

praesĭdĭŭm, -ī, *garrison, defence.*

praestō, -stārĕ, -stĭtī, -stĭtŭm or -stătŭm, to *stand before, excel;* to *furnish.*

praesŭm, -essĕ, -fuī, -fŭtūrŭs, to *be ahead, be first, be present, be in command of.*

prĭdiē (adv.), *on the day before.*

prīmŭs, -ă, -ŭm (Gr. [123]), *first.*

princeps, -cĭpĭs, *leading, chief;* as a noun, princeps, a *chief.*

princĭpātŭs, -ūs, *leadership; highest office.*

prĭŏr, -ĭŭs (Gr. [123]), *former.*

prĭstĭnŭs, -ă, -ŭm, *ancient.*

prĭŭs quăm,or priusquăm(conj.), *sooner than, before.*

prō (prep. w. abl.), *before, for, in behalf of, in proportion to.*

prŏbō,-ārĕ,-āvī,-ātŭm, to *prove.*

prōcēdō, -cēdĕrĕ, -cessī, -cessŭm, to *go forward, advance, proceed.*

Procillŭs, -ī, *Procillus.*

prōdeō, -īrĕ, -iī, -ĭtŭm, to *come out, go forth.*

prōdūcō, -dūcĕrĕ, -duxī, -ductŭm, to *lead out, lead forth.*

proelĭŭm, -ī, *battle.*

prŏfectĭō, -ōnĭs, *departure, start.*

prŏfĭciscŏr, -fĭciscī, -fectŭs, to *start, set out, advance.*

prŏfŭgĭō, -fŭgĕrĕ, -fūgī, to *flee.*

prohĭbeō, -hĭbĕrĕ, -hĭbuī, -hĭbĭtŭm, to *keep out, prohibit, stop.*

prōjĭcĭō, -jĭcĕrĕ, -jēcī, -jectŭm, to *throw.*

prŏpĭŏr, -ĭŭs (Gr. [123]), *nearer.*

LATIN INDEX.

proptĕr (prep.), *on account of.*
proptĕreā (adv.), *for this reason;*
proptĕreā quŏd, *for the reason that, because.*
prōsŭm, prōdessĕ, prōfuī, prōfūtūrŭs (Gr. [269)], *to be useful, be advantageous.*
prōvincĭă, -ae, *province.*
proxĭmŭs, -ă, -ŭm (Gr. [123]), *nearest, next;* proximum iter, *shortest route.*
pugnŏ, -āre, -āvī, -ātŭm, *to fight.*
Pӯrēnaeī montēs, the *Pyrenees.*

Q.

quaerŏ, quaerĕrĕ, quaesīvī, quaesītŭm, *to ask, inquire.*
quālĭs, -ĕ, *such as; what kind of, what.*
quăm (conj. and adv.), *than;* with superlatives it emphasizes the meaning; quăm maxĭmŭs, *the very greatest, the greatest possible.*
quamdiū (conj.), *as long as, while.*
quartŭs, -ă, -ŭm, *fourth.*
quattuŏr, *four.*
-quĕ (conj.), *and.*
quĕrŏr, quĕrī, questŭs, *to complain.*
quī, quae, quŏd (Gr. 138), *who, which, that, what.*
quĭd (adv.), *why?*
quīdĕm (adv.), *even;* ne . . . quīdĕm, *not even.*
quĭn (conj.), *that, but that.*
quindĕcĭm, *fifteen.*
quinquĕ, *five.*
quintŭs, -ă, -ŭm, *fifth.*
quĭs, quae, quĭd (Gr. 139), *who? which? what?* (Gr. 140); *any one, any thing.*
quisquăm, quicquăm, or quidquăm (Gr. 141), *any one, any thing.*
quisquĕ, quaequĕ, quidquĕ (Gr. 141), *every, each.*
quŏd (conj.), *because.*

quŏquĕ (adv.), *also.*
quŏtīdiānŭs, -ă, -ŭm, *daily.*
quŏtīdiē (adv.), *daily.*

R.

rătĭs, -ĭs, *raft.*
rĕcĭpĭŏ, -cĭpĕrĕ, -cēpī, -ceptŭm, *to take back, receive;* sē rĕcĭpĕrĕ, *to betake one's self, retreat.*
rĕdeŏ, -īrĕ, -iī, -ĭtŭm, *to go back, return.*
rĕdĭmŏ, -ĭmĕrĕ, -ēmī, -emptŭm, *to buy, purchase.*
rĕdĭtĭŏ, -ōnĭs, *return.*
rĕdūcŏ, -dūcĕrĕ, -duxī, -ductŭm, *to bring back.*
rĕfĕrŏ, rĕferrĕ, rettŭlī, rĕlātŭm, *to carry back;* pĕdĕm rĕferrĕ, *to retreat.*
rĕgĭŏ, -ōnĭs, *region, country.*
regnŭm, -ī, *kingdom, kingly power.* [*rest of.*
rĕlĭquŭs, -ă, -ŭm, *remaining; the*
rĕmĭniscŏr, -scī (Gr. 280), *to remember, recall, call to mind.*
rĕnuncĭŏ, -ārĕ, -āvī, -ātŭm, *to announce, tell, bring word.*
renuntio = renuncio.
rĕpellŏ, rĕpellĕrĕ, reppŭlī, repulsŭm, *to drive back, drive off, repulse.*
rĕpĕrĭŏ, rĕpĕrīrĕ, reppĕrī, rĕpertŭm, *to find, gain; to find out, learn.*
rĕpugnŏ, -ārĕ, -āvī, -ātŭm, *to oppose, be opposed to.*
rēs, rēī, *thing, matter, circumstance;* res militaris, *warfare.*
rescindŏ, -scindĕrĕ, -scĭdī, -scissŭm, *to break down, destroy.*
resciscŏ, -sciscĕrĕ, -scīvī, or -scĭī, -scĭtŭm, *to learn, find out.*
respondeŏ, -spondĕrĕ, -spondī, -sponsŭm, *to answer.*
restĭtuŏ, -uĕrĕ, -uī, -ūtŭm, *to restore, re-establish.*

LATIN INDEX. 99

rĕtĭneō, -tĭnĕrĕ, -tĭnuī, -tentŭm, to *keep, retain.*
rĕvertō, -vertĕrĕ, -vertī, -versŭm, to *return* (also pass. rĕvertŏr, with the same meaning).
Rhēnŭs, -ī, the *Rhine* (river).
Rhŏdănŭs, -ī, the *Rhone* (river).
rīpă, -ae, *bank* (of a river).
rŏgō, -ārĕ, -āvī, -ātŭm, to *ask, ask for.*
Rōmă, -ae, *Rome.*
Rōmānŭs, -ă, -ŭm, *Roman;* pl. Rōmānī, the *Romans.*

S.

saepĕ (adv.), *often.*
sălŭs, -ūtīs, *safety.*
sanguĭs, -ĭnĭs (M.) (Gr. [115]), *blood.*
Santŏnēs, -ŭm, the *Santones.*
sătĭs (adv. and indeclinable adj.), *enough.*
sătĭsfactĭō, -ōnĭs, *excuse.*
scĭō, scīrĕ, scīvī, scītŭm, to *know.*
sĕcundŭs, -ă, -ŭm, *second.*
sĕd (conj.), *but.*
sēdĕcĭm, *sixteen.*
sēdĭtĭōsŭs, -ă, -ŭm, *seditious, quarrelsome.*
sĕmĕl (adv.), *once;* sĕmĕl atquĕ ĭtĕrŭm, *once and again, repeatedly.*
sēmentĭs, -ĭs, *sowing* (of grain).
sĕnātŭs, -ūs, *senate.*
sĕnex, sĕnĭs (Gr. [115]), *old.*
sĕnĭŏr (Gr. [123]), *older.*
septentrĭō, -ōnĭs, *north* (usually pl.).
septĭmŭs, -ă, -ŭm, *seventh.*
sĕpultūră, -ae, *burial.*
Sēquănă, -ae (F.), *Seine* (river).
Sēquănŭs, -ă, -ŭm, *Sequanian;* pl. Sēquănī, the *Sequanians.*
sĕquŏr, sĕquī, sĕcūtŭs, to *follow;* to *be inflicted* (said of punishment).

servīlĭs, -ĕ, *of slaves;* servīlĭs tŭmultŭs, *slave insurrection.*
servītŭs, -ūtĭs, *slavery.*
sescentī, -ae, -ă, *six hundred.*
sex, *six.*
sī (conj.), *if.*
sīcŭt (conj.), *as, just as.*
sĭlvă, -ae, *wood, forest.*
sĭn (conj.), *but if.*
sŏcĭŭs, -ī, *friend, ally.*
sōl, sōlĭs, *sun.*
sōlum (adv.), *only;* nōn sōlŭm ... sĕd ĕtĭăm, *not only ... but also.*
sōlŭs, -ă, -ŭm (Gr. 71), *alone.*
spătĭŭm, -ī, *space, distance; time.*
spectō, -ārĕ, -āvī, -ātŭm, to *look, look at, see.*
spērō, -ārĕ, -āvī, -ātŭm, to *hope, expect, hope for.*
spēs, spěī, *hope;* ĭn spĕm vĕnīrĕ, "*come into hope,*" *entertain a hope.*
stătuō, -uĕrĕ, -uī, -ūtŭm, to *decide, determine.*
stīpendĭārĭŭs, -ă, -ŭm, *tributary.*
stŭdĭŭm, -ī, *zeal, friendship.*
sŭb (prep. w. acc. and abl.), *under.*
subdūcō, -dūcĕrĕ, -duxī, -ductŭm, to *withdraw, draw off.*
subsĭdĭŭm, -ī, *reinforcement, help.*
subsŭm, -essĕ, -fuī, -fŭtūrŭs, to *be near, be at hand.*
subvehō, -vehĕrĕ, -vexī, -vectŭm, to *bring up.*
Suēvī, -ōrum, the *Suevi, Swabians.*
suī (Gr. 125), *himself, herself,* etc.; *themselves;* intĕr sē; *see* inter.
Sullă, -ae, *Sulla.*
sŭm, essĕ, fuī, fŭtūrŭs (Gr. 221), to *be.*
summŭs, -ă, -ŭm (Gr. [123]), *highest;* summŭs mons, *top of the mountain;* so in similar expressions.
sūmō, sūmĕrĕ, sumpsī, sumptŭm, to *take.*

sŭpĕrŏ, -āre, -āvī, -ātŭm, to *overcome, conquer.*
sŭpersŭm, -essĕ, -fuī, -fŭtŭrŭs, to *be left over, survive.*
sŭpĕrŭs, -ă, -ŭm (Gr. [123]), *upper.*
suppĕtŏ, -pĕtĕrĕ, -pĕtīvī, -pĕtītŭm, to *be on hand, be in store.*
suscĭpĭŏ, -cĭpĕrĕ, -cēpī, -ceptŭm, to *undertake; sibi suscipere, to take on one's self.*
suspīcĭŏ, -ōnĭs, *suspicion.*
sustĭneŏ, -tĭnērĕ, -tĭnuī, -tentŭm, to *hold out against, withstand.*
suŭs, -ă, -ŭm, *his own, his, her, its,* etc.

T.

T. = Titus.
tăceŏ, tăcērĕ, tăcuī, tăcĭtŭm, to *keep silent, hold one's peace.*
tandĕm (adv.), *at last, at length.*
tēlŭm, -ī, *missile, javelin.*
tempĕrŏ, -ārĕ, -āvī, -ātŭm, to *refrain.*
tempŭs, -ŏrĭs, *time.*
tĕneŏ, tĕnērĕ, tĕnuī, tentŭm, to *hold.*
tentŏ, -ārĕ, -āvī, -ātŭm, to *try, attempt, test.*
tergŭm, -ī, *back.*
tertĭŭs, -ă, -ŭm, *third.*
testāmentŭm, -ī, *will.*
Teutŏnī, -ōrŭm, the *Teutoni.*
tĭmŏr, -ŏrĭs, *fear, panic.*
Tolōsātēs, -ĭŭm, the *Tolosates.*
tŏtĭdĕm (indeclinable adj.), *as many, the same number of.*
tōtŭs, -ă, -ŭm (Gr. 71), *whole, all.*
trādŏ, -dĕrĕ, -dĭdī, -dĭtŭm, to *give over, surrender.*
trănŏ, -ārĕ, -āvī, -ātŭm, to *swim across.*
trans (prep. w. acc.), *over, across, beyond.*

transdūcŏ, -dūcĕrĕ, -duxī, -ductŭm (Gr. [268]), to *lead over, transport.*
transeŏ, -īrĕ, -iī, -ĭtŭm, to *go over, cross.*
trēs, trĭă (Gr. 118), *three.*
trībūnŭs, -ī, *tribune.*
trībuŏ, -uĕrĕ, -uī, -ūtŭm, to *assign, attribute.*
trĭduŭm, -ī, *three days.*
trĭgintă, *thirty.*
triplex, -ĭcĭs (Gr. [108]), *triple.*
tū (Gr. 125), *thou, thee;* often translated by Eng. *you.*
tŭm (adv.), *then.*
tŭmultŭs, -ūs, *uproar, broil; insurrection.*
tuŭs, -ă, -ŭm, *thy, thine.*

U.

ŭbī (conj.), *where, when.*
Ubĭī, -ōrŭm, the *Ubii.*
ultĕrĭŏr, -ĭŭs (Gr. [123]), *farther, later.*
ultĭmŭs, -ă, -ŭm (Gr. [123]), *farthest, last.*
ultrā (prep.), *beyond.*
undĕ (conj.), *whence, from which.*
undēvīgintī, *eighteen.*
undĭquĕ (adv.), *on all sides, from all sides.*
ūnŭs, -ă, -ŭm (Gr. 71), *one, only, alone.*
urbs, -bĭs, *city.*
usquĕ ăd, *up to, until.*
ūsŭs, -ūs, *use, experience, advantage;* dat. ūsuī (Gr. [272]), *advantageous, useful.*
ŭt (conj.), *as;* w. subj., *in order that, that, so that.*
ŭtĕr, -tră, -trŭm (Gr. 71), *which (of two).*
ŭtī (conj.), *as; that* (the same as ut).
ūtŏr, ūtī, ūsŭs (Gr. [297]), to *use, employ, enjoy.*

LATIN INDEX. 101

utrimquĕ (adv.), *on both sides*.
uxŏr, -ōrĭs, *spouse; husband or wife*.

V.

văcŏ, -ārĕ, -āvī, -ātŭm, *to be empty, be vacant*.
vădŭm, -ī, *shoal, ford*.
văgŏr, -ārī, -ātŭs, *to wander*.
văleŏ, vălērĕ, văluī, vălĭtŭm, *to be strong, be able, have influence*.
Vălĕrĭŭs, -ī, *Valerius*.
vehĕmentĕr (adv.), *greatly, strongly*.
vĕl (conj.), *or;* vĕl... vĕl, *either ...or*.
vēlox, -ōcĭs, *swift*.
vĕnĭŏ, vĕnīrĕ, vēnī, ventŭm, *to come*.
verbŭm, -ī, *word*.
vergŏ, vergĕrĕ, *to slope, extend*.
vertŏ, vertĕrĕ, vertī, versŭm, *to turn*.
vērŭs, -ă, -ŭm, *true*.
vescŏr, vescī (Gr. [297]), *feed on, eat*.

Vĕsontĭŏ, -ōnĭs, *Vesontio*.
vespĕr, -ī (Gr. [115]), *evening*.
vestĕr, -tră, -trŭm, *your, yours*.
vĕtŭs, -ĕrĭs, *old, ancient*.
vĭă, -ae, *way, road, path, journey*.
victōrĭă, -ae, *victory*.
vīcŭs, -ī, *village*.
vĭdeŏ, vĭdērĕ, vīdī, vīsŭm, *to see; pass*. vĭdērī, *to seem*.
vĭgĭlĭă, -ae, *watch*.
vĭgĭntī, *twenty*.
vinclŭm = vinculum.
vincŭlŭm, -ī, *chain, fetter*.
vīnŭm, -ī, *wine*.
virtūs, -ūtĭs, *manhood, merit, courage*.
vĭs, vīs (Gr. [115]), *violence, force;* pl. vīres, *strength*.
vŏcŏ, -ārĕ, -āvī, -ātŭm, *to call*.
Vŏcontĭī, -ōrŭm, *the Vocontii*.
vŏlŏ, vellĕ, vŏluī (Gr. 225), *to wish, be willing*.
vŏluntās, -ātĭs, *wish, consent*.
vŏluptās, -ātĭs, *pleasure*.
vox, vōcĭs, *voice, talk, words*.
vulnŭs, -ĕrĭs, *wound*.

ENGLISH INDEX.

A.

a (not expressed in Latin).
able; to be able, *possum, posse, potui; valeo, valēre, valui.*
about (adv.), *circiter;* prep. *circum; de* (= concerning).
absent, to be absent, *absum, abesse, afui, afutūrus.*
accomplish, *conficio, -ficĕre, -fēci, -fectum.*
according to (expressed by abl. case).
account; on account of, *ob; propter.*
accuse, *accūso, -āre, -āvi, -ātum.*
across, *trans.*
admit, *recipio, -cipĕre, -cēpi, -ceptum.*
advantageous, to be adv., *prosum, prodesse, profui.*
affirm, *confirmo, -āre, -āvi, -ātum.*
after (conj.), *postquam;* often expressed by abl. abs.
after (prep.), *post.*
afterward, *postea.*
again, *rursus.*
against my will, *me invito.*
aid (noun), *auxilium, -i.*
aid (verb), *sublĕvo, -āre, -āvi, -ātum.*
all, *totus, -a, -um* (Gr. 71); *omnis, -e.*
ally, *socius, -i.*
Allobroges, *Allobrŏges, -um.*
allow, *do, dare, dedi, datum;* allow to surrender = receive into surrender, *accipĕre in dedıtiōnem.*
almost, *paene.*

alone, *solus, -a, -um* (Gr. 71).
Alps, *Alpes, -ium* (F.).
ambassador, *legātus, -i.*
among, *in* w. abl., *apud.*
an (not expressed in Latin).
and, *et; -que; atque* or *ac.*
announce, *nuntio, -āre, -āvi, -ātum; enuntio, renuntio.*
another, *alius, -a, -ud;* one another; see one.
answer, *responsum, -i.*
any, *aliquis, -qua, -quid;* after *si, nisi, ne, num; quis, qua, quid;* in neg. sentences, *quisquam* or *ullus.*
anything, *aliquid;* after *ne,* etc., *quid* (Gr. [140]).
Aquitania, *Aquitania, -ae.*
Arar, *Arar, -ăris.*
Ariovistus, *Ariovistus, -i.*
arms, *arma, -ōrum.*
army, *exercitus, -us.*
around, *circum.*
arrival, *adventus, -us.*
arrive, *venio, -īre, vēni, ventum; pervenio.*
artifice, *insidiae, -ārum.*
Arverni, *Arverni, -ōrum.*
as (rel. pr.), *qui, quae, quod.*
as possible, *quam,* w. superl.
ask for, *rogo, -āre, -āvi, -ātum; postŭlo, -are, -āvi, -ātum.*
assemble, *convenio, -ire, -vēni, -ventum.*
assign, *tribuo, -uĕre, -ui, -ūtum.*
assizes, *conventus, -uum.*
at, expressed by abl. or loc. case;
at home, *domi;* (= to) *ad.*

ENGLISH INDEX.

attack, *adgredior, -grĕdi, -gressum; impĕtum facio, facĕre, feci, factum,* w. prep. *in* w. acc.
attempt (verb), *conor, -āri, -ātus.*
attempt (noun); make any attempt = attempt anything, *quicquam conāri.*
attribute, *tribuo,-uĕre,-ui,-ūtum.*
auxiliaries, *auxilia, -ōrum.*
avoid, *rito, -āre, -āvi, -ātum.*
await, *expecto, -āre, -āvi, -ātum.*
aware, *conscius, -a, -um.*
away, be away, *absum, abesse, afui, afutūrus*; **take away**; see **take.**

B.

back, *tergum, -i.*
back (adv.); see **lead, bring,** etc.
bad, *malus, -a, -um.*
baggage, *impedimenta, -ōrum.*
bank, *ripa, -ae.*
battle, *proelium, -i.*
be, *sum, esse, fui, futūrus;* **be, able, advantageous, absent,** etc.; see under **able,** etc.
bear, *fero, ferre, tuli, latum.*
because, *quod* (Gr. [328]); expressed also by abl. abs.
before (prep.), *ante.*
before (conj.), *prius . . . quam.*
beg, *obsĕcro, -āre, -āvi, -ātum.*
begin [*coepio, coepĕre*], *coepi, coeptum;* **begin** (battle), *committo, -mittĕre, -misi, -missum.*
beginning, *initium, -i.*
Belgians, *Belgae, -ārum.*
best, *optĭmus, -a, -um* (Gr. [123]).
betake one's self, *se recipio, -cipĕre, -cēpi, -ceptum.*
better, *melior, -ius* (Gr. [123]).
between, *inter.*
beyond, *ultra;* (= **across**), *trans.*
Bibracte, *Bibracte, -is* (N.).
bid, *jubeo, jubēre, jussi, jussum.*

blame, *accūso, -āre, -āvi, -ātum; incuso.*
blame, free from; see **free.**
blood, *sanguis, -ĭnis* (Gr. [115]).
boat, *linter, -tris* (c.).
body, *corpus, -ŏris.*
Boii, *Boii, -ōrum.*
boldly, more boldly, *audacius.*
boldness, *audacia, -ae.*
both, *uterque, -trăque, -trumque.*
brave, *fortis, -e.*
breadth, *latitūdo, -ĭnis;* **in breadth,** *in latitudĭnem.*
bring, *fero, ferre, tuli, latum, refĕro;* **bring together,** *confĕro;* **bring back,** *redūco, -ducĕre, -duxi, -ductum;* **bring** (= **induce**), *addūco;* **bring up** (a river), *subveho, -vehĕre, -vexi, -vectum;* **bring word,** *nuntio, -āre, -āvi, -ātum;* **bring over,** *transporto, -āre, -āvi, -ātum.*
broad, *latus, -a, -um.*
broken, *fractus, -a, -um.*
brother, *frater, -tris.*
build, *perdūco, -ducĕre, -duxi, -ductum.*
burial, *sepultūra, -ae.*
burn, *cremo, -āre, -āvi, -ātum.*
business, *negotium, -i.*
by, *a, ab* (to denote the doer); often expressed by abl. case.

C.

Cæsar, *Caesar, -ăris.*
call, *appello, -āre, -āvi, -ātum; voco, -āre, -āvi, -ātum;* **call together,** *convŏco.*
camp, *castra, -orum.*
can, *possum, posse, potui.*
canton, *pagus, -i.*
care, *cura, -ae.*
cause (noun), *causa, -ae.*
cause (verb), *committo, -mittĕre, -misi, -missum;* followed by a result-clause, *ut* w. subj.

ENGLISH INDEX. 105

cavalry, *equitātus, -us.*
cease, *desisto,-sistĕre,-stĭti,-stĭtum.*
Celts, *Celtae, -ārum.*
centurion, *centurio, -ōnis.*
chance, *casus, -us.*
change, *converto, -vertĕre, -verti, -versum.*
character, *natūra, -ae.*
charge, *procurro, -currĕre, -curri, -cursum.*
cheer, *confirmo, -āre, -āvi, -ātum.*
chief, *princeps, -ĭpis;* chief men, *princĭpes.*
children, *libĕri, -ōrum.* [*tum.*
choose, *delĕgo, -legĕre, -lēgi, -lec-*
circumstance, *res, rei.*
city, *urbs, -bis.*
come, *venio, -īre, veni, ventum;*
 come together, *convenio;*
 come up to, *succēdo, -cedĕre, -cessi, -cessum,* w. prep. *sub;*
 come nearer, *propius accēdo;*
 come to pass, *fio, fĭĕri, factus.*
coming, *adventus, -us.*
command, be in command of, *praesum, -esse, -fui, -futūrus* (Gr. [269]).
compasses; see pair.
compel, *cogo, cogĕre, coēgi, coactum.*
complain, *queror, queri, questus.*
conference, *colloquium, -i.*
conquer, *vinco, vincĕre, vici, victum.*
consent, *voluntas, -ātis.*
Considius, *Considius, -i.*
conspiracy, *conjuratio, -ōnis.*
construct, *perdūco,-ducĕre,-duxi, -ductum.*
consul, *consul, -ŭlis.*
contend, *contendo,-tendĕre,-tendi, -tentum.*
corn, *frumentum, -i;* or pl. *frumenta.*
council, *concilium, -i.*
country, *fines, -ium.*

courage, *anĭmus, -i; virtus, -ūtis.*
course, *iter, itinĕris* (Gr. [115]).
cross, *transeo, -ire, -ii, -ĭtum.*
crush, *opprĭmo, -primĕre, -pressi, -pressum.*
culture, *humanĭtas, -ātis.*
custom, *institūtum, -i.*

D.

daily (adv.), *quotidie;* (adj.) *quotidiānus, -a, -um* (or *cotidianus*).
danger *pericŭlum, -i.*
dangerous, *periculōsus, -a, -um.*
dare, *audeo, -ēre, ausus* (Gr. [216], (g)).
daughter, *filia, -ae.*
day, *dies, -ēi* (c.); two days, *biduum, -i.*
daybreak, *prima lux.*
death, *mors, -rtis.*
decide on, *statuo, -uĕre, -ui, -ūtum.*
deep, *altus, -a, -um.*
defeat, *calamĭtas, -ātis.*
deliver (a speech), *habeo, -ēre, -ui, -ĭtum.*
demand, *flagĭto, -āre, -āvi, -ātum.*
depart, *discēdo, -cedĕre, -cessi, -cessum.*
departure, *profectio, -ōnis.*
depend, *nitor, niti, nisus* or *nixus.*
depth, *altitūdo, -ĭnis.*
deserter, *perfŭga, -ae.*
desire, *cupidĭtas, -ātis.*
desirous, *cupĭdus, -a, -um.*
differ, *diffĕro, -ferre, distŭli, dilātum.*
difficult, *difficĭlis, -e* (Gr. 121).
discuss, *jacto, -āre, -āvi, -ātum.*
dismiss, *dimitto, -mittĕre, -misi, -missum.*
distant, to be distant, *absum.*
district, *pagus, -i.*
disturb, *perturbo,-āre,-āvi,-ātum.*
ditch, *fossa, -ae.*
Divico, *Divico, -ōnis.*

divide, divĭdo, -vidēre, -vīsi, -vī-
sum.
Divitiacus, Divitiăcus, -i.
do, facio, facĕre, feci, factum; (as
an auxiliary, not expressed in
Latin).
doubt (noun), there is no doubt,
non est dubium.
doubt (verb), dubĭto, -āre, -āvi,
-ātum.
draw, circumdūco, -ducĕre, -duxi,
-ductum; draw up (troops), in-
strŭo, -struĕre, -struxi, -structum.
drive back, rejicio, -jicĕre, -jēci,
-jectum.
Dubis, Dubis, -is.
Dumnorix, Dumnŏrix, -ĭgis.
dwell, habĭto, -āre, -āvi, -ātum;
incŏlo, -colĕre, -colui, -cultum.

E.

each, uterque, -trăque, -trumque
(Gr. 71); to each other, inter se.
eagerly, most eagerly, cupidis-
sĭme.
eagerness, cupidĭtas, -ātis.
earlier than, prius ... quam.
early, early in the night, prima
nocte.
east, oriens sol.
easy, facĭlis, -e.
effeminate, effemĭno, -āre, -āvi,
-ātum.
eighty, octoginta.
elated, sublātus, -a, -um.
empty, to be empty, vaco, -āre,
-āvi, -ātum.
encourage, cohortor, -āri, -ātus.
end, finis, -is (c.).
endure, perfĕro,-ferre,-tŭli,-lātum.
enemy, hostis, -is.
envoy, legātus, -i.
equal, par, -is (Gr. [108]).
even, etiam.
exact, sumo, sumĕre, sumpsi,
sumptum.

excellence, bonĭtas, -ātis.
except, praeter.
extend, pateo, -ēre, -ui.

F.

fact, res, rei; often expressed also
by neut. adj., e.g., haec, these
facts.
faith, fides, -ĕi.
far (adv.), longe.
farther, ulterior, -ius.
father, pater, -tris.
favor, indulgeo, -gēre, -lsi (Gr.
[269]).
feelings, anĭmus, -i.
few, pl. of paucus, -a, -um.
fifteen, quindĕcim.
fight, pugna, -ae.
fight, pugno, -āre, -āvi, -ātum;
contendo, -tendĕre, -tendi, -ten-
tum.
fill, compleo, -plēre, -plēvi, -plētum.
find, find out, reperio, -ire, rep-
pĕri, repertum.
finish, perficio, -ficĕre, -fēci, -fec-
tum.
fire, ignis, -is.
first, primus, -a, -um (Gr. [123]);
at first, primo.
five, quinque.
fix, confirmo, -āre, -āvi, -ātum.
flank, latus, -ĕris; right flank,
latus apertum (open side).
flee, fugio, fugĕre, fūgi, fugĭtum;
profugio.
flight, fuga, -ae.
flow, fluo, -uĕre, -uxi.
follow, sequor, sequi, secūtus.
following, postĕrus, -a, -um.
for (on account of), ob; for the
sake, see sake; in behalf of,
pro.
forces, copiae, -ārum.
forced marches = great marches.
forefathers, majōres, -um.
forest, silva, -ae.

ENGLISH INDEX. 107

forget, *obliviscor, -livisci, -litus* (Gr. 280).
form, *facio, facĕre, feci, factum.*
former, *prior, -ius* (Gr. [123]).
fort, *arx, arcis.*
fortify, *munio, -ire, -ivi, -itum; ·communio.*
forty, *quadraginta.*
four, *quattuor.*
fourth, *quartus, -a, -um.*
free from blame, *purgātus, -a, -um.*
friend, *amīcus, -i.*
friendly, *amicus, -a, -um.*
friendship, *amicitia, -ae.*
frighten, *perterreo, -ēre, -ui, -itum.*
from, *de;* (away from), *a, ab;* (out from), *e, ex;* from which, *unde;* from one another, *inter se.*
front, in front of, *pro.*
fugitive, *fugitivus, -i.*
furnish, *facio, facĕre, feci, factum.*
future, for the future, *in reliquum tempus.*

G.

gain, *concilio, -āre, -āvi, -ātum;* gain a request, *impĕtro, -āre, -avi, -ātum.*
Garonne (river), *Garumna, -ae.*
Gaul, *Gallia, -ae.*
Gaul, a Gaul, *Gallus;* the Gauls, *Galli.*
German, *Germānus, -a, -um;* the Germans, *Germani.*
get, get possession of, *potior, -iri, -itus* (Gr. [297]); get used, *consuesco, -suescĕre, -suēvi, -suētum.*
give, *do, dare, dedi, datum.*
glory, *gloria, -ae.*
go, *eo, ire, ivi,* or *ii, itum; se confĕro, -ferre, -tŭli, -lātum;* proficiscor, *-ficisci, -fectus;* go on = be carried on, pass. of *gero, gerĕre, gessi, gestum.*
god, *deus, -i* (Gr. 68).
good, *bonus, -a, -um* (Gr. [123]).
grain, *frumentum, -i;* or pl., *frumenta.*
great, *magnus, -a, -um* (Gr. [123]).
greatly, *vehementer.*
greediness, *cupidĭtas, -ātis.*

H.

habit, be in the habit, complete tenses of *consuesco, -suescĕre, -suēvi, -suētum.*
Hæduan, *Haeduus, -a, -um.*
half, half way up the hill, *in colle medio;* a mile and a half = "one thousand and five hundred paces."
hand, *manus, -us* (F.).
happen, *accĭdo, -cidĕre, -cĭdi.*
hard, *difficĭlis, -e* (Gr. [123]).
harm, *maleficium, -i.*
Harudes, *Harudes, -um.*
haste, make haste = hasten.
hasten, *contendo, -dĕre, -di, -tum; matūro, -āre, -āvi, -ātum.*
have, *habeo, -ēre, -ui, -itum;* expressed also by dat. of possessor; have to (= must), expressed by pass. periphr. conj.; I had rather, *malo, malle, malui.*
he, *is, ille,* &c.; in nom. usually expressed by the verb-ending.
height, *altitūdo, -inis.*
help, *auxilium, -i.*
Helvetian, *Helvetius, -a, -um;* the Helvetians, *Helvetii.*
high, *altus, -a, -um.*
hill, *collis, -is* (M.).
himself, *ipse,* &c. (ref.) *sui,* &c.
hire, *mercēde arcesso, -essĕre, -essivi, -essitum;* (lit. summon by pay); gen. of *is, ille,* &c. (ref.) *suus, -a, -um.*

hither, Hither Gaul, *Gallia citerior.*
hold, *teneo, -ēre, -ui, -tum;* (hold assizes), *ago, agĕre, egi, actum.*
home, *domus, -us* (Gr. [115]); at home, *domi;* homeward, *domum.*
honor, *honor, -ōris.*
hope, *spes, spĕi.*
hope, hope for, *spero, -āre, -āvi, -ātum.*
horseman, *eques, -itis.*
hostage, *obses, -ĭdis.*
hostile, *inimicus, -a, -um.*
house, *domus, -us* (Gr. [115]).
huge, *ingens, -ntis.*
hundred, *centum.*
hurt, *offendo, -fendĕre, -fendi, -fensum.*

I.

I, *ego* (Gr. 124); often expressed by the verb-ending.
import, *importo, -āre, -āvi, -ātum.*
important, most important, *summus, -a, -um* (highest).
in, *in* w. abl.; often expressed by abl. or loc. case.
incredible, *incredibĭlis, -e.*
induce, *adduco, -ducĕre, -duxi, -ductum.*
inflict, *infĕro, -ferre, -tŭli, -lātum;* **inflict punishment on,** *supplicium sumĕre de* (exact punishment from).
influence, *auctorĭtas, -ātis;* to have influence, *possum.*
inhabit, *incŏlo, -ĕre, -ui.*
inhabitant, *incŏla, -ae.*
injury, *injuria, -ae.*
intend = have in mind, *esse alicui in anĭmo;* also expressed by act. periphr. conj.
intercessor, *deprecātor, -ōris.*
interests, *res, rerum.*

interval, *intervallum, -i.*
intervene, passive of *intermitto, -mittĕre, -misi, -missum.*
into, *in* w. acc.
it, *sui; is, ea, id; ille,* &c.
itself, *ipse, ipsa, ipsum.*

J.

javelin, *pilum, -i.*
join (battle), *committo, -mittĕre, -misi, -missum.*
journey, *iter, itinĕris* (Gr. [115]).
Jura, *Jura, -ae.*

K.

keep, keep out, *prohibeo, -ēre, -ui, -ĭtum;* **keep in,** *contineo, -tinēre, -tinui;* (= **stay**), *se teneo, -ēre, -ui, -tum.*
know, *cognosco, -noscĕre, -nōvi, -nĭtum.*
known, to make known, *nuntio, -āre, -āvi, -ātum.*
kill, *interficio, -ficĕre, -fēci, -fectum.*
kind, *genus, -ĕris.*
kindness, *beneficium, -i.*
king, *rex, regis.*
kingdom, *regnum, -i.*
kingly power, *regnum, -i.*

L.

Labienus, *Labiēnus, -i.*
lack, *inopia, -ae.*
lake, *lacus, -us* (Gr. [110]).
land, *ager, -gri;* **lands** (= country), *fines, -ium.*
language, *lingua, -ae.*
lapse, after a lapse of three days, *triduo intermisso.*
large, *magnus, -a, -um.*
larger, *major, -us* (Gr. [123]).
largest, *maxĭmus, -a, -um* (Gr. [123]).
last, then at last; see then.

ENGLISH INDEX. 109

lately, *nuper*.
law, *lex, legis*.
lay waste, *popŭlor, -āri, -ātus*.
lead, *duco, ducĕre, duxi, ductum;*
lead forth or out, *ēdūco;* lead back, *redūco;* lead (= induce), *indūco*.
leadership, *principātus, -us*.
learn, *comperio, -perire, -pĕri, -pertum; intellĕgo, -legĕre, -lexi, -lectum; cognosco, -noscĕre, -nōvi, -nĭtum*.
least, *minĭmus, -a, -um;* (adv.) *minĭme*.
leave, *relinquo, -linquĕre, -liqui, -lictum;* (= go away) *decēdo, -cedĕre, -cessi, -cessum*, w. prep. *de; discēdo; egredior, -grĕdi, -gressus*, w. prep. *c*.
left, *relĭquus, -a, -um*.
legion, *legio, -ōnis*.
length, *longitūdo, -ĭnis;* in length, *in longitudinem*.
less (adj.), *minor, -us*.
less (adv.), *minus*.
let, in hortatory sentences; expressed in Latin by the subj.
levy, *impĕro, -āre, -āvi, -ātum*.
line (of battle), *acies, -ēi*.
Lingones, *Lingŏnes, -um*.
Liscus, *Liscus, -i*.
lost, *sublātus, -a, -um* (taken away).

M.

make, *facio, facĕre, feci, factum;* make (war), *infĕro, gero;* make use of, *utor, uti, usus;* make (= render, cause to be), *efficio, -ficĕre, -fēci, -fectum;* make a stand; see stand.
man, *homo, -ĭnis; vir, viri*. "Men" is often expressed by using a masculine adjective.
many, pl. of *multus, -a, -um*.
march (noun), *iter, itinĕris* (Gr. [115]).

march (verb) = make a march; *iter facio, facĕre, feci, factum*.
marriage, *matrimonium;* in marriage, *in matrimonium*.
marry, *in matrimonium duco, ducĕre, duxi, ductum;* also *duco* alone.
matter, *res, rei*.
may, in wishes expressed by subj.; may (= one is permitted), *licet, licēre, licuit, licĭtum*.
mean, *designo, -āre, -āvi, -ātum*.
meanwhile, *intĕrim*.
Messala, *Messāla, -ae*.
Mettius, *Mettius, -i*.
mile, *mille passuum*.
mind, *mens, -ntis*.
missile, *telum, -i*.
month, *mensis, -is*.
more, *plus* (Gr. [92] and [123]).
most, to be most powerful, *plurimum possum*.
mountain, *mons, -ntis*.
move, *moveo, -ēre, movi, motum; commoveo*.
much, *multus, -a, -um;* much (= many things), *multa*.
multitude, *multitūdo, -ĭnis*.
must, expressed by pass. peri. conj.
my, *meus, -a, -um*.

N.

name, *nomen, -ĭnis*.
narrow, *angustus, -a, -um*.
nation, *popŭlus, -i*.
nature, *natūra, -ae*.
nearer, *citerior, -ius* (Gr. [123]).
nearer (adv.), *propius* (Gr. [123]).
nearest, *proxĭmus, -a, -um* (Gr. [123] and [268]).
necessity, from necessity, *necessario* (adv.).
neighbor, *finitĭmus, -i*.
neighboring, *proxĭmus, -a, -um* (Gr. [123]).

neither, *neque* or *nec*.
new, *novus, -a, -um*.
next (following), *postĕrus, -a, -um*; *proxĭmus, -a, -um*; on the next day, *postridie* or *postridie ejus diēi* (Gr. [285]).
no, *nullus, -a, -um*; no one, *nemo, -ĭnis; nullus*.
nobility, *nobilĭtas, -ātis*.
noble, *nobĭlis, -e*.
nor, *neque* or *nec;* neither ... nor, *neque ... neque* or *nec ... nec*.
not, *non*; not yet, *nondum*.
nothing, *nihil* (indecl.).
notice, *anĭmum adverto, -vertĕre, -verti, -versum*, or *animadverto*.
number, *numĕrus, -i;* large number, *magna copia*.
numerous, *multi, -ae, -a*.

O.

oath, *jusjurandum, jurisjurandi;* take an oath, *juro, -are, -avi, -atum*.
occupy, *occŭpo, -āre, -āvi, -ātum*.
of, expressed by gen. case.
off, shut off; see shut.
often, *saepe*.
old, *vetus, -ĕris; senex, senis*.
on, *in* w. abl.; often expressed by abl. or dat. case; on the right wing, *a dextro cornu*.
one, *unus, -a, -um* (Gr. 71); the one ... the other, *alter ... alter;* one another, with, for, to, &c., one another, *inter se*.
only, *unus, -a, -um* (Gr. 71).
opportunity, *facultas, -ātis*.
or, *aut*.
order, *jubeo, -ere, jussi, jussum*.
Orgetorix, *Orgetŏrix, -ĭgis*.
other, *alius, -a, -ud;* the other (of two), *alter, -a, -um*.
ought, *debeo, -ēre, -ui, -ĭtum;* also expressed by pass. periph. conj.

our, *noster, -tra, -trum*.
out, out of, out from, *e* or *ex;* go out, *exeo, exīre, exii, exĭtum*.
over, cross over = cross.
overlook, *neglēgo, -legĕre, -lexi, -lectum*.
own, *suus, -a, -um;* also expressed by gen. case of *ipse*.

P.

pace, *passus, -us*.
pair of compasses, *circĭnus, -i*.
panic, *timor, -ōris*.
pardon, *ignosco, -noscĕre, -nōvi, -nōtum* (Gr. [269]).
part, *pars, -rtis*.
party, *factio, -ōnis*.
pass, come to pass, *fio, fĭĕri, factus*.
passage, *iter, itinĕris* (Gr. [115]).
peace, *pax, pacis*.
people (a nation), *popŭlus, -i*.
perfectly, expressed by superlative.
perform, *facio, facĕre, feci, factum; conficio, perficio*.
permit, it is permitted, *licet, licēre, licuit, licĭtum*.
persuade, *persuadeo, -ēre, -suāsi, -suāsum*.
phalanx, *phalanx, -ngis*.
Piso, *Piso, -ōnis*.
pitch (a camp), *pono, ponĕre, posui, posĭtum*.
place, *locus, -i* (Gr. [116]).
plenty, *copia, -ae*.
popularity, *gratia, -ae*.
position, *locus, -i* (Gr. [116]).
possession, get possession; see get.
possible, as possible, *quam* w. superl.
post, *constituo, -uĕre, -ui, -ūtum*.
power, *potestas, -ātis;* (= sway, upper hand), *potentātus, -us;* kingly power, *regnum*.

ENGLISH INDEX. 111

powerful, to be powerful, *possum, posse, potui.*
prefer, *malo, malle, malui.*
prepare, *compăro, -āre, -āvi, -ātum.*
prepared (= ready), *parātus, -a, -um.*
present, *praesens, -ntis;* **to be present,** *adsum.*
prevent, *prohibeo, -ēre, -ui, -ĭtum.*
prisoner, *hostis captus; captīvus, -i.*
privilege, *facultas, -ātis.*
prolong, *duco, ducĕre, duxi, ductum.*
promise, *polliceor, -ēri, -ĭtus.*
proper, it is proper, *oportet, oportēre, oportuit.*
province, *provincia, -ae.*
punishment, *supplicium, -i.*
pursue, *sequor, sequi, secūtus; insĕquor.*
put, put an end = make an end; **put around,** *circumdo, -dăre, -dĕdi, -dătum* (Gr. 226).

R.

raft, *ratis, -is.*
rather; see **have.**
ready, *parātus, -a, -um.*
reason, *causa, -ae.*
receive, *capio, capĕre, cepi, captum; accipio.*
record, *tabŭla, -ae.*
reduce, *redĭgo, -ĭgĕre, -ēgi, -actum.*
refinement, *cultus, -us.*
refrain, *tempĕro, -āre, -āvi, -ātum.*
region, *regio, -ōnis.*
remain, *supersum, -esse, -fui, -futūrus.*
remaining, *relĭquus, -a, -um.*
report, *nuntio, -āre, -āvi, -ātum; enuntio, renuntio.*
repulse, *propulso,-āre,-āvi,-ātum.*

request, gain a request, *impĕtro, -āre, -āvi, -ātum.*
rescue, *eripio, -ripĕre, -ripui, -reptum.*
resist, *subsisto, -sistĕre, -stĭti, -stĭtum.*
resolve, he resolved = it pleased him, *placuit ei.*
rest of, *relĭquus, -a, -um.*
retreat, *pedem refĕro, -ferre, -tŭli, -lātum.*
return, *reditio, -ōnis.*
return, *redeo, -īre, -ii, -ĭtum; revertor, -verti, -versus;* also act. *reverto; se recipio, -cipĕre, -cēpi, -ceptum.*
revolution, *res novae.*
Rhine (river), *Rhenus, -i.*
Rhone (river), *Rhodănus.*
right, right flank; see **flank.**
ripe, *matūrus, -a, -um.*
river, *flumen, -ĭnis.*
road, *via, -ae.*
Roman, *Romānus, -a, -um.*
Rome, *Roma, -ae.*
room, *spatium, -i.*
rouse up, *incĭto, -āre, -āvi, -ātum.*
route, *iter, itinĕris* (Gr. [115]).
royal power, *regnum.*
run up, *accurro, -currĕre, -curri, -cursum.*

S.

sake, for the sake, *causā.*
same, *idem, eădem, idem.*
save, *eripio, -ripĕre, -ripui, -reptum.*
say, *dico, dicĕre, dixi, dictum.*
second, *alter, -a, -um.*
see, *video, -ēre, vidi, visum; conspicor, -āri, -ātus.*
seek, *appĕto, -petĕre, -petīvi, -petītum.*
seize, *occŭpo, -āre, -āvi, -ātum.*
senate, *senātus, -us.*
send, *mitto, mittĕre, misi, missum.*

112 ENGLISH INDEX.

Sequanian, *Sequănus, -a, -um.*
set, *constituo, -uĕre, -ui, -ūtum;*
set out, *proficiscor, -ficisci, -fectus.*
seventh, *septĭmus, -a, -um.*
severe, *gravis, -e;* severest (= greatest), *summus, -a, -um.*
severely, *gravĭter, vehementer.*
ship, *navis, -is* (Gr. [99]).
shortest, *proxĭmus, -a, -um.*
shut off, *interclūdo, -cludĕre, -clūsi, -clūsum.*
signal, *signum, -i.*
situation, *locus, -i* (Gr. [116]).
six, *sex.*
six hundred, *sescenti, -ae, -a.*
sixteen, *sedĕcim.*
size, *magnitūdo, -ĭnis.*
slain, the slain, *occĭsi, -ōrum.*
slaughter, *internecio, -ōnis.*
slay, *interficio, -ficĕre, -fēci, -fectum;* *concīdo, -cidĕre, -cidi.*
small, *parvus, -a, -um.*
smaller, *minor, -us* (Gr. [123]).
so, *ita.*
soil, *solum, -i.*
soldier, *miles, -ĭtis.*
some, *nonnullus, -a, -um;* some
... others, *alii ... alii.*
son, *filius, -i.*
sorrow, *dolor, -ōris.*
space, *spatium.*
speak, *loquor, loqui, locūtus.*
speech, *oratio, -ōnis.*
spirit, *anĭmus, -i.*
spring up, *innascor, -nasci, -nātus.*
stand, make a stand, *insto, -stāre, -instĭti;* take a stand, *consisto, -sistĕre, -stĭti, -stĭtum.*
start, *proficiscor, -ficisci, -fectus.*
state, *civitas, -ātis.*
stone, *lapis, -ĭdis* (c.).
stop, *prohibeo, -ēre, -ui, -ĭtum;* (= make an end), *finem facio, facere, feci, factum.*
strongly, *gravĭter.*

successive, *continuus, -a, -um.*
sudden, *subĭtus, -a, -um.*
suddenly, *repente.*
Suevi, *Suevi, -ōrum.*
suitable, *idoneus, -a, -um.*
summon, *voco, -āre, -āvi, -ātum.*
sunset, *solis occāsus, -us.*
supply (noun), *copia, -ae.*
supply (verb), *supporto, -āre, -āvi, -ātum.*
surrender, *deditio, -ōnis.*
surround, *cingo, cingĕre, cinxi, cinctum.*
survive, *supersum, -esse, -fui, -futūrus.*
suspect, *suspĭcor, -āri, -ātus.*
suspicion, *suspicio, -ōnis.*
sway, *imperium, -i;* *dicio, -ōnis.*
swiftly, *celerĭter.*
sword, *gladius, -i.*

T.

take, *capio, capĕre, cepi, captum;* take away, *aufĕro, -ferre, abstŭli, ablātum;* *tollo, tollĕre, sustŭli, sublātum;* take an oath, *juro, -āre, -āvi, -ātum.*
teach, *instituo, -uĕre, -ui, -ūtum.*
tear, *lacrĭma, -ae.*
tell, *nuntio, -āre, -āvi, -ātum;* *enuntio, renuntio;* (= order), *jubeo, jubēre, jussi, jussum.*
ten, *decem.*
tenth, *decĭmus, -a, -um.*
territories, *fines, -ium.*
than, *quam;* also expressed by abl. case.
that (demon.), *is, ea, id; ille, illa, illud; iste, ista, istud;* (relat.), *qui, quae, quod.*
that (conj.), *ut, quin;* that not, *ne;* but that, *quin.* The English conj. *that* in indirect quotations is omitted in Latin, where the infin. is used.
the, omitted in Latin.

their, *suus, -a, -um;* when not reflexive, expressed by the gen. case of a pronoun, *eōrum, illōrum,* &c.
themselves, *sui; ipse.*
then, *tum;* then at last, *tum demum.*
there (introductory), not expressed in Latin.
there (adv. = in that place), *ibi.*
these; see this.
thing, *res, rei;* often expressed by a neuter adjective; e.g. *haec,* these things; *multa,* many things.
think, *existimo, -āre, -āvi, -ātum.*
third, *tertius, -a, -um.*
thirteen, *tredĕcim.*
this, *hic, haec, hoc; is, ea, id.*
those, *ii, eae, ea,* &c.; *illi, illae, illa,* &c.
thousand, *mille* (Gr. [118]).
three, *tres, tria;* three days, *triduum.*
through, *per.*
throw, *jacio, jacĕre, jeci, jactum; conjicio, -jicĕre, -jēci, -jectum.*
thus, *ita.*
Tigurinus, *Tigurīnus, -i.*
time, *tempus, -ŏris.*
to, *ad, in;* often expressed by dat. or acc. case.
together, usually expressed by *con-;* e.g. *convŏco,* call together, &c.
too, expressed by comparative.
top, expressed by *summus* in agreement.
torture, *cruciātus, -us.*
toward, *ad.*
town, *oppĭdum, -i.*
trader, *mercātor, -ōris.*
train, *exerceo, -ēre, -ui, -ĭtum.*
treat, *ago, agĕre, egi, actum;* treat as enemies = hold in the number of enemies.

tribe, tribe by tribe, *generātim* (adv. "tribewise").
trickery, *dolus, -i.*
troops, *copiae, -ārum.*
trust, *confido, -fīdĕre, -fīsus,* w. dat. (Gr. [269]) or abl. (Gr. 295).
try, *conor, -āri, -ātus.*
turn, *verto, vertĕre, verti, versum;* turn away, *averto.*
twenty, *viginti.*
two, *duo, -ae, -o* (Gr. 72); two days, *biduum, -i.*
two hundred, *ducenti, -ae, -a.*

U.

Ubii, *Ubii, -orum.*
under, *sub;* under the sway, in *diciōne.*
undergo, *subeo, -īre, -ii, -ĭtum.*
undertake, *suscipio, -cipĕre, -cēpi, -ceptum.*
unfavorable, *aliēnus, -a, -um.*
unwilling, *invītus, -a, -um;* to be unwilling, *nolo, nolle, nolui.*
upbraid, *incūso, -āre, -āvi, -ātum.*
use, *utor, uti, usus* (Gr. [297]).
used, get used; see get.
useful, to be useful, *prosum, prodesse, profui, profutūrus.*

V.

Verbigenus, *Verbigenus, -i.*
very, expressed by the superlative.
victory, *victoria, -ae.*
vigorously, *acrĭter.*
village, *vicus, -i.*
violence, *vis, vis* (Gr. [115]).
visit, *commeo, -āre, -āvi, -ātum;* w. prep. *ad.*

W.

wage, *gero, gerĕre, gessi, gestum.*
wait, *moror, -āri, -ātus.*
wall, *murus, -i.*

wander, *vagor, -āri, -ātus.*
war, *bellum, -i.*
warn, *moneo, -ēre, -ui, -itum.*
waste, lay waste; see lay.
watch, *vigilia, -ae.*
way, *via, -ae*; half way up; see half.
we, *nos*; often expressed in verb-ending.
weaken, *effemīno, -āre, -āvi, -ātum.*
what, *qualis, -e*; *qui, quae, quod.*
which (relat.), *qui, quae, quod*; from which, *unde.*
while, *dum*; often expressed by abl. abs.
who (rel.), *qui, quae, quod*; (interrog.), *quis? quae? quid?*
whole, *totus, -a, -um* (Gr. 71); *omnis, -e.*
will (vb.), expressed by future tense).
will, against my will, = I [being] unwilling, abl. abs.
wine, *vinum, -i.*
wing, *cornu, -us.*
winter, *hiĕmo, -āre, -āvi, -ātum.*
wish, *volo, velle, volui.*

with, *cum, apud*; often expressed by abl. case.
within, *intra* (time within which expressed by abl. case).
without, *sine.*
witness, *testis, -is.*
word, *verbum, -i*; bring word; see bring.
work, *opus, -ĕris.*
wound, *vulnus, -ĕris.*
wrong, *injuria, -ae.*

Y.

year, *annus, -i.*
yet, not yet, *nondum.*
you, *tu, te* or *vos*; often expressed by verb-ending.
younger, *junior* (Gr. [123]).
your, *tuus, -a, -um*; *vester, -tra, -trum.*
yourselves, *vos.*

Z.

zeal, *alacrĭtas, -ātis.*

J. S. CUSHING & CO., PRINTERS, 115 HIGH STREET, BOSTON.

[For Allen & Greenough's Cæsar; four books with vocabulary.]

PARALLEL REFERENCES TO BLACKBURN'S "ESSENTIALS OF LATIN GRAMMAR."

[Unbracketed references are to the head matter. The corresponding note should always be read also, and the illustrations studied. Bracketed references are to the notes. When a note contains more than one paragraph, a small figure at the right is used to show the paragraph referred to.]

BOOK I.

Chap. I. est divisa, [344]. — lingua, 300. — dividit, [257]². — horum, 283. — effeminandos, 340, [349]². — Germanis, 271. — qua de causa, 443. — quam . . . dictum est, [322]², 337.
Chap. II. Messala, etc., 487, 307. — civitati persuasit, [269]³. — ut exirent, [325]⁷. — cum praestarent, [328]. — imperio, [297]². — hoc, 298. — id, [269]³. — fiebat, [309]³. — ut . . . possent, [326]⁵. — bellandi, [288]. — adficiebantur, [12] (ƒ).
Chap. III. quae pertinerent, [322]⁵. — comparare, 338. — ut occuparet, [325]⁷, [269]³, [311]². — perfacile factu, 352. — non esse dubium quin, [326]¹. — regno occupato, 307, [346]. — Galliae, [290].
Chap. IV. ut cremaretur, [326]⁵. — igni, [99]⁴. — die constituta, 60, 301. — causae, 288. — cum conaretur, [330]¹.
Chap. V. arbitrati sunt, [330]¹. — domum, 265. — receptos, [346].
Chap. VI. possent, 316. — singuli, [118]. — locis, [299]. — a. d. v. Kal. Apr., [268]², 496.
Chap. VII. qui dicerent, 325. — sibi, 270. — ut liceat, [325]⁷. — Cassium . . . occisum, 338. — concedendum, [348]. — animo, 305. — itineris faciundi, 349. — dum convenirent, [330]⁴. — reverterentur, 324.
Chap. VIII. quo . . . possit, 325, [325]³. — si . . . possent, 323.
Chap. IX. novis rebus, [269]³.
Chap. X. ut haberet, [326]⁴, [326]⁵.
Chap. XI. depopulatis agris, [346].
Chap. XII. flumen, [268]. — Ararim, [99]¹. — mandarunt, 215.
Chap. XIII. pontem faciendum, [349]². — intelligerent, [330]¹. — diebus, 301. — incommodi, 280.
Chap. XIV. eo . . . quo, [298]². — quod si, [267]. — vexassent, 322. — cum, [329].
Chap. XVI. cotidie,[12]². — Haeduos frumentum,[262]⁵.— flagitare, 342.
Chap. XVII. ne . . . conferat, [325]². — dubitare quin, [326]. — Haeduis, [269]².
Chap. XIX. conaretur, [330]⁵.
Chap. XX. futurum uti, 476. — faciat, [325]⁵. — tanti, 274.
Chap. XXI. qui cognoscerent, 325.
Chap. XXII. milia, 266.   Chap. XXIII. dici, [285]³.
Chap. XXIV. qui sustineret, 325.   Chap. XXV. impedimento, 272.
Chap. XXVI. coniciebant, [12] (c). — Lingonas, [74]².
Chap. XXXI. Caesari, [269]. — adamassent, 215. — quo minus essent, [325]³. — hanc consuetudinem, 440. — vicerit, 322. — quin sumat, [326]¹. — Rhenum, [268].
Chap. XXXII. Sequanis, 270.
Chap. XXXIII. curae, 272. — ut fecissent, 333. — quibus rebus, [269]⁴.
Chap. XXXVI. qui faceret, [328].
Chap. XXXVII. qui . . . essent, 322. — resisti, 234, [235], end.
Chap. XXXIX. quam diceret, [322]⁵. — ut . . . posset, [325]⁷.

Chap. XL. cur ... judicaret, 317, 472. — sibi persuaderi, 234, [235], end. potuerint, [312].
Chap. XLI. imperatoris, [285].
Chap. XLII. equitibus, [269]². — si quid, [267]. — facto, [297]³.
Chap. XLIV. si remittatur, 331, 460.
Chap. XLVI. omni Gallia, 294.
Chap. XLVII. uti constitueret, [325]⁷. — quin conicerent, [326]. — civitate, 297.
Chap. L. utrum ... necne, 432, 433.
Chap. LII. phalangas, [74]².

BOOK II.

Chap. I. vererentur, 322. — novis imperiis, [269]³.
Chap. III. opinione, [296] (d). — ex Belgis, [284]⁴. — potuerint, [312].
Chap. V. rei publicae, 291.
Chap. VII. subsidio, 272. — potiundi oppidi, 340, [297]². — omnibus copiis, 304. — amplius, 266 or [296] (e).
Chap. X. convenirent, [325]⁵.
Chap. XVII. ex ... Gallis, [284]⁴.
Chap. XIX. hostis, [99]⁵.
Chap. XXI. posset, [326]². — defuerit, [312].
Chap. XXVII. quo praeferrent, [325]³.
Chap. XXX. contemptui, 272.
Chap. XXXII. ne quam, [140].
Chap. XXXIII. pellibus, 297.

BOOK III.

Chap. V. pugnaretur, [300]².
Chap. VI. sui colligendi, [348]².
Chap. VII. mare, [268]³.
Chap. VIII. quam acceperant, 478.
Chap. IX. ut acciderent, [321]².
Chap. X. retentorum equitum, 347.
Chap. XI. adeat, [325]⁵.
Chap. XXVI. prius ... quam ... posset, [330]⁵.

BOOK IV.

Chap. I. premebantur, [309]².
Chap. II. desiderent, [322]⁵, compare [333].
Chap. IV. prius quam fieret, [330]⁵.
Chap. V. consuetudinis, [285].
Chap. XII. amplius octingentos, [296] (e).
Chap. XIV. -ne ... an ... an, [314]⁴.
Chap. XVII. deiciendi operis, [349]².
Chap. XIX. uti convenirent, [325]⁷.
Chap. XXI. qui polliceantur, 325. — dare, 335. — magni, [274]. — auderet, [311]².
Chap. XXIII. convenirent, [330]⁴. — ut quae haberet, [328].
Chap. XXIV. copiis, 304. — generis, [288].
Chap. XXVII. ignoscere, [338].
Chap. XXX. hoc, 297.
Chap. XXXII. geruntur, [309]¹. — ventitaret, [247]¹.
Chap. XXXIV. quae continerent, [326]².
Chap. XXXV. tanto spatio, 302.

[For Allen & Greenough's Cicero.]

PARALLEL REFERENCES TO BLACKBURN'S "ESSENTIALS OF LATIN GRAMMAR."

[Unbracketed references are to the head matter. The corresponding note should always be read also, and the illustrations studied. Bracketed references are to the notes. When a note contains more than one paragraph, a small figure at the right is used to show the paragraph referred to.]

DEFENCE OF ROSCIUS.

1. Mirari... surrexerim, etc., 468–475; for the order, see 479–482. cum sedeant, [328]. sim, [333]. defendere, 335. ut adsint, [326][5]. — 2. istius, 440. sim, 316. aliis, [269][2]. me, 485. Rosci, 67. reciperem, 325, [311][1]. fecisset, 327. — 3. dixero, [331]. concedi, 234. ignosci, [269][3]. — 4. petitum sit, 316. ut dicerent, [325][7]. ut arbitrarentur, 326, [311]. ci... qui, 440. debeam, [326][2]. causae, 269. ut ne, [325][2]. — 5. ereptum, [346]. — 6. rectum [esse] se pugnare, 38, 337. proscriberentur, [330][1]. — 7. isti, 440. quod sciam, [267]. — 8. judicatote, [315][3]. — 9. Ameriam, 265. — 10. tris, [99][5]. Tiberim, [99][1]. ne teneam, [325][6]. — 12. despexerit, 333. ut moliantur, 325. quamvis felix sit, [321][2]. qui habeat, [326][2]. — 13. qui solvisset, [326][2]. cicit, [12] (c). qui fuisset, [326][2]. domum, 265. auferebat, [309][3]. urbe tota, [299]. — 15. nobilis, [99][5]. qui peterent, 325. vellem, 322. — 17. domo, [293]. — 18. ut pugnarent, [326][5]. de parricidio [284][3]. cum jugulandum, [349][2]. — 19. pater occisus, 347. ut optet, [326][5]. qui dicat, 325. — 21. si postularet, 331, 312. auditum sit, 450. — 22. major, [296] (e). de luxuria, [284][3]. — 30. venisses, [320]. — 32. tibi, 269. veniat, [325][5]. — 33. poterat, 449. possis, 316. — 41. diem, 60. — 42. pernicii, [58][2]. — 43. ut componeretur, [326][5]. retineretur, 316. — 45. verear, [328]. — 48. quod, quia, [328]. — 50. quasi nescias, [327][3]. — 54. condemnaretis, [311]. — 55. an vero, 434. — 57. hominibus, 269.

IMPEACHMENT OF VERRES.

3. judicaveritis, [331]. — partim, [101], [248], [267]. devitaverim, 333. — 4. dictitat, [247][1]. — 5. cadit, [309][2]. — 10. constitueret, [326][5]. — 14. commemorare, 335. — 24. agere, 335. — 29. expediat, [326][2]. — 31. Nonae, 406. — 44. fuisse desideraturos, 460. — 56. fuisse, 465.

PLUNDER OF SYRACUSE.
1. hanc, illo, 440. — 12. cat, 321.

CRUCIFIXION OF A ROMAN CITIZEN.
1. dicam, [309]². quae sint, [326]². tenerem, [311]. — 2. nescio qua, [323]⁴. — 6. quemquam, 444. — 10. induatur, 154, [267]². — 12. quod velit, [326]².

THE MANILIAN LAW.
3. lactandum, 234, [235], end. mihi, 270. — 13. commendetis, [326]³. — 19. memoria, 299. amiserant, [330]. — 22. dum contigunt, [309]¹. — 27. haberetis, 320. superarit, [326]². — 38. existimetis, 317. — 49. quin conferatis, [326]¹. — 50. erat diligendus, 455. — 53. an, 434. — 57. ne legaretur, 325. utrum ... an, 432. — 59. cum quaereret, [330]. quo ... hoc, [208]². — 64. parendum, 234, [235], end. — 66. idoneus, etc., [326]³. quasi non videamus, [327]³. — 70. putem, 322. — 71. videar, 326.

CATILINE I.
2. oportebat, [309]². — 5. fateatur, [326]². — 6. recognoscas, [325]⁵. — 7. in ante diem, [208]². sui conservandi, [348]². cum. dicebas, [330]¹. — 8. quam te, 477. — 8. ullo, 444. — 9. gentium, [283]. — 10. id temporis, [283]. desiderant, [309]². — 11. videbam, [309]³. — 18. mihi, [269]². — 22. duint, [226]. est tanti, [274]. — 27. mactari, 338. — 31. nescio quo pacto, [323]⁴. — 33. arcebis, [315]².

CATILINE II.
3. accuset, [326]². — 4. videretis, 333. eduxisset, 320. mihi, 269. — 5. mallem, 316. eduxisset, [325]⁵. — 7. ejecerit, [331]. conceperit, [326]². tota Italia, [299]. — 9. possitis, 325. — 11. nescio quod, [323]⁴. — 13. ei, [270]. — 14. ciciebam, [309]³. velint, [326]². — 18. sis, 317. — 19. non vident, 430.

CATILINE III.
7. deferrem, [322]⁵. — 8. ut uteretur, [325]⁷. — 9. defuturas, 468. — 15. occideret, [325]³. — 20. conlocandum, [340]². — 22. quo, [208]². si dicam, [331].

CATILINE IV.
6. jam pridem videbam, [309]². — 9. mea, [201]. — 12. huic, [269]. — 17. futurum fuit, 440, 455.

ARCHIAS.
4. urbe, [254]². — 25. civitate, 297. — 31. quae comprobetur, [326]².

[For Allen's Latin Composition.]

PARALLEL REFERENCES TO BLACKBURN'S "ESSENTIALS OF LATIN GRAMMAR."

[The unbracketed references are to the head matter in coarse print. They should be carefully memorized, and the notes and illustrations to them should be carefully studied and mastered.
Bracketed references are to the notes. When only a part of the note is included in the reference, the paragraph is indicated by a small figure at the right. References in the foot-notes are indicated as there by a, b, c, etc.]

1. 254, 255, 257.
2. 262. Notes: c, adjectives are often used substantively as in English; f, "*inter se*"; g, "remaining Gauls"; h, 300; i, [308]^5.
3. 426–434. Comp. [314]. Notes: b, 431; c, 429; d, 432; a, 273, 299.
4. 435–445, 256, [257]^2. Notes: a, "in which day"; c, [298]^2; f, *quod* to agree with "head."
8. 262, [268]. Notes: a, [116]; b, use prep. a; g, 254.
9. 269, 234.
10. 277, 280, 281, 289, 290, 291, [297]^2. Note: a, *capitis*, [289].
11. [285], [288], [290]. Notes: c, [288]; e, [285].
12. 271. For the dat. with adjs. a prep. is often used in the same sense.
13. 294, 296, 297, 298, [290], [300], [303]. Notes: a, [296] (c), the same is true of adverbs also; b, [296] (e).
14. 264, 267. Note: g, [267]^2.
15. 269, 270, 272. Note: a, "to [you] entering."
16. 295, 297, 300, 303, 305, 306, [274]. Note: b, [300], [303].
17. 265, 266, 273, 284, 293, 299, 301, 487, [268]. Notes: a, [309]^1; b, [254]^2; c, 490; i, [273]^1.
18. 213, 345, 348, 349. Note: a, 270.
19. 316, 317, 318–321, [315]. Note: a, [296], end.
20. 311, 312.
21. 327, 331, 448. Notes: a, 450; d, [332], 452.
22. 328, 330. Note: a, [309]^1.
23. 325, 326, 351, [346]. Note: e, [309]^5.
24. 337, 338. The tenses of the infinitives and participles denote time, present, past, or future, relative to the time of the verb on which they depend. Note: b, [340]^2.

27. 323, 324, 469–472.
28. 323. Notes: c, 139; e, [311][2].
29. [325][7], [326][5].
30. 281, 291.
31. [255][5], [285].
33. 315, 318–321.
34. 346.
35. 270, 351, 352. Note: a, make the relative agree with *Argei*, [256].
37. [254].
38. 283, 284, 286, 288, [285]. Notes: e, [288]; h, [325][7].
39. 277, 280, 281, 291.
40. [269]. Note: f, *coepi* takes the passive form when followed by a passive infinitive.
44. 274, 294, 296, 298, 303, [297][2], [297][3], [300].
45. 266, 301, 490–493.
46. 265, 266, 273, 284, 293, 299, [297][4].
47. [255], [257][2].

Adjs. are often used substantively, the masc. denoting persons; the neut., things.

Certain adjs. designate a part; *e.g.*: *summus mons* = top of the mountain; *media nox* = midnight.

An adj. limiting the subject often has the same force as an adv. limiting the verb.

alius ... alium = one another; *alter ... alterum* = each other.

49. 441, 442.
52. Note: c, [274].
54. 327, 449–452, [332][2].
55. 346, [316], [321][2].
56. 329, [321][2], [327][3], [330][3].
57. [309], [330].
58. [329], [330].
60. 325.
61. [325][3], [325][4], [326].
62. [326][2], [326][3], [328]. A clause of characteristic or of result is found after *quam*, than; *e.g.*: *sollertior est quam qui* (or *ut*) *decipi possit*, he is too shrewd to be tricked.

www.ingramcontent.com/pod-product-compliance
Lightning Source LLC
Chambersburg PA
CBHW031345230426
43670CB00006B/444